C000065827

ROBERT BURNS (1759–96) was born in Alloway, Ayrshire, the son of a tenant farmer. He was raised and educated there, and at Mount Oliphant and Lochlie. Burns worked as a flax dresser in Irvine between 1781 and 1782, returning to farming at Lochlie and, from 1784 at Mossgiel, with his brother Gilbert. After the success of the Kilmarnock edition of *Poems, Chiefly in the Scottish Dialect* (1786), Burns spent a period of time in Edinburgh; the Edinburgh edition followed in 1787. After the Border and Highland tours of 1787 he returned to Edinburgh, and began contributing to James Johnson's *Scots Musical Museum* (1787–1803) and, later, to George Thomson's *Collection of Original Scottish Airs* (1793–1841). In 1788 Burns moved to Ellisland in Dumfriesshire, holding the lease until 1791, when he took up an Excise post in Dumfries. His colourful biography and complex love-life – from early romances with Betty Paton and 'Highland Mary' Campbell, later liaisons with women including, possibly, Agnes McLehose, to his marriage to Jean Armour – has often distracted attention from his work, as has Henry Mackenzie's characterisation of Burns (with which the poet collaborated) as the 'Heaven-taught ploughman'. However, Burns's role as Scotland's 'National Bard' is balanced by his international reputation. His poetry and songs, expressed in the Scots and English languages, include humorous pieces, often based on Scottish traditions, like 'Tam o' Shanter'; dismissals of religious hypocrisy, like 'Holy Willie's Prayer'; compassionate pieces like 'Westlin Winds' and 'To a Mouse'; considerations of working class life, like 'The Cotter's Saturday Night' and lyrics of love in its various moods, from 'A Red red rose' to 'The Banks o' Doon'. Politicised pieces, reflecting the complexity of his opinions, range from 'For a' that and a' that' to 'The Rights of Woman'. *The Merry Muses of Caledonia* was published posthumously, without Burns's authorisation.

JAMES BARKE (1906–58) was born in Torwoodlee, Galashiels and raised in Tulliallan in Fife, with strong connexions to rural Galloway. He worked in Glasgow, became a full-time novelist and dramatist, associated with the Unity Theatre, and ran a hotel in Ayrshire, returning to Glasgow in 1955. Barke's novels include *The World his Pillow* (1933), *Major Operation* (1936) and *The Land of the Leal* (1939). He is best known for his five-part historical novel about the life of Robert Burns, *The Immortal Memory* (1946–54), including *The Wind that Shakes the Barley* (1946), *The Song in the Greenthorn Tree* (1947), *The Wonder of All the Gay World* (1949), *The Crest of the Broken Wave* (1953) and *The Well of the Silent Harp* (1954), with an accompanying novel on Jean Armour *Bonnie Jean* (1959). He also edited *Poems and Songs of Robert Burns* (1955) and was an expert on *piobaireachd*.

SYDNEY GOODSIR SMITH (1915–75) was born in Wellington, New Zealand, and moved in 1928 to Edinburgh, where his father was Chair of Forensic Medicine at the University. Educated at the Universities of Edinburgh and Oxford, he is best known for his poetry in Scots, including his masterpiece on love, *Under the Eildon Tree* (1948). Other poetry includes *The Deevil's Waltz* (1946), *So Late into the Night* (1952) and *Figs and Thistles* (1959). His plays include *The Wallace* (1960), performed at the Edinburgh Festival, and *The Rut of Spring* (1949–50). Other work includes the comic novel *Carotid Cornucopius* (1947) and, as editor, *Robert Fergusson 1750–1744* (1952) and *Hugh MacDiarmid: a Festschrift* (1962) with Kulgin Duval. In addition to *The Merry Muses*, he edited *A Choice of Burns's Poems and Songs* (1966), and he was a talented artist, art critic, and translator of writers including Alexander Blok.

JOHN DeLANCEY FERGUSON (1888–1966) was born in Scottsville, New York. His father, a veteran of the Civil War, was rector of Grace Episcopal Church, and an immigrant from Portadown, Northern Ireland; his mother was the daughter of immigrants from Lurgan. Raised in Plainfield, New Jersey, he was educated at Rutgers University and Columbia University, publishing his PhD thesis *American Literature in Spain* (1916). Ferguson taught at Heidelberg College, Ohio Wesleyan and was a professor at Brooklyn College, New York, retiring in 1954. He is probably best known for his edition of the *Letters of Robert Burns* (1931), revised in 1985 by G. Ross Roy, and for his biography *Pride and Passion: Robert Burns, 1759–1796* (1939). His publications include *Mark Twain, Man and Legend* (1965), *Theme and Variation in the Short Story* (1938) and, as editor, *RLS: Stevenson's Letters to Charles Baxter* (1956), with Marshall Waingrow.

VALENTINA BOLD was born in Edinburgh in 1964, grew up in Balbirnie in Fife, and was educated at the University of Edinburgh, Memorial University of Newfoundland and the University of Glasgow. She has worked at the University of Glasgow's Dumfries campus since it opened in 1999, heading the Scottish Studies programme and running the taught M.Litts in 'Robert Burns Studies' and 'Scottish Cultural Heritage'. Her publications include a CD-rom *Northern Folk: Living Traditions of North East Scotland* (1999), with

Tom McKean; *Smeddum: A Lewis Grassic Gibbon Anthology* (2001) and *James Hogg: A Bard of Nature's Making* (2007). She is currently editing James Hogg's *The Brownie of Bodsbeck* for the Stirling–South Carolina *The Collected Works of James Hogg* edition, and *The Kitty Hartley Manuscript: Scots Songs from Scotch Corner*, and is general editor of 'The History and Culture of Scotland' series for Peter Lang.

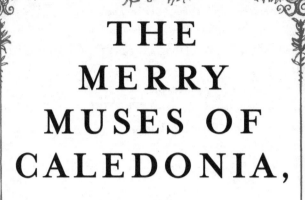

THE MERRY MUSES OF CALEDONIA,

BY ROBERT BURNS.

EDITED BY

JAMES BARKE

AND

SYDNEY GOODSIR SMITH,

with a Prefatory Note and some authentic Burns
Texts contributed by

J. DeLANCEY FERGUSON.

a new Introduction and some music score
annotations by

VALENTINA BOLD,

and illustrations by

BOB DEWAR.

PUBLISHED BY THE LUATH PRESS.

MM,IX.

First published c.1799

Bicentenary edition edited by James Barke and Sydney Goodsir Smith,
with a Prefatory Note and some authentic Burns Texts contributed by
J. DeLancey Ferguson, first published by Macdonald Printers,
Edinburgh in 1959

Luath edition 2009
ISBN: 978-1-906307-68-4

The paper used in this book is sourced from renewable forestry
and is FSC credited material.

Mixed Sources
Product group from well-managed
forests and other controlled sources
www.fsc.org Cert no. SA-COC-1565
© 1996 Forest Stewardship Council
FSC

Printed and bound by MPG Books Ltd., Cornwall

Design by Tom Bee

Typeset in 12 point Mrs Eaves by 3btype.com

(7)

CONTENTS

III OLD SONGS USED BY BURNS FOR POLITE
   VERSIONS

(ii)

ACKNOWLEDGEMENTS

I AM grateful to Alasdair Barke, Kitty Pal, John Calder and Jane Ferguson Blanshard for their kind permission to include copyright material from the 1959 edition of *The Merry Muses of Caledonia*, edited by James Barke, Sydney Goodsir Smith and John DeLancey Ferguson, along with the glossary by Sydney Goodsir Smith, and to Tessa Ransford on behalf of M. Macdonald. I would like to thank The Mitchell Library, who gave permission to include manuscript references from the 'James Barke Papers' in Special Collections; the National Library of Scotland, for permission to quote from the 'Sydney Goodsir Smith' Papers; Edinburgh University Library for permission to quote from the 'Sydney Goodsir Smith' Collection; the University of Delaware's department of Special Collections, for permission to quote from the 'Sydney Goodsir Smith' Papers; Broughton House, for permission to quote from the Ewing correspondence and the Andrew Carnegie Library, Dunfermline, for permission to cite the Ewing transcript of the 1799 edition of *The Merry Muses of Caledonia*.

I would particularly like to thank the following people, who offered me valuable assistance in locating and consulting library materials: Jim Allen of the Hornel Library, Broughton House, Kirkcudbright; Sally Harrower and George Stanley of the National Library of Scotland; Ruth Airley and Neil Moffat of the Ewart Library, Dumfries; Tricia Boyd of Edinburgh University Library; Christine Henderson of the Mitchell Library; Iris Snyder of Special Collections at the University of Delaware's library; Janice

Erskine at the Andrew Carnegie Library, Dunfermline; Nancy Groce and Steve Winnick of the American Folklife Center at Library of Congress; Larissa Watkin of the Library at the Grand Masonic Temple in Washington, as well as my colleagues Avril Goodwin, Jan O'Callaghan and John Macdonald at the University of Glasgow's Dumfries Campus Library.

Ross Roy, Gerry Carruthers, John Manson, Ed Cray and Tom Hall all helped in substantial ways. I am grateful, too, to the Globe Inn, Dumfries, which kindly lent me its copy of the 1911 edition, and particularly to Maureen McKerrow and Jane Brown. I would like to thank Fred Freeman, Sheena Wellington and Karine Polwart for sharing their insights into musical aspects of Burns's songs; all the misunderstandings, of course, are wholly my own. I would like to thank David Nicol, Alice Bold, Aileen McGuigan and Carol Hill for their encouragement and supportiveness, along with Gavin MacDougall, Leila Cruickshank, Catriona Wallace and all of the team at Luath. The one missing person from this list is my father, Alan Bold, whose scholarship and kindness is a lasting source of inspiration.

INTRODUCTION: THE ELUSIVE TEXT

The Merry Muses of Caledonia is, potentially, one of the most significant works which purports to be by Robert Burns. Equally, and particularly from the point of view of its editors, it is singularly challenging. The text of this new Luath edition is taken from the 1959 edition of *The Merry Muses*, published by Callum Macdonald in Edinburgh. It is accompanied by the original headnotes and essays from that edition, by James Barke, Sydney Goodsir Smith and J. DeLancey Ferguson. Smith's glossary, which appeared in the 1964 American edition, with the same editors, is included. Three illustrations from the 1959 edition have been omitted: the title page of the first edition, 'Ellibanks' and an illustration by Rendell Wells of the Anchor Close, where the Crochallan Fencibles, early editors of *The Merry Muses*, met in Dawney Douglas's tavern. This loss is more than compensated for by the inclusion of evocative new illustrations, drawn especially for the present edition, by Bob Dewar. For the first time, too, the music of the songs by Burns has been included: this fulfils the desire of the 1959 editors, thwarted by the untimely death of James Barke. In my Introduction, I seek to complement the work of Barke, Smith and Ferguson by discussing the development of their edition, and reviewing the peculiar history and characteristics of this elusive set of songs.

It could be argued that *The Merry Muses* has a life and a validity of its own, independent of any of its authors and editors. It is a conglomerate, and arguably amorphous, mass of songs. Although associated with Burns from an early stage in its life, it was first published after Burns's death and without his approval. Neither is there any extant proof that he personally amassed these items, or composed them, with the intention to publish. Contrary to popular expectations, only certain of the texts, as the 1959 editors note, are verifiably Burns's, or collected by Burns, because of their existence in manuscript, or publication elsewhere.

While some of *The Merry Muses'* contents are indisputably by the poet, or collected and amended by him, many more were bundled into 19th century editions by their editors, in an attempt to add weight through the association with Burns. It could even be said that *The Merry Muses* has a significance which is independent of Burns, revealing cultural expectations about bawdy song during its period of publication, from the late 18th century to, now, the early 21st. However, the main *frisson* attached to *The Merry Muses* is, of course, its long association with Burns.

Previous editors have worked from the premise that *The Merry Muses's* value is in rounding off the poet's corpus, allowing readers to appreciate the full range of Burns's output as songwriter and collector. The contents, too, are supposed to represent Burns as we hope he was: openly sexual, raucously humorous, playful yet empathetic to women. The existence of the *Muses* panders to the premise that Burns was the quintessential poet of love in all its forms, from the most sentimental to the most graphic. As Frederick L. Beaty noted in the 1960s, 'to him sexual attraction was the most natural and inspiring justification for existence [...] from this basic premise [...] stemmed the related attitudes expressed throughout his poetry'.[1]

---

[1] Frederick L. Beaty, 'Burns's Comedy of Romantic Love', *PMLA* 2 (May, 1968): 429–38.

Seen from that viewpoint, *The Merry Muses* offers tantalising glimpses of Burns's poetry at its rawest and bawdiest, at the extreme end of the spectrum of his love lyrics.

These are texts which require imaginative readjustments on the part of the 21st century reader, particularly for those who are unfamiliar with the bawdy or its modern erotic equivalents. At first glance, many of these songs seem odd, in ways which can range from the puerile to the mildly shocking. However, as Barke suggests in his essay, it is necessary to temporarily suspend preconceptions and enter into a worldview which, arguably, has persisted from the 18th century onwards, changing subtly along the way. Equally, it is essential to rid oneself of the 'residual shame' attached to erotica that Alan Bold identified in *The Sexual Dimension in Literature*: 'to judge from the evidence available, few people willingly admit to an enjoyment of erotic literature. They claim to read it for scholarly, for historical, for critical reasons but rarely for fun though in other areas it is accepted that entertainment can be combined with enlightenment'.[2] Burns, of course, was working within a rich and varied tradition of bawdry, in written and oral forms, in Scotland and beyond. At the more sophisticated end of the scale Dunbar comes to mind, like Chaucer in England and Boccaccio in Europe, for his knowing suggestions of women's enjoyment of sex, in poems like 'The Tua Mariit Wemen and the Wedo'. In terms of oral tradition, Scotland, as Barke indicates, has a rich and lively bawdry background, which is still extant. Bearing these

---

[2] Alan Bold, *The Sexual Dimension in Literature* (London: Vision Press, 1982): 7.

factors, and Barke's essay, in mind, it becomes possible to appreciate the songs, within their bawdy context, for their good humour, verbal playfulness, and disresp-ectfulness towards standard social mores.

THE CONTEXT OF BAWDRY

This was certainly the way in which they were enjoyed in the late 18th century. As DeLancey Ferguson explains in his essay, Burns circulated specific bawdy items in letters to trusted friends, like Provost Maxwell of Lochmaben, or by lending his now lost 'collection' to those he treated with self-conscious empathy, such as John McMurdo of Drunlanrig. These tantalising glimpses of his bawdy work, through references to it and the inclusion of selected pieces, suggest that Burns sought to flatter his friends by hinting at their gentlemanly broad-mindedness and their ability to enjoy without being corrupted. In this way, he could present himself as the poetic equal of the gentry by showing a common interest, sometimes expressed by the gentry through the possession of libertine literature and membership of erotic clubs. Burns was also indicating his own status as a gentlemanly collector, linked in a 'cloaciniad' way to his enthusiastic role in the *Scots Musical Museum*.

It is in context of the 'fraternal' enjoyment of the bawdry, to quote Robert Crawford, that *The Merry Muses* must be viewed.[3] It certainly represents the worldview of the 18th century drinking club. First published as *The Merry Muses of Caledonia: A Collection of Favourite Scots Songs, Ancient and Modern;*

---

3 See Robert Crawford, *Robert Burns & Cultural Authority* (Edinburgh: Polygon, 1999):13.

Selected for use of the Crochallan Fencibles,[4] its apparent editors were a group of drinking and carousing companions. Its members included William Dunbar, one of its founders, and the presiding officer (also a member, like Burns, of the Canongate Kilwinning Lodge of Freemasons); Charles Hay, Lord Newton (the group's 'major and muster-master-general') and Robert Cleghorn who was particularly involved with the 'cloaciniad' verses which interested the club. Burns refers to his membership of the group in writing, for instance, to Peter Hill, in February 1794, where he wishes to be remembered to his 'old friend, Colon [*sic*] Dunbar of the Crochallan Fencibles'.[5]

Male clubs, ranging from those who shared intellectual ideas to those who shared more insalubrious experiences were, of course, common in Scotland at this period, as the 1959 editors mention here; several seem to have attitudes to sexuality which were active, imaginative and relatively unabashed. Burns himself had, as is well known, been part of the intellectually active 'Tarbolton Bachelors'. The Crochallan group were, presumably, more sexually-orientated: they certainly enjoyed erotic and bawdy songs although they were, perhaps, less practically sexual than other, more colourful organisations such as the Beggar's Benison — a club whose tastes ran to masturbatory rituals, and the detailed inspection of naked, very young women

---

4 *The Merry Muses of Caledonia; A Collection of Favourite Scots Songs, Ancient and Modern; Selected for use of the Crochallan Fencibles* (no publisher, no printer: 1799).

5 See *The Letters of Robert Burns* 2 vols, 2nd edition, ed J. DeLancey Ferguson and G. Ross Roy (Oxford: Clarendon, 1985) vol II, no.614.

(Burns's acquaintances included at least one member of the Benison, Sir John Whitefoord).[6]

Viewed from an 18th century gentlemanly perspective — although less *Fanny Hill* and more, as Barke puts it, 'tap-room story' — the songs become titillating rather than obscene, designed to elicit a chuckle (or, perhaps, a belly laugh). These are a relatively tame group of texts, playfully designed for consumption by a male audience. They are heterosexual in orientation, focussed on consensual sex in familiar positions, and with a strong focus on what used to be quaintly referred to as the male and female pudenda.[7] They operate according to their own rules — perhaps not as codified as those identified for other song forms, such as the ballad, but nevertheless apparent. They exhibit, too, most of the characteristics Bold identified in bawdy verse, in the introduction to his *The Bawdy Beautiful*:

> They invariably utilise obvious hand-me-down rhymes, except when suggestive rhymes are implied. They rely on regular, thumping rhythms that crudely parallel the steady rhythm of the sexual act [...] [They] are thematically predictable — boy meets girl; boy is had by girl — so the

---

6 See David Stevenson *Beggar's Benison. Sex clubs of Enlightenment Scotland* (Phantassie, East Linton: Tuckwell, 2001).

7 See, for instance, Gershon Legman *The Horn Book, Studies in Erotic Folklore and Bibliography* (New York: University Books, 1964); Alan Bold *The Sexual Dimension in Literature* (London: Vision Press, 1982); G.S. Rousseau and Roy Porter, eds., *Sexual Worlds of the Enlightenment*. Manchester: Manchester University Press, 1987; Evelyn Lord, *The Hell-Fire Clubs. Sex, Satanism and Secret Societies* (New Haven: Yale University Press, 2008) and, for background information, David Foxon, *Libertine Literature in England. 1660–1745* (New York: University Books, 1965).

structural bond of the verse need only be sound enough to carry the undemanding narrative.[8]

Another typical characteristic is the way in which *The Merry Muses* employs easily-understood euphemisms for sexual experiences. 'Nature's richest joys', for instance, are recalled in 'To Alexander Findlater'. Then there is the statement in 'Ye Hae Lien Wrang, Lassie', based on farming experiences (like many of the metaphors here), 'Ye've let the pounie o'er the dyke, / And he's been in the corn, lassie'. This is hammered home, in case there was any misunderstanding (these pieces are not subtle), with an overt description of the symptoms of pregnancy, 'For ay the brose ye sup at e'en / Ye bock them or the morn, lassie'. So, too, obvious images are used for the penis and vagina: the 'chanter pipe' which women play in 'John Anderson My Jo'; the burrowing 'Modiewark'; the 'Nine Inch will please a Lady' versus the women's 'dungeons deep' in 'Act Sederunt of the Session' or 'Love's Channel' (reminiscent of Cleland) in 'I'll tell you a Tale of a Wife'. Some, of course, are much more explicit, like 'My Girl She's Airy', expressing appreciation for her 'breath [...] as sweet as the blossoms in May' and a longing, 'For her a, b, e, d, and her c, u, n, t'.

The Merry Muses, at other times, is a self-conscious display of Burns's ability in diverse poetic styles, within the context of bawdry. In 'Act Sederunt of the Session', for instance, he applies satirical techniques to suggest the ridiculousness of contemporary kirk attitudes to sex, suggesting a new law

---

8 Alan Bold *The Bawdy Beautiful. The Sphere Book of Improper Verse* (London: Sphere, 1979): xxii.

which makes sex compulsory. The punitive attitudes of the clergy to extra, or premarital, affairs are, similarly, soundly rejected in 'The Fornicator'. Burns is — with humorous intention — engaging with the serious issue of contemporary church practices towards those who engaged in premarital sex which could range from the annoying and unpleasant to the inhumane.[9] Then there is the bawdy mock-pastoral of 'Ode to Spring'.

Burns's bawdry, too, reflects an interest in the oral traditions of erotica with which he was familiar and which, as Barke indicates, persisted and developed in Scotland in the 1950s, just as they do today. Burns's interest in collecting bawdry, reflected here in pieces like 'Brose an' Butter' and 'Cumnock Psalms', is part of his wider interest in traditional songs. In this he parallels other collectors with bawdy material (often unpublished in their lifetimes) within their wider collected repertoire, including David Herd and Peter Buchan. Burns collected, amended and composed bawdy songs in oral traditional styles. Examples here include the explicit, if rather mannered, voice of his collected 'John Anderson My Jo': no doubt an adapted and improved version of that in oral circulation in contemporary Scotland. As with much of his work, he reflects different aspects of sexuality, too: from the open enjoyment of sex, in many of these pieces, to a sympathetic awareness of its possible consequences for women, in 'Ye hae Lien Wrang, Lassie', humorously yet sensitively illustrated by Bob Dewar in this edition.

9 See Christopher Whatley, 'Burns: Work, Kirk and Community in Later Eighteenth-Century Scotland' in Burns Now, ed Kenneth Simpson (Edinburgh: Canongate Academic, 1994): 92–116.

PERFORMANCE TEXTS

A major factor which has to be considered with *The Merry Muses* is that it is, primarily, a collection of songs for performance, rather than designed to be read either silently, or aloud, as poems on the printed page. With the exception of one or two items, which are designed for recitation rather than singing, this is a collection which really comes to life when it is used as it was originally presented: *'for use of the Crochallan Fencibles'*, as a source text for singers. As Cedric Thorpe Davie said, considering Burns as a 'writer of songs': 'but for the tunes, the words would never have come into existence, and it is absurd to regard the latter as poetry to be read or spoken aloud'.[10] This observation has particular validity for *The Merry Muses*.

They have, of course, been recorded before, most successfully as a group on Ewan MacColl's *Songs from Robert Burns's Merry Muses of Caledonia* (1962), which owes an openly-acknowledged debt to the 1959 edition. This useful set of 24 *Merry Muses* includes scholarly and appreciative sleeve-notes by Kenneth S. Goldstein, and certainly merits re-issue and wider distribution.[11] It features proclamatory and appropriate performances in MacColl's distinctive style, which suit *The Merry Muses* very well. 'The Jolly Gauger', for instance, is performed in a pacy, assertive and thoughtful manner, slowing down slightly for the section where the

---

[10] Cedric Thorpe Davie, 'Robert Burns, Writer of Songs', in Donald A. Low, ed, *Critical Essays on Robert Burns* (London: Routledge & Kegan Paul, 1975): 157.

[11] Ewan MacColl, *Songs from Robert Burns' Merry Muses of Caledonia*. Sung by Ewan MacColl. Edited and annotated by Kenneth S. Goldstein. (np: Dionysus, 1962). D1.

girl is laid down 'Amang the broom', and with the verse
where she lays 'blessings' on the gauger for his actions.
'The Trogger', equally, stresses the strong rhythmic qual-
ities of the piece, with a drawn-out 'trogger' and 'troggin',
enhancing the humour. MacColl shows an awareness,
too, of the sophistication of other items. 'The Bonniest
Lass', set here to 'For a' that, an' a' that', starts in a gentle
manner then shifts, appropriately, to a more aggressive —
and sympathetic — performance style, building towards a
venomous ending, speaking out against 'canting stuff'.

More recently, Gill Bowman, Tich Frier *et al*'s *Robert Burns
— The Merry Muses* (1996) have demonstrated that the songs
still stand well as performance texts.[12] Notable inter-
pretations include Davy Steele's 'Wad ye do that?', which
skilfully captures the wistfulness and appeal of the lover, as
he pleads with the 'Gudewife, when your gudeman's frae
hame' to let him in to her bedchamber, as well as his
intended's couthiness of response: 'He f—s me five times
ilka night, / Wad ye do that?'. The deceptive softness of
the tune, 'John Anderson, My Jo', is highly appropriate.
Equally, Gill Bowman's 'How can I keep my Maidenhead'
shows an awareness of how the light tune, 'The Birks o'
Abergeldie', can adeptly underline the flirtatious opening,
and underwrite the humour of the explicit ending. Other
recordings worth mentioning include the driving version
of 'Brose an' Butter' on *Eddi Reader Sings the Songs of Robert
Burns*,[13] featuring Ian Carr, Phil Cunningham, Boo

12 Gill Bowman, Tich Frier et al, *Robert Burns — The Merry Muses*
(Glasgow: Iona Records, 1996) IRCD035: 10, 14.

13 Eddi Reader, *Eddi Reader sings the songs of Robert Burns* (London:
Rough Trade Records, 2003) RTRADE CD 097 : 5.

Hewardine and John McCusker in an engaging arrangemement. The farming-based euphemisms — the mouse and the 'modewurck' paralleled with 'the thing / I had i' my nieve yeſtreen'; the 'Gar'ner lad' desired 'To gully awa wi' his dibble' — have humorous emphasis from the pacy performances.

Jean Redpath, too, included several of *The Merry Muses* on her series of recordings with Serge Hovey.[14] 'The Fornicator',[15] with a rapid and, at times, almoſt harsh accompaniment, and a drawn out 'fornicator', is an intelligent performance, using the rhythm of the tune self-consciously to add emphasis to the text. The pairing of a rather formal setting, with piano and flute, to 'Nine Inch will Please a Lady' is highly appropriate, with a pause before the firſt punchline, underlining the paradoxical pairing of the 'lady' and 'koontrie c—t' aspects of the piece, its humour underlined by Redpath's characteriſtically polished tradıtional ſtyle.[16]

The comprehensive and groundbreaking Linn record series of *The Complete Songs of Robert Burns,* too, features several of *The Merry Muses*.[17] Janet Russell's unaccompanied 'O

---

[14] Jean Redpath, *Songs of Robert Burns*. Arranged by Serge Hovey, 7 vols. Firſt published 1976–1990. Rereleased on 4 CDs (USA: Rounder; Cockenzie: Greentrax, 1990–1996), CDTRAX 114–16 and 029.

[15] Redpath, *Songs of Robert Burns*, vol 5 and 6: 16.

[16] Redpath *Songs of Robert Burns*, vol 1 and 2: 16.

[17] *Robert Burns. The Complete Songs*. 12 vols. Various artiſts. Ed Fred Freeman (Glasgow: Linn Records, 1995–2002) Linn Records CDK 047, 051, 062, 083, 086, 099, 107, 143, 156, 199, 200 and 201.

wha'll mow me now', for instance, emphasises the wryness of this woman's reflections on her predicament, left pregnant by 'A sodger wi' his bandileers'. The cry of the refrain, 'wha'll m—w me now', is genuinely regretful and deeply humorous. Russell's knowing interpretation takes full account of its nuances. Ian Benzie's intelligent version of 'Green sleeves' has a jaunty and yet urgent accompaniment which is well-suited to the words: Jonny Hardie on the fiddle emphasises the chorus line addressed to the true love: 'I shall rouse her in the morn, / My fiddle and I thegither' and Marc Duff, on bodhran, holds the whole together rhythmically. The bouzouki, played by Jamie McMenemy, and the recorder, from Duff again, add additional charm to this light-hearted song; it is cleverly paired, too, with a song with the less overtly erotic dialogue of love: 'Sweet Tibbie Dunbar'.[18]

It is unsurprising that *The Merry Muses* should receive such sophisticated treatments on the Linn series. Fred Freeman, its director, is acutely aware both of Burns's musicality, and of the characteristics of *The Merry Muses*. In a recent discussion, for instance,[19] he drew my attention to the fact that the texts reflect 18th century notions of the grotesque, as a device for social satire, and as an antidote to, as Burns put it, 'cant about decorum'. Freeman identifies, in *The Merry Muses,* the ways in which Burns both 'good naturedly airs these views' with his intellectual peers and, simultaneously, 'asserts himself, like a jolly beggar, before the upper classes'. Like Legman, Freeman sees

---

[18] *Robert Burns. The Complete Songs*, vol 5: 22.

[19] The quotations here are from telephone conversations between Fred Freeman and Valentina Bold, in late 2008, quoted with permission from Fred Freeman.

these songs as expressing aspects of female experience —
these are not, solely, pieces for male consumption:

> In many of the songs the female is the superior sexual
> partner as she sooples the beſtial male again and again:
> poking fun at his impotence ('the laîthron doup' in 'Come
> Rede Me Dames' ('Nine Inch will Please a Lady') or
> deflating him, literally, in 'The Reels of Bogie'). Then,
> too, she is so often the dispassionate observer — observing
> the male 'fodgeling his arse' in 'Andrew an' his cutty Gun',
> or pronouncing boaſtfully 'his ba's'll no be dry the day'
> ('Duncan Davidson'). She is his equal in the battle of the
> sexes (e.g., 'As I lookît ower yon caſtle wa', ['Cumnock
> Psalms']), and she can laugh at her own predicaments.[20]

As well as appreciating the playfulness, and wryness, of the
texts, Freeman is acutely aware of Burns's thoughtfulness
in matching texts to tunes:

> For Burns, the medium is the message. The tunes have
> everything to do with his idea of a unîty of effect;
> everything to do with his intent. Practically speaking, this
> means that if his theme is purely playful or feſtive,
> normally with reference to dancing for joy, he will use a jig
> or slip jig. If he wishes to portray breathless excîtement, as
> with the rising randy thoughts of his characters, or, indeed,
> of sexual action îtself, he will use a reel, which is an
> unremîtting, breathless form. If his poking fun has a level
> of pointed satire or jibe to ît, he will use a ſtrathspey, which
> is always punctuated wîth îts Scots snaps.

Commenting in particular on the tunes (reproduced at
the end of the present edîtion) of the 1959 edîtors' A

---

[20] This quotation, and those which follow, are from an e-mail from
Fred Freeman to Valentina Bold, 16 December 2008, quoted
with permission from Fred Freeman.

texts, Freeman is particularly impressed by the matching of words and tunes:

> Not only are his tunes engaging and interesting in them-
> selves but, again, he has adhered to his principle of a
> successful marriage of form and content: for example,
> breathless action or anticipation of action (reel – 'The
> Fornicator', 'Ode to Spring'); poking fun at legislators
> (strathspey – 'Act Sederunt'); high jinks, celebration (jig –
> 'My Girl She's Airy' – 'she dances, she glances'; 'Nine Inch'
> – joy of sex; 'When Princes' and 'While Prose' – sex as
> great happy leveller); (slip jig – 'I'll tell you a tale' – as with
> 'Brose an' Butter' which is also a mischievous tale); (Borders
> double hornpipe – 'O Saw ye my Maggie' – uses this [...]
> as archetypal characters of love, like 'Wee Willie Gray').

Freeman, equally, admires the use of 'somewhat baroque' tunes in pieces like 'There Was Twa Wives' and 'Bonie Mary', which allows Burns 'to set his content into relief [...] as he implicitly thumbs his nose at propriety, upper class drawing rooms and polite conversation'.

Freeman, finally, sees strong parallels between the songs of *The Merry Muses* and those of *The Jolly Beggars*, as did Cedric Thorpe Davie. Davie notes that *The Merry Muses* pairs texts and melody with skill, in the particular case of 'I'll Tell you a Tale of a Wife' and the tune 'Auld Sir Symon'; it does not distract: 'the listener is not much concerned with the tune so long as he can fasten on the lewd lines'. This, says Davie, is a much weaker pairing when the same tune is used in *The Jolly Beggars* for 'Sir Wisdom's a fool when he's fou'.[21] The musical choices of *The Merry Muses*, then, as Freeman's observations indicate, are often done with care,

---

21 Cedric Thorpe Davie, 'Robert Burns, Writer of Songs', in Donald A. Low, ed, *Critical Essays on Robert Burns* (London: Routledge & Kegan Paul, 1975): 176.

thoughtfulness, and with full knowledge of the relation-
ships between text and air.

Other singers express their open appreciation of *The Merry
Muses,* including Sheena Wellington.[22] When I asked her
how the texts stand up in performance, she drew attention
to the diversity of quality, and character, among the
pieces; while some are 'just your dirt dirty and that fair
enough group' others are 'very clever'. Wellington
particularly admires 'Nine inch will Please a lady' because
'you can get a really good laugh out of that one'. Other
pieces, according to Wellington, have 'that thread o
humanity that he couldnae help himself in doing';
examples include 'Wha'll Mow me Now': 'he obviously
despises the lad that's leaving this lassie'. Another
particular favourite is 'O saw ye my Maggie?', for its
pairing of words and tune.[23] Karine Polwart, equally,
admires Burns's songs in *The Merry Muses,*[24] particularly for
the ways in which they depict women: 'he writes about
them genuinely as real people, not as superficial, pretty
objects, just of his desire. They're kind of complicated
people. Equally, like Freeman, and influenced by the
experience of working on his Linn Records series, Polwart

---

[22] Taken from a transcript of a recorded telephone conversation of
Sheena Wellington and Valentina Bold, 12 December 2008,
quoted with permission from Sheena Wellington.

[23] Jo Miller notes that often 'popular choices by women singers
include 'Dainty Davie' and 'John Anderson my Jo' in her article
'Burns's Songs: A Singer's View', *Burns Now*, ed Kenneth Simpson
(Edinburgh: Canongate Academic, 1994): 193–207.

[24] Karine Polwart, interviewed by Valentina Bold during the first
Dumfries 'Burns Song' festival, on 25 January 2005, the Station
Hotel, Dumfries, and quoted here with her permission.

finds the way in which Burns used dance tunes, in particular, something of a 'revelation': 'they're great tunes […] I think they're absolutely fantaſtic language […] and completely untranslatable […] because the whole reason for the words is the rhythm and the sound and the percussive nature of the words, so you can't juſt slot in another word […] they're amazing liſtle songs'. Polwart particularly likes the songs which show women in 'more ſtroppy moods', like 'O can ye Labour lee, young man': 'iſt's basically a taunt, iſt's a woman taunting a man about whether […] he can really hold his own in the sack basically, that's the whole point of iſt, and the dance songs were a good format for Burns to be cheeky, quiſte saucy, quiſte satirical, but quiſte pointed at the same time'.

The songs, as Polwart suggeſts, are of various types, wiſth great diversiſty of tone and attiſtude. Many adopt, as Polwart suggeſts, and as Gershon Legman noted both in *The Horn Book* and his *The Merry Muses*, a perspective which is broadly sympathetic to women, if not quiſte female: these are women as men like to think they are: ready for, or thinking about, intercourse moſt of the time, as in 'Ellibanks', and measuring their men by their sexual prowess (passim). Their women certainly have a voice, if not much willpower: in 'Let me in this Ae Night', for inſtance, male persiſtence triumphs, although the women is allowed to express her regrets, humorously. Certainly, there is the implicît notion throughout that women deserve not to be abandoned when pregnant as in, again, 'Ye Hae Lien Wrang'.

Ignoring or pruning this aspect of Burns's work, as was routinely done in the 19th century, diſtorts the reader's views of the poet. In *Bawdy Burns. The Chriſtian Rebel*, Cyril

Pearl makes a strong case for defying the 'effrontery' of editors in ignoring, or even suppressing, Burns's erotica. As an example, he cites the changes William Scott Douglas made in his published version of 'Green Grow the Rashes O', where he replaced, 'A feather bed is no sae saft, / As the bosoms o' the lasses' for Burns's original, 'The lasses they hae wimple bores, / The widows they hae gashes O.'[25] Changes like these remove the smeddum of the original, and replace it with something both less potent and more pedestrian.

The Merry Muses, then, offers another facet to the construction of Burns's poetic *persona*, counterbalancing Henry Mackenzie's fantasy (with which, of course, the poet willingly collaborated): the clean-cut, 'heaven-taught ploughman'.[26] Equally, it could be argued that the work represents an attempt to present Burns as another fantasy creature, partly based in fact, and one which he actively fostered: the highly-sexed, unrepentantly bawdy, boozing — and, crucially, irresistible — womaniser. If Burns had not written *The Merry Muses*, they would have to have been invented. This is where the book is problematic: there is a distinct probability that many items — particularly those of the late 19th and early 20th century editions — are neither by Burns nor were they familiar to him.

---

[25] Cyril Pearl *Bawdy Burns. The Christian Rebel* (London: Frederick Muller, 1958): 151.

[26] See Henry Mackenzie, review of the Kilmarnock edition in *The Lounger*, 97 (9 Dec 1786), reprinted in *Robert Burns, The Critical Heritage*, ed Donald A. Low (London, Routledge: 1974): 66–71.

THE TEXTUAL HISTORY

The textual history of *The Merry Muses* is extremely complicated. Although many, or moſt, of its texts were no doubt familiar to the Crochallan members, *The Merry Muses* was not itself published as a book until three years after Burns's death, in 1799, without being attributed to Burns in the book itself, and without his permission or approval. This volume has no specific reference to Burns and his precise involvement with its production would seem to be minimal if any. However, *The Merry Muses* was linked to the poet through his association with the Crochallans.

According to a literary legend which was, as Ferguson notes here and discusses elsewhere, firſt recorded by Robert Chambers, the 1799 volume was compiled after Burns's death, based on a manuscript allegedly inveigled out of the grieving Jean Armour.[27] This manuscript is no longer extant, or at leaſt its location is unknown; in 1959 Ferguson revised his earlier opinion that it might have been deſtroyed. Related to the literary legend, the 1799 ediſion was long thought to have been published in Dumfries; modern scholars, including Ferguson, think it more likely that it was published in Edinburgh. Moreover, until the later 19th century, and not conclusively until the publication of the 1959 ediſion, the exiſtence of the Crochallan volume was itself based on rumour. The one copy occasionally available to later 19th century ediſors, such as William Scott Douglas and, later, W.H. Ewing, was that which passed through the hands of William Craibe

---

27 See J. DeLancey Fergusson, 'The Suppressed Poems of Burns', *Modern Philology* 30 (1): 1932: 53–60 and 'Burns and The Merry Muses', *Modern Language Notes*, Nov 1951: 471–73.

Angus and which, by 1959, was in the personal collection of the former Liberal Prime Minister, the Earl of Rosebery. The Rosebery copy, which is very slightly damaged, lacks a date, and so the only way of dating *The Merry Muses* was to use the watermarks on its paper. These placed the volume at around 1800 or earlier. Ross Roy's copy is dated 1799,[28] but, given the watermarking issue, it is still impossible even to date the book exactly. A microfilm copy of the Rosebery volume was made accessible to the 1959 editors, and is now available for consultation in the National Library of Scotland.[29]

It is possible, given Burns's historical associations with erotica, that the manuscript alluded to, as discussed by Ferguson, or at least selected texts from it, was used by the Fencibles. Probably it had been seen by at least some of its most prominent members. However, it is equally likely that, if the Crochallans were indeed the authors (and, again, there is no absolute certainty), the songs were remembered from performances. This could be one explanation of why the texts by Burns intermingle with other items from the Club's oral repertoire.

To complicate matters, *The Merry Muses* has been in constant flux and development since its first appearance. Even the 1799 edition, recently reprinted by the University of South Carolina Press, is based, in parts at least, on memories: the Burns manuscript that it is associated with has never

---

[28] See *The Merry Muses of Caledonia*. Facsimile edition (Columbia, South Carolina: University of South Carolina Press for the Thomas Cooper Library, 1999).

[29] Microfilm, *The merry muses of Caledonia: a collection of favourite Scots songs, ancient and modern; selected for the use of the Crochallan Fencibles* (Edinburgh?: 1799) Mf 1059.

been found although there are traces of it in various letters and references. Ferguson discusses this ably here in his 'Sources and Texts of the Suppressed Poems'. Since 1799, *The Merry Muses* has passed through various incarnations; there were over 30 editions or printings, all with minor or major variations, up to 2000. There are concentrated clusters too: at least seven editions which can be tentatively dated between 1900 and 1911, and a minimum of 10 more, including a US printing, between 1962 and 1982. There is a gap between around 1843 and 1872 and, again, between 1930 and 1959, possibly reflecting attitudes to erotic texts, and censorship, at these times. It is recommended that readers with a particular interest in the textual history consult Gershon Legman's 1965 edition of *The Merry Muses*, which includes a detailed bibliography.

THE 1959 EDITION

The decision I made to present the texts from the 1959 edition was taken for several reasons. First of all, the 1959 is an honest attempt to strip out extraneous texts which had been included alongside those of the 1799 edition. Barke, Smith and Ferguson's endeavour was pioneering in that it was not caught up in the 1827 sequence (of which more presently), but drew directly on holograph texts where it was at all possible. The description of the texts as '*The Merry Muses of Caledonia*, edited by James Barke and Sydney Goodsir Smith, with a Prefatory note and some authentic Burns Texts contributed by J. DeLancey Ferguson', is a far more accurate description than those in most of the 19th and 20th century editions, where the explicit attribution, 'by Robert Burns', usually appears.

The 1959 edition is valuable in that it groups the texts by their provenance: as songs in Burns's holograph (by him or collected by him); songs from printed sources (by or attributed to Burns, or used by Burns for 'polite versions', many of which will be immediately familiar to readers) and those collected by Burns, as well as a final section of what they term 'Alien Modes', along with the related text of 'The Libel Summons'. Smith explains this system fully, along with his reasons for excluding items from previous editions, in his '*Merry Muses* Introductory'. Perhaps paradoxically, because the 1959 editors adopted such a rational system of presentation and organisation, and because they preferred holograph or verifiable texts to others, it could even be argued that Burns himself might have approved of this edition in a way which is unlikely with earlier issues of the work. The editors had good reasons, which they explain, to believe that these songs were collected, amended, or written by Burns himself. However, a cautionary note should be raised: even some of the texts indisputably by Burns were designed for private consumption among friends rather than for publication. This is not Burns as he might have wished to have been remembered or, in all cases, at his most polished. Finally, the 1959 edition was chosen rather than, for instance, the 1965 re-issue (which has minor changes from 1959), because it was the only version of their edition which Barke, Smith and Ferguson were all able to approve, although Barke, sadly, died before the final corrections of the proofs.

The 1959 edition was presented under the auspices of Sydney Goodsir Smith's Auk Society, for which a subscription of two guineas bought a 'free' copy, anticipating the possibility of prosecution by publishing it openly for sale. This was, of course, still a real, or at least perceived, danger for erotic publications – even those of the relatively mild, heterosexual consensual type of *The Merry Muses* – prior to the *Lady Chatterley* trial of 1960, unsuccessfully prosecuted under the Obscene Publications Act of 1959.[30] High profile cases were within living memory of the editors. Examples included Radclyffe Hall's *The Well of Loneliness,* tried in 1928 over the fears it might encourage lesbianism, and the 1933 American trial of *Ulysses* – even if the latter was not judged to be pornographic. During the former trial, the Chief Magistrate insisted, 'art and obscenity are not disassociated'[31] and this notion discouraged open publication of *The Merry Muses* even in the 1950s. There was, too, the long shadow cast by the 'Hicklin judgement' of 1868, which sought to determine 'whether the tendency of the matter charged as obscenity is to deprave and corrupt those whose minds are open to such immoral influences'. No doubt all these factors caused the 1959 editors to err on the side of caution. A wish to anticipate being questioned along such lines lay behind the statement, too, 'not for maids, ministers or striplings', which is found on the title pages of most of the 19th century editions of *The Merry Muses*.

While attitudes to censorship have, of course, changed since 1959, and scholarship on Burns, too, has moved on immensely, it has to be said that criticism of *The Merry Muses*

---

30 See C.H. Rolph, ed., *The Trial of Lady Chatterley: Regina v Penguin Books Ltd.* (Harmondsworth: Penguin, 1961).

31 Quoted in Jonathan Dollimore, *Sex, Literature and Censorship* (Cambridge: Polity Press, 2001): 100.

is still in its preliminary stages. Ferguson, Smith and Barke were among the first editors to consider the book seriously, as a collection which included significant work by, or recorded by, Burns. Their scholarly articles, drawing attention to the situations where the songs first appeared as well as to their contexts, particularly the comments in the headnotes, are extremely useful. Here, there is much more detailed commentary on the history of the texts than, say, the 1911 notes by M'Naught, writing under the pseudonymn of 'Vindex' for the Burns Federation edition (of which more soon).

The discrete essays by each editor are also illuminating. Ferguson contributes an overview of the history of the various editions and, in particular of the holograph sources he argued were essential in establishing Burns's authorship or at least that the pieces had passed through his hands, whether authored or collected. He makes modest claims for the edition, based on the admirable admission that so much is still unknown about its provenance. Barke's piece, on 'Pornography and Bawdry' is a spirited discussion of erotic material, from the class-room to the barnyard, in early to mid 20th century Scotland, along with a humorous apologia for Burns's forays into the genre: he puts Burns into context, both in terms of his contemporary bawdry climate, and also within the early 20th century, when several of the editions were published. Incidentally, Barke had researched this subject with care, as the Mitchell Library's holdings show, collecting contemporary erotic broadsheets like 'It Happened one Night' and a euphemistic piece using meta-phors around the radio (an 'aerial erected', for instance); his own localised version of 'The Ball of Kirriemuir',

'The Ball of Borevaig' (using chanter-pipe metaphors, reminiscent of 'John Anderson, My Jo'), is quite imaginative.[32] Sydney Goodsir Smith completes the set of essays, with a scholarly discussion of the characteristics of each section. He stresses, too, the importance of making the texts available in a controlled environment, as here, based on the premise outlined above: 'we cannot know Burns completely without them'.

While some of *The Merry Muses* appeared, often in expurgated forms, in editions of Burns's complete poetry or works — most notably in the Aldine edition of 1893 and William Scott Douglas's[33] — the 1959 editors worked primarily from selected key texts of *The Merry Muses* itself: the 1799 Rosebery edition and J.C. Ewing's transcription of it in particular, as well as using the 1911 Burns Federation edition. I have chosen, therefore, to focus on them. The 1959 edition is, in the main, composed of items from the 1799 edition and, for the purposes of comparison, I would like to make some comments on the items they share in common. Incidentally, as this section is, inevitably, rather detailed and dry, the general reader may prefer to skip through the next part of the introduction and move straight on to the following essays.

THE 1799 EDITION

In total, 97 texts appear in the 1959 edition as compared to 86 in the 1799; of these texts, 76 feature in both volumes,

---

[32] The Barke Papers, The Mitchell Library, Box 10B; Box 3A.

[33] See *The Poetical works of Robert Burns*, ed George A. Aitken, 3 vols (London: Aldine, 1893) and William Scott Douglas *The complete poetical works of Robert Burns*, 2 vols (London: Swan Sonnenschein, 1890).

although often with references to slightly different versions. These are indicated in the 1959 headnotes: where a holograph exists, the 1959 editors prefer it to the 1799 version. The 1959 choice of titles shows an intriguing difference with the original edition in that titles are often those of the chorus lines – in other words, the ones the audience would join in on – while the 1959 editors prefer more literary titles. Perhaps this indicates a greater respect for the whole, by the 1799 editors, as performance texts. The 1959 scholars arguably, being more used to dealing with words, treat the texts more as fixed on the page, than as musical possibilities. Barke as a piper, of course, was the exception, but sadly his untimely death meant he had no opportunity to apply that knowledge to the songs.

To be specific, of the 12 songs in the 1959 Section I 'Songs in Burns's Holograph' Part A (by Burns), for instance, seven are also in the 1799: their provenance is listed in the headnotes for individual songs. The omissions from the 1959 edition are intriguing. Sometimes it seems that a song is omitted for not being bawdy enough, although associated with Burns directly. For instance 'Anna' (1799: 8–10), better known as 'Yestreen I had a pint o' wine', is omitted in the 1959 edition. In the 1799 version, Anna's locks are 'raven', rather than the better known 'gowden', and there is an additional two verse 'Postscript by another hand', observing: 'The kirk and state may gae to h—ll, / An' I shall gae to Anna' and that 'Had I on earth but wishes three, / The first should be my Anna'. Similarly, 'My Wife's a wanton wee thing' (1799: 116–7) is omitted by Barke *et al*. 'I am a bard', best known as 'I am a bard of no regard' of *The Jolly Beggars*, in the 1799, is also excluded from 1959, perhaps because its relative innocuousness – even with its euphemisms and playfulness – do not sit well alongside the other items. Equally other pieces are, perhaps, seen as distracting from the Burnsian emphasis of the 1959 edition and, therefore, not used. Therefore, while the 1959 editors include the 'original set' of 'The Mill, Mill-o' from 1779, they omit the version below it, starting 'Beneath a green shade I fand a green maid' (1799: 73–4) which is in Ramsay's *Tea Table Miscellany* of 1724.

Other items which appear in 1799 are not included in 1959, perhaps on the grounds that they have the ring of raw traditional song, as opposed to being the tidied up versions of traditional lyrics which Burns's own compositions, as a whole, seem to be. This might explain the exclusion of pieces like 1799's 'He Till't and she Till't' (1799: 116), set to 'Maggie Lauder'. This is close to a nonsense rhyme about sex: 'He till't, and she till't, / An' a' to mak a lad again'; then he 'dang' and 'bor'd' while she 'flang' and 'roar'd' together, 'An' couldna mak a lassie o't.' Some items are, perhaps, omitted on aesthetic grounds: some certainly are of the 'added in' variety, alluded to above. 1799's 'Johnie Scott' (1799: 112–14), for instance, is excluded. Here, maidens resolve to 'twine' 'your c—t-hair, and [..] my c—t-hair', and to 'cowe our a—e' if that is not enough, to make a coat, and a kilt too, for the hero. A similar dismissal perhaps accounts for the loss of 'My auntie Jean held to the shore' (1799: 13), set to 'John Anderson, my Jo'; she bought a feather bed for 'twenty and a plack' and made 'fifty mark' within it subsequently, 'O! What a noble bargain / Was auntie Jeanie's bed!'

Within the texts, there are instances of quite substantial differences between the holograph versions and the 1799, most of which are drawn to the reader's attention by the 1959 editors, but some of which are not. For instance, with 'Green Grow the Rashes O (A)' (1799: 28–9), the 1799 version lacks the first verse of that in 1959, starting 'In sober hours I am a priest'. It might be suggested that the Fencibles forgot one of the verses in the song, or that Burns added a verse in his version for John Richmond, in 1786, from which Ferguson has taken the text. Nevertheless, the omission alters the meaning somewhat, focussing on the sexual interaction rather than the musings of its narrator and, arguably, making it more direct and preferable for performance, in the way oral transmission usually works.

The Rosebery copy is in itself intriguing, partly because it includes manuscript notes by William Scott Douglas, as Ewing notes in his own set of notes on this copy, now in Dunfermline's Carnegie Library, and discussed below.[34] The Scott Douglas notes are useful, and are cited throughout the 1959 edition headnotes, particularly by Ferguson, as appropriate. They include attributions of the songs — those Scott Douglas considered to be 'by Burns', and those he thought were 'old' (indicated by his notes at the song title). Broadly speaking, the editors of the 1959 edition agree with his ascriptions noting, for instance, with 'Godly Girzie', that this was 'ascribed to Burns by Scott Douglas'. More usually, though, their use of Scott Douglas's notes

---

[34] It is possible to verify that the notes on the 1799 were by Scott Douglas, too, by comparing his handwriting here in other known sources of his writing. See, for instance, his notes in NLS MS 2074. I am grateful to George Stanley of the National Library of Scotland for bringing this to my attention.

on the 1799 Rosebery copy is implicît rather than ftated. For inftance, Scott Douglas notes 'Wad ye do that' (1799 Rosebery copy: 14) is 'old, wîth revisions'; the 1959 edîtors note ît is the 'Original of Burns's song 'Lass, when your mîther is frae hame'.' Sometimes, they omît the notes; for inftance at the end of 'The Bower of Bliss', Scott Douglas notes 'Laft ftanza only by Burns'; this is not referred to in 1959.

More importantly, Scott Douglas also includes variants on some of the songs although, unfortunately, in moft cases, he does not say what his sources are (these were, of course, working notes). There are minor textual changes, for inftance in 'Comin' o'er the Hills o' Coupar' (1799 Rosebery copy: 37—8), the 'Graipît' of the firft verse is changed, in Scott Douglas's hand, to 'Measured' and 'Highland hand' to 'Highland wand' (a change the 1959 edîtors do not support, or even mention); the second change does seem more appropriate, but whether ît is based on Scott Douglas's consultation of specific addît-ional sources is unclear. Wîth 'Daintie Davie' (1799: 67—8; the 1959's A text) in the fourth verse the line 'And, splash! Gaed out his gravy' is scored out and, by hand, 'creeshd them weel wi' gravy' is wrîtten in. In 'The Modiewark' (1799: 68-9) the second line, 'And below my apron has biggît a hill', is changed by Scott Douglas to 'And below my apron has biggît our hills'.

There are changes, too, at times, wîth the tunes: for 'Anna' (not included, as mentioned, in 1959), Scott Douglas suggefts 'The Deareft of the Quorum' and notes, 'In April 1793 Burns "sent this song" to Thomson – to suît "the Banks of Banna" – "Made a good while ago"'. Wîth

'Muirland Meg' (1799 Rosebery copy: 16) the tune title of 'Eppy Macnab' is scored out and 'The Campbells are coming' written in instead; the 1959 editors stick with the tune 'Saw ye my Eppie McNab'. The original tune is in the *Scots Musical Museum* for song 336 and, in his notes to this song, Dick points out it appears in various places including *Curious Scots Tunes* of 1742, *The Caledonian Pocket Companion* of 1754, *Bremner's Reels* of 1768 and *Aird's Airs* of 1782.[35] It is quite different from the march-like 'Campbells are Coming' and so its use would significantly change the reception of the song; it is unclear why Scott Douglas preferred his choice, or on what grounds.

There are significant textual additions too, for instance, in the cases of 'Ellibanks' and 'When Princes and Prelates' ('Poor bodies do naething but m—w' in 1799). These are both acknowledged by DeLancey Ferguson in his headnotes, although in the second instance he merely says they are 'Interpolated stanzas', rather than pointing out they appear in the Rosebery copy in Scott Douglas's hand. Nor do the 1959 editors, particularly in the first section, always refer to the Scott Douglas notes, presumably reflecting the likelihood that DeLancey Ferguson did not see them first-hand. For instance, with respect to 'the Fornicator' (1799 Rosebery copy: 4), Scott Douglas offers a variant reading for the last two lines of the second verse: 'Those hills of snow which wyled me so / To be a fornicator'. There is an alternate reading, too, for the fifth and sixth lines of the fourth verse: 'my sweet wee girl', rather than 'roguish boy', with a following, related change from 'his sake' to 'her sake'.

---

[35] James C. Dick, *Songs of Robert Burns, now first printed with the melodies for which they were written* (London: Henry Frowde, 1903): 489.

Some of Scott Douglas's notes of alternative versions do show substantial differences both from the 1799 edition, and from the 1959 reprinted versions. This is exemplified by 'John Anderson, My Jo', where he offers a number of alternate readings. For the line, 'Frae my tap-knot to my toe, John', for instance, Scott Douglas suggests, 'My skin frae tap to' toe' — giving a more sensual feeling. 'I'm like' becomes 'Is like' in the third verse of 1799, giving the verse more of a coherence. The fourth verse of 1799, opening 'O it is a fine thing', which the 1959 editors include, is deleted by Scott Douglas, with the comment 'delete this verse as not in keeping' (a comment which the 1959 editors do not include). With verse 5, opening 'When you come on before John', opposite the line, 'See that you grip me fine', Scott Douglas has written in, 'And aft requires my helpin hand / John Anderson, my Jo'. The manuscript also includes variations on the verses; for verse 3, for instance, there are variant lines, 'When we were young and yauld, John / We've lain out-ower the dyke'. As well as offering alternative readings, some of Scott Douglas's notes are highly informative. Regarding 'Nae hair on't', for instance (1799: 87), he writes 'This is in the Dublin collection 1769'; his note is transcribed, verbatim, into the 1959 headnote for this item. Similarly, with reference to 'Poor Bodies Do Naething but M—w' (1799: 80–83; 1959's 'When Princes and Prelates'), Scott Douglas's hand-written notes include: 'the poet sent a copy of this to Graham of Fintry in his letter of 5. Janry 1793'; 'July 1794 in letter to Geo. Thomson' and 'A copy forwarded by the poet from Sanquhar to Cleghorn, Saughton Mills, 12 Decr 1792'. The 1959 editors do not include the information on the people featured in the piece which Scott Douglas notes.

Some are fairly obvious ('Br—nsw—ck', for instance, glossed as 'Brunswick', 'Pr—ss—a' as 'Prussia') but some are useful. He notes, for instance, beside the name of Brunswick, the forces, on 'July 3, 1792, arrived at Coblentz with the combined armies of Austria & Prussia' and, at the third verse, opening 'Out over the Rhine', notes this alludes to '[The defeat of the Austrians at Jemappas by Domourier, Nov 1792] near Mons (Austria)'. Much of this information, but not all, is incorporated in the 1959 headnotes.

More substantially, 'The Court of Equity' is handwritten in to the book, including, again, variant readings. This is quite different from Hecht's *Archiv* collated version, as used by Sydney Goodsir Smith in 1959; as Hecht's is composite, and Scott Douglas was rejected by the 1959 editors, it is impossible to offer detailed comparison, but there are substantial differences in phraseology and the ordering of specific lines and sections; some lines in this manuscript are not in the 1959 version. In addition to the manuscript additions, the Rosebery copy includes pasted in items relating to the history of the text; it is unclear if these were added by Scott Douglas or, as is probably more likely given that it was his copy, by the Earl of Rosebery. One, for instance, is a letter regarding 'Burns' Merry Muses' / To the Editor of the *North British Daily Mail*', from James McKie, Kilmarnock, dated 30 August 1871 and it is worth quoting some of this here, as it reflects late 19th century attitudes in general towards *The Merry Muses*. McKie draws attention to his own, forthcoming, two volume edition of Burns's poetry and songs, 'profusely annotated, and prefaced by a chronological memoir of the poet by a fully qualified biographer and editor. Information regarding many productions hitherto attributed to Burns, but now proved to be the work of others, is contained in these volumes'. He draws attention, too, to recent correspondence relating to *The Merry Muses* in the *Mail*, referring to coverage in *The Spectator* regarding 'the coarseness and refinement of Burns's writings and [...] his share in the production of that work.' McKie fumes:

> No such work was ever written or published by Burns. He indeed, form for his own use, a MS. collection of old songs — too free in language, as a whole, for general publication. The very few of his own pieces included in that collection are either taken from his *Jolly Beggars* or are found in 'Johnson's Museum', yet, although free enough for their way, they are by no means considered very gross, Burns is in no way responsible for the publication of the rubbish which has been privately printed since his death.

Such remarks indicate both an awareness of Burns's minimal role in the production of *The Merry Muses*, and the desire of polite society to outwardly condemn such examples of 'grossness'. Of course, for other readers, or perhaps the same readers under different circumstances, the 'grossness' was a large part of their appeal.

THE '1827' EDITIONS

The volume generally languished in obscurity for much of the 19th century, with the possible exception of the early 'Dublin' version,[36] at least until the publication of the '1827' edition. This, it has been argued by Gershon

---

[36] *The merry muses : a choice collection of favourite songs* (Dublin: Printed for the booksellers, [1804?]).

Legman and reiterated by Ross Roy,[37] was probably published in 1872 in London for John Hotten, with the publication numerals reversed, to confuse the perceived censors. It is difficult to be precise in tracing the '1827' text's history, but it spawned a variety of private editions, based on its contents. Most of these appeared, in all probability, from the third quarter of the 19th century into the early 20th century. It is possible that some editors directly consulted the 1799 volume, but more likely, as Roy implies, that they are a self-generating set of texts, based on an assumed provenance going back to the Crochallans, and to Burns.

There are, then, multiple variants of this edition, with more or less minor variations. The publication information they include cannot be trusted, even when they are dated or placed. Some of the dates are blatantly inaccurate and designed as attempts to frustrate any attempts at prosecution for obscenity. When a place of publication is indicated it is usually within Scotland, England or Ireland: Edinburgh, Dublin, Belfast and London are all noted but, again, these locations are not certain, because of the wish to confuse censors. These were limited editions, often stating that they consisted of 90, or 99 copies.

Many, if not all, of the existing '1827' volumes are surveyed by G. Ross Roy in his extremely helpful article on this set of publications, which updates M'Naught's earlier

---

37 See Gershon Legman, *The Horn Book* (New York: University Books, 1964): 148–9 and *The Merry Muses of Caledonia* (New York: University Books, 1965): lxii, Ross Roy, 'The "1827" edition of Robert Burns's *Merry Muses of Caledonia*, *Burns Chronicle* 4th series: XI (1986): 32.

attempt to present the various versions of *The Merry Muses* chronologically. Where M'Naught finds seven versions post the Crochallan edition, noting that most are related, Roy identifies 17 variations on the 1827 text, with estimated dates ranging from 1872 to 1920 (using techniques such as tracing library accession dates to determine the latest possible date of publication).[38] Roy, very helpfully, also gives illustrations of most title pages, allowing the easy identification of individual copies.

---

[38] G. Ross Roy, 'The "1827" Edition of Robert Burns's *Merry Muses of Caledonia*', *Burns Chronicle* 4th series: XI (1986): 32–44; D. M'Naught, 'The Merry Muses of Caledonia', *Burns Chronicle* III (1894): 24–45. There are additional copies which Ross Roy did not have access to at the time of writing. There is, for instance, a substantial number of editions in Edward Atkinson Hornel's collection, available for public consultation in the Hornel Library, Broughton House, Kirkcudbright. Hornel was assisted in purchasing these items by James Cameron Ewing and their correspondence relating to the building of this collection is cited below. Within the Broughton House collection there are copies of Ross Roy's 1 (Su 151–6 and Su 151–7); 3 (Su151–10) which includes manuscript notes by J.C. Ewing; 5 (Su 151-8); 6 (Su 151–5), 10 (Su 151–4), 12 (Su 151–9) along with a 'Dublin' edition of '1830?' (Su 151–12) and a related 'London' edition of '1843' (Su 151–11). The Ewart library in Dumfries also holds an 1827 edition, Ross Roy's 7, at Shelfmark Db151 (821 BUR). There is also an NLS copy of no 7, unlisted by Roy, at NLS HI.77653. Since Ross Roy published his article, there are now several photographic copies of the 1827 available on the internet, for instance, at the time of writing, there were multiple editions, including some from the '1827' sequence, along with Gershon Legman's modern edition, for instance, at http://www. drinkingsongs.net/html/books-and-manuscripts/1700-1799/1799-merry-muses-of-caledonia/index.htm.

In the '1827' editions, items from the 1799 volume mingle with other pieces apparently by Burns and with a selection of other erotic pieces of varying quality, many of them similar to broadside literature, then in circulation. M'Naught is particularly dismissive of their contents: 'edition after edition of 'Merry Muses', more or less spurious, was issued from the disreputable press in all parts of the kingdom, and sold privately for dishonourable gain. These, for the most part, are merely filthy receptacles for the floating obscenity of their periods' with minimal relation to the Crochallan volume. While the language is, perhaps, a little strong — M'Naught claimed to feel 'nausea — trending closely on the physical' in the reading[39] — the statement is largely correct.

As well as many additional items to the 1799 printing, which are soon classified into sections of 'Scottish', 'English' and 'Irish' themed texts, at the end, too, there is a set of bawdy 'Toasts and Sentiments'. Most of this new material has nothing directly to do with Burns, and more to do with the perceived activities, and proclivities, of 18th century British drinking clubs, and their creative descendants. Burns is explicitly named as author on the first Ross Roy text, assumed to be the earliest of around 1872, and thereafter. The '1827' usually includes a preface, which is reprinted from one edition to the next, with occasional variations in the later reprints, explaining the Burns credentials of the whole, and putting the texts into some sort of bawdy context. It also includes two letters: the one from Burns to Robert Ainslie of 3 March

---

39 M'Naught 1894: 31.

1788, describing a sexual encounter with Jean Armour at Mauchline and the letter to James Johnson of 25 May 1788 relating to the marriage to Jean Armour. There is also a copy of the 'Libel Summons' or 'The Court of Equity'. It is not completely clear what all the sources for the '1827' edition were: it is possible it makes reference to the lost Burns manuscript, or the 1799 edition, or to previously published items, or to a combination of all of these, but they follow 19th and early 20th century editing practices, rather than modern standards for collation.

There are two intriguing missing links to all of this. The first is the Allan Cunningham manuscript copy of *The Merry Muses*, discovered by Gershon Legman but, sadly, not available to the 1959 editors (although Smith makes reference to it in later editions). It is contained within an '1825 Dublin' edition of *The Merry Muses* held within the British Museum, with additional items reprinted in Legman's *The Horn Book* and discussed very fully again in his edition of *The Merry Muses of Caledonia*.[40] Interested readers should consult Legman's edition directly for further information. Its main value lies in pointing out Burns's authorship in one or two instances, as Smith notes in the second edition of the Barke, Smith and Ferguson version, where certain texts (as mentioned below) are transferred between sections in the book on the strength of Legman's statements.

---

[40] See Gershon Legman *The Horn Book* (New York: University Books, 1964): 129–69; Gershon Legman *The Merry Muses of Caledonia* (New York: University Books, 1965), particularly 271–3.

THE EWING TRANSCRIPT

Another intriguing aside is the abortive edition planned
by the art dealer and bibliophile William Craibe Angus
(1830–1899), based on the Crochallan volume and to be
edited by William Ernest Henley (1849–1903), based on
a transcription from the 1799 edition, by J.C. Ewing.
This volume, as Smith points out in his 'Merry Muses
Introductory' was consulted by M'Naught while he
prepared the 1911 Burns Federation edition and at some
point beforehand, as he mentions in the 1894 article cited
above. Barke and Smith consulted this directly, and it
played an influential role on their developing under-
standing of the textual history. Ewing made two copies of
his transcription. One of these, which Barke and Smith
saw, and made Ferguson aware of, is still held by the Local
Studies department of the Andrew Carnegie Library in
Dunfermline, within the Murison collection. It is
probable that the other, as Legman speculates from an
informed position, was made available by Henley to John
S. Farmer, who made a serious attempt to rehabilitate *The
Merry Muses* in his *Merry Songs and Ballads* of 1895, including
several texts from the 1799 edition.[41]

The transcript now in Dunfermline, which I would like to
consider because of its effect on the 1959 edition, is a
monumental piece of work. Bound in a fine volume with
a handwritten black and red title page, it includes a note,
dated Glasgow, 21 September 1912, by Ewing. Here he
explains that he made two copies around 1893 for Craibe

---

[41] Gershon Legman, *The Merry Muses of Caledonia* (New York:
University Books, 1965), p.268.

Angus for the Henley edition, based on Scott Douglas's annotated 1799 edition (the copy now in the National Library of Scotland and considered above): 'that intention, however, was never carried out'.[42]

Ewing includes two pasted-in letters from Henley to Angus; the first is dated 19 of March 1892, and states Henley's desire to see 'the edition of '41'. He promises to discuss a reprint with Bruce (R.T. Hamilton Bruce, 'who acquired the original edition from Mr W.C. Angus' according to Ewing's handwritten note here); Henley adds, 'I hope to pull it off'. A second letter was evidently enclosed when this volume was being returned: 'Here is the book: one of the most astonishing, I think, in English. Please don't part with it till we can arrange a reprint: to which I propose to contribute a prefatory note. And let me have it back as soon as is convenient'. Henley evidently had serious intentions, noting that there were, 'several points to be elucidated in the matter of this first edition: but each of these anon.' It is likely that the project was stymied by the death of Henley, and Angus, before the close of the 19th century, although it is likely that it informed Henley and his co-editor T.F. Henderson's choices, in their 1896 Centenary edition of *The Poetry of Robert Burns*.[43]

Barke and Smith consulted the Ewing transcription at an early stage of their work, having been alerted to its exist-

---

42 'The Merry Muses of Caledonia', bound volume including transcript and notes by J.C. Ewing, Andrew Carnegie Library, Local Studies, 1247a.

43 *The Poetry of Robert Burns*, 4 vols, ed W.E. Henley and T.F. Henderson (London: Caxton, 1896).

ence by Maurice Lindsay. Equally, they made Ferguson aware of its existence, although until quite a late stage of the editorial process he doubted the existence of the 1799 (thought to be 1800 at this stage) edition itself. The Ewing transcript, as can be seen in the editor's correspondence, played a major role in the early preparations for the 1959 editions. Barke made a partial transcript of some of Ewing's introductory notes but, more importantly finding it — again through the aid of Lindsay — allowed the team to establish the existence and whereabouts of the 1799 volume. However, by the time of the publication of their edition, the 1959 editors, having seen the Rosebery volume, were less convinced of the value of Ewing's transcript. In his 'Merry Muses Introductory', Smith indicates that the text was not wholly accurate, and that its existence had damaging consequences. He points out it was copied for J.S. Farmer, to publish and sell in a limited edition; the inaccuracies are compounded, Smith states, by being adopted by M'Naught in his 1911 edition.

Certainly, there are shortcomings to the Ewing transcription, particularly by modern editorial standards. However, its existence gives some insight into how Henley might have presented the text, had he lived to see it through to completion. It seems likely this edition might have been close to the facsimile edition of 1999, in drawing on the 1799 edition as closely as possible, albeit with Scott Douglas's interpolations incorporated into the text, along with some pre-editorial changes made by Ewing.

Ewing is respectful towards the 1800 text, and towards the notes that Scott Douglas had left on his own copy. He transcribes the text itself in black on the right hand pages of the volumes, noting Scott Douglas's manuscript attributions (to Burns, beginning with 'The Fornicator',[44] or to 'old' songs) and alternate tunes for the settings. He leaves the left hand pages of the transcript volume blank in the main, but notes alternate readings, where Scott Douglas has indicated them, in red there, with superscript referencing, also in red, at the appropriate places on the right hand texts. To use the example of 'The Fornicator' again, at the end of the second verse, for instance, an alternative reading for 'Those limbs so clean, where I between / Commenced Fornicater' is given: 'Or – Those hills of snow that wyled me so / To be a Fornicator'; in verse 4 an alternative reading for 'My rogish boy, his mother's joy' is indicated: 'My sweet wee girl, her mother's pearl' and, for the 'his *pater*' and 'his sake', 'her' in both instances. Other examples of songs where alternative wordings are given, include 'Yon, yon lassie' (pp.55–6 in the transcript, pp.46–7 in 1799).

This is certainly not a literal transcription in the modern sense. Occasionally, Ewing omits one of the Scott Douglas notes. For instance, with 'Our Gudewife's sae modest' there is no note, as in the Rosebery copy, of 'By Burns'. It is difficult to know, in such an instance, if the omission is deliberate – did Ewing disagree? – or, as is more likely, a copyist's error. In other words, the transcript – as Smith indicates – is not always wholly reliable. Ewing's preparatory editing, in several places, is evident. He appears, as he goes along, to be rationalising the text for the planned edition, while he is transcribing. Some of his amendments are relatively minor. For instance, Ewing does not use

---

[44] pp.1–4 of the Ewing transcript; pp.3–4 of the 1799 *The Merry Muses.*

capital letters for each word in the titles as the 1800 edition or for the descriptive 'TUNE' but, instead, uses standard sentence capitalisation. Nor does he have capitals on the first, or first two, words of the song, as was the practice in 1799, using run-on sentences instead. He is usually faithful to the punctuation of the original — for instance the three exclamation marks used in verse 3 of 'For A' That and A' That' — but occasionally changes a colon into a semi-colon for line-endings. In a more interventionist manner, in places Ewing changes the spelling of the 1799 text, possibly for what he saw as rationalisation. For instance, where the 1799 edition has 'The Fornicater', Ewing has changed this to 'Fornicator'.[45] Barke, Smith and Ferguson also follow this spelling, incidentally, and it may be that Ewing, like the 1959 editors, is basing his change here on his knowledge of Burns's holographs; Ferguson's source text is 'the Davidson Cook transcript, from the Honresfield Manuscript, which is the 1959 editors' source text. In the same song, 'quarintine' in the 1799 is corrected to 'quarantine' by Ewing as it is, too, by Barke, Smith and Ferguson. In other cases, spelling changes are evidently intended as corrections to what might be read, from a 19th century perspective, as mistakes in the original. For instance in 'The Jolly Gauger',[46] 'An[d] weel gang nae mair a rovin'' in the original becomes 'An' we'll gang nae mair a rovin'' in Ewing's version, as in 1959.

Unlike Barke, Ferguson and Smith, Ewing fills in the blanks in the 1799 edition, perhaps on the grounds that his

---

45 The Ewing transcript: 1–4; in the 1799 *The Merry Muses of Caledonia*: 3–4.

46 The Ewing transcript: 33–4; in the 1799 *The Merry Muses of Caledonia*: 31–2.

contemporaries will not be overly shocked or possibly for ease of reading: 'm—w', therefore becomes 'maw' through-out, 'a—e' 'arse', 'p—e' 'pintle', 'c—t' 'cunt', 'f—g' 'fucking' and, 'd—d' 'damn'd'. If, however, Ewing is unsure which word is missing, he leaves the blank in place. In 'Errock Braes', for instance, while 'arse' and 'pintle' both appear, for 'b—s' Ewing has 'b ?', presumably as he is not sure about the missing word. In a responsible way, in 'The case of Conscience', although 'cunt' is filled in, the ambiguous 'xxx' and 'xxx' of the original (and p.25 of the transcript) are left in this form by Ewing.

Sometimes, it seems as if Ewing is feeling the burden of writing all this out by hand. On (28) of the transcript (the 1799 edition: 27), for instance, after the second verse he writes out the chorus in full, but with the third, writes 'Chorus, as above'. On the other hand, where the 1799 edition usually abbreviates the choruses after their first appearances, writing out the initial phrase and then an '&c', Ewing more usually writes out the chorus in full. On occasion, there are more substantial changes involving the ordering of choruses and verses. Ewing, for instance, some-times re-orders the song verses and choruses from the standard practices used in the 1799 edition. Where the original usually prints the chorus first, before the first verse, and then repeats the chorus throughout the text, Ewing likes to start with the first verse and follow this verse with the chorus's first appearance. This is his practice, for instance, in 'The Reel of Stumpie'.[47] While this might seem rational it is, arguably, a significant change, perhaps altering perfor-

---

47 The Ewing transcript: 27; *The Merry Muses of Caledonia*: 26.

mance practices reflected in the 1800 text and followed by the Crochallan Fencibles. Similarly, the removal of quotation marks, in inſtances like 'The Patriarch', change the emphasis on dialogue which is often such a characteriſtic feature of tradiſtional song. The Ewing/ Henley ediſtion would, perhaps, have had minimal awareness of performance issues, focussing on the texts as poems rather than as songs.

THE 1911 EDITION

The firſt ediſtion of the *Muses* which made any effort to reſtrict its content to Burns's own compoſitions and collected pieces was the 1911 Burns Federation ediſtion, compiled anonymously — under the pseudonym of 'Vindex' — by Duncan M'Naught, of the *Burns Chronicle*.[48] Described as the 'original ediſtion', with the claim it is 'A Vindication of Robert Burns in connection with the above publication and the spurious ediſtions which succeeded it', it includes an introduction by M'Naught, which includes the main findings of his 1894 article.[49] It summarises responses to *The Merry Muses* from other readers, including Wordsworth, who saw *The Merry Muses,* probably in its 1799 form, and found it full of 'low, tame and loathsome ribaldry', thinking it to be 'an abominable pamphlet' and adding, although possibly not with the thoughtfulness that the remark implies, 'the truth is […] there is not one verse

---

[48] *The Merry Muses of Caledonia (Original Ediſtion). A Collection of Favouriſte Scots Songs Ancient and Modern; Selected for use of the Crochallan Fencibles* (no place of publication: the Burns Federation), 1911.

[49] See D. M'Naught , D., 'The Merry Muses of Caledonia', *Burns Chronicle* III (1894): 24–45 and 'The "Merry Muses" Again', *Burns Chronicle* XX (1911): 105–19.

in that miscellany that was ever publicly acknowledged by Burns, nor is there above a single page that can be traced to his manuscript'.[50] Finally, M'Naught makes eight points about the 1799 text which can be summarised thus: that Burns made the collection for his own use, and for that of the Crochallan Fencibles; that he saw it as 'a historical and literary curiosity' to be kept discretely; that 'it was filched from his wife on false pretences after his decease'; that it was printed in Dumfries, c.1800; that 85 songs appeared, without Burns's name attached; that only 40 of these were reprinted in subsequent editions; that a Dublin collection was printed before 1827 with *The Merry Muses* title but no reference to Burns; that the '1827' edition appeared, including the letters mentioned.[51] M'Naught follows the 1799 edition fairly closely, with some minor title changes. The 1799 title of 'I rede you beware of the ripples', for instance, becomes 'Beware of the Ripples'; the untitled song which follows on 'Our Gudewife's Sae Modest', and is set to the tune of 'John Anderson, my Jo', indexed in 1799 by its first line, is given the title by M'Naught of 'My Auntie Jean'. As an appendix, he gives 'The Court of Equity; or, The Libel Summons', collated from the British Museum copy and from other sources, including Scott Douglas's version and, as I have above in relation to the 1959 copy, he gives variations between these two versions, along with that in the 1827 *Merry Muses* and in the expurgated version which appeared in the 1863 Aldine edition of Burns's works, edited by G.A. Aitken.[52]

---

[50] Quoted *The Merry Muses of Caledonia (Original Edition)* 1911: xxvi.

[51] *The Merry Muses of Caledonia (Original Edition)* 1911: xxix.

[52] *The Poetical works of Robert Burns*, ed George A. Aitken 3 vols, (London: Aldine, 1893).

There are useful, albeit brief, headnotes by M'Naught too; by comparing these with the 1959, it can be seen that the modern editors had made explicit reference to M'Naught or, at least, approached the text with similar interests in mind. For instance, with the first piece, 'The Fornicator', M'Naught's note makes similar points to Ferguson's, although the earlier writer is slightly fuller, offering observations on the song:

> This is an early production of Burns, and refers to the public rebuke administered to him by the Kirk Session, in the Autumn of 1784, following on the birth of 'his dear-bought Bess', whose mother was Elizabeth Paton, a servant of the family while in Lochlea. An altered version will be found in Scott Douglas's Kilmarnock edition (vol ii., p.420). Burns usually draws upon his imagination when writing in this vein. The 'roguish boy', for instance, was of the opposite sex in reality.[53]

Similarly, the second item in M'Naught , 'Beware of the Ripples', has a headnote which is almost identical to Smith's, in the 1959 section II. Compare Smith's observations there to M'Naught's: 'This is an old song, on which Burns modelled 'The Bonnie Moor-Hen', which Clarinda advised him not to publish "for your sake and mine", in a letter dated January 30, 1788'. Smith and M'Naught only diverge on their second sentence, where M'Naught has, 'Scott Douglas published it in his Kilmarnock Edition, with a quotation from the old version in his introductory note (Vol. II., p.275). In other notes, as might be expected, the two editions are somewhat different. For instance, in Section IV with 'Jockey was a

---

53 *The Merry Muses of Caledonia (Original Edition)* 1911: 33.

bonny lad', M'Naught merely states, 'an old song which appears in the Appendix to Herd's collection',[54] where the 1959 editors note, in addition, that 'the changes are all improvements poetically and were almost certainly made by Burns when transcribing the song'. However, the 1959 editors evidently used M'Naught as a major source for their own work, both there and in the subsequent editions which used the 1959 as their source text.

POST 1959

After the Federation edition, there were rather fewer publications of the *Muses*, up to the time the present copy text was published. There were various offshoots from the 1959 edition itself. Smith and Ferguson oversaw the second edition, which was the US one, appearing in 1964 with G.P. Putnam's Sons, New York. Basically, this follows the 1959 text, using the same illustrations and ordering of the texts. One substantial change, though, is that Robert Burns is now credited on the title page; there is also the addition of new glossary by Sydney Goodsir Smith.[55] Smith notes, too, in an additional paragraph to the foreword, dated Edinburgh, January 1964, that Gershon Legman had recently discovered Allan Cunningham's manuscript in the British Museum Library, 'which suggests

---

54 *The Merry Muses of Caledonia (Original Edition)* 1911: 97.

55 Robert Burns *The Merry Muses of Caledonia*. Edited by James Barke and Sydney Goodsir Smith. With a Prefatory Note and some authentic Burns Texts contributed by J. DeLancey Ferguson (New York: G.P. Putnam's Sons, 1964). Although the glossary is not credited to Smith, its manuscript existence in the National Library of Scotland, at NLS ACC 10397/44 shows that he was the primary author, and corrector, of this.

(or even, I believe, proves) that six songs in Section III originals' are actually Burns and indicates 'the purified versions of these in the Aldine edition of 1839 are in fact forged expurgations by Cunningham himself.'[56] This affects 'Ye Hae Lien Wrang,' 'Comin' O'er the Hills o' Coupar', 'How Can I Keep my Maidenhead?', 'Wad Ye Do That?', 'There Cam a Cadger' and 'Jenny Macraw'. The songs, however, remain in Section III at this point.

When the edition went into its third incarnation, and through its third publisher, printed in 1965 in London, for W.H. Allen, it now had a pleasant cameo, presumably of Pan playing his pipes, or a satyr, impressed on the front cover.[57] The new Foreword is slightly rephrased — dated Edinburgh, August 1964 — based on the fact that Legman's work had now appeared. Making the same observation about Cunningham's contribution as before, this time Smith moves the six songs at question into section IV, 'Collected by Burns'. The notes to these songs, too, are amended accordingly. Where 'Ye Hae Lien Wrang', for instance, in 1959 and in 1964, has 'From MMC. Original of Burns's fragmentary song of same name' (*Ald* 1839, II, 155) in 1965 it is now 'From MMC. Attributed to Burns by GL', in 1965 (p.106). Similarly, with 'How can I keep my Maidenhead', there is a change: the second sentence, giving

56 Robert Burns *The Merry Muses of Caledonia*. Edited by James Barke and Sydney Goodsir Smith. With a Prefatory Note and some authentic Burns Texts contributed by J. DeLancey Ferguson (New York: G.P. Putnam's Sons, 1964): 6.

57 Robert Burns *The Merry Muses of Caledonia*. Edited by James Barke and Sydney Goodsir Smith. With a Prefatory Note and some authentic Burns Texts contributed by J. DeLancey Ferguson (London: W.H. Allen, 1965).

the songs as the 'original' of Burns's 'I met a lass, a bonnie lass' is excised, and a new sentence is added at the end 'Attributed to Burns by GL'. In the note to 'How can I keep my Maidenhead', the second sentence is deleted and, instead, Smith adds, 'Another version, almost certainly by Burns, in the Cunningham MS is printed in *The Horn Book* (GL, 137). In the respective headnotes to 'Wad ye do that?' and 'There Cam a Cadger', the second sentence of each is deleted, and replaced with 'Attributed to Burns by GL'. In the headnote to 'Jenny Macraw' the second sentence goes again, and is replaced by 'Attributed to Burns in Cunningham MS' (GL, 185). Aside from those changes, the edition is identical to the 1959. This volume was reprinted by Panther, in London, in 1970, as a paperback, adopting the same changes as in 1965.[58] The only shift is from hardback to paperback, with a period-specific cover wrap-around illustration by Graham Percy, in reds and yellows. This includes glimpses, for the first time, of bared breasts in what appears to be either a very liberal tavern, or brothel. A tartan curtain hints at the Scottish connotations and a strap line is added: 'A collection of bawdry by Scotland's earthiest poet'. To round off the set with its original publisher *The Merry Muses* came out, finally, with Macdonald, in 1982.[59]

---

[58] Robert Burns *The Merry Muses of Caledonia*, edited by James Barke and Sydney Goodsir Smith with a prefaratory note and some authentic Burns texts by J. DeLancey Ferguson (London: Panther, 1966), reprinted 1970.

[59] *The merry muses of Caledonia. Robert Burns*, edited by James Barke and Sydney Goodsir Smith; with a prefatory note and some authentic Burns texts contributed by J. DeLancey Ferguson (Edinburgh: Macdonald Publishers, 1982).

Most modern editions, with various editors and pub-
lishers, usually draw strongly on the 1959 text and its
descendants. They include the uncredited version of Barke,
Smith and Ferguson in *Bawdy verse and folksongs written and
collected by Robert Burns*, introduced by Magnus Magnusson.
Magnusson's edition unashamedly uses the Barke, Smith
and Ferguson text, following the 1965 ordering, without
giving them credit.[60] Minor changes include titling the
first section 'From Burns's Manuscripts' (presumably to
attract a more popular audience than 'Songs in Burns's
Holograph' might do), then the text follows the 1965
edition of the 1959 text exactly, using the same section
titles, with two exceptions: for II, the two parts of the first
editors' title is reversed, into 'By or attributed to Burns —
from printed sources', and the sixth section becomes
simply 'The Libel Summons'; the glossary of the
American edition, and the 1965, is also included.
Magnusson's Introduction is purposely pitched at the
popular audience: useful in its way, characterising the
songs as 'boisterous', 'down-to-earth' and 'fun'. He
includes a capsule biography of Burns, commentary on
some of his other poems, like 'To a Mouse', a summary of
his personal liaisons, and brief remarks on the Crochallan
Fencibles. DeLancey Ferguson, Barke and Smith's
headnotes have been removed, along with their essays.
Magnusson, implicitly, is presented as editor, even if the
title page says only that the work is 'introduced' by him.

---

[60] Magnus Magnusson *Bawdy Verse and Folksongs. Written and Collected by
Robert Burns* (London: Macmillan, 1982) first published 1965 as
The Merry Muses of Caledonia (W.H. Allen & Co, Ltd.)

The Paul Harris edition, as *The Secret Cabinet of Robert Burns*,[61] is much more overtly, and skilfully, edited. The selection is smaller than that in the 1959 edition and those which follow on from it, with 61 texts in total, with glossaries, helpfully, with each individual text. The ordering of texts is somewhat different from the 1959: the first four items, for instance, are in the 1959 section IV (Collected by Burns) and additional texts are included, like 'Wat ye what my minnie did' but the vast majority of texts in the Harris edition also appear in 1959, and often appear to use the 1959 edition as their source. The new headnotes, though, are extremely useful, scholarly and sometimes go beyond the 1959 editors, who are fully acknowledged where used. Critical commentary is offered on the songs as literary works; this is more detailed than in the 1959, and cross-referenced with later editions, such as Legman's. An in-depth knowledge of Burns is evident, with references to J.C. Dick and other scholars, along with prototype texts, like those in Allan Ramsay's *Tea-Table Miscellany*.[62] Other significant editions include Eric Lemuel Randall's, of 1966, which includes very full headnotes which owe a debt to Legman, a generalist's essay and illustrations.[63] Finally, the 1999 facsimile edition of the 1799, by Ross Roy and with a useful accompanying essay on the significance of *The Merry Muses*,[64] takes the set to its starting point, providing a

---

[61] *The Secret Cabinet of Robert Burns. Merry Muses of Caledonia* (Edinburgh: Paul Harris, 1979).

[62] See, for instance, 'Andrew An' his Cuttie Gun' in *The Secret Cabinet of Robert Burns*: 35.

[63] *The Merry Muses Illustrated*, edited by Eric Lemuel Randall (London: Luxor Press, 1966).

[64] *Robert Burns and The Merry Muses*, (Columbia, SC: University of South Carolina Press for the Thomas Cooper Library: 1999).

reliable text for the earliest known version of *The Merry Muses*.

THE 1959 EDITORS

The 1959 edition, ultimately, represents a labour of scholarship as well as a labour of love: the letters give some indication of the gargantuan effort involved, and one which yielded very tangible results. This edition is as much, if not more, their creation than Burns's. At the time of editing Barke was at the height of his fame as the acclaimed novelist – albeit with some dissenting voices – of the *Immortal Memory* of Burns, the multi-parted novel which follows the poet from birth to death. He had researched the life in great depth, as the Mitchell papers document fully, although the depth of his research on Burns has still not been fully recognised.[65] Smith, equally, was making his reputation as a poet and editor, having recently published on *Robert Fergusson*'s poetry.[66] He brought considerable *elan* and scholarship to the project. Ferguson was the most scholarly of the three, well respected for his Burns *Letters* and the biography *Pride and Passion* (1939). Sadly, Barke died before the edition was seen through to completion. The making of the edition, too (which took a mammoth 11 years to complete) was beset with problems.

---

[65] There is still no major study of Barke as a novelist, or scholar on Burns, although it is hoped that the proceedings of the conference on his centenary, which took place in Glasgow at the Mitchell Library in 2005, will be forthcoming in the future, co-edited by Valentina Bold and David Borthwick.

[66] Sydney Goodsir Smith, ed., *Robert Fergusson, 1750–1774* (Edinburgh: Nelson, 1952).

The essays and notes accompanying the 1959 text offer only an overview of the immense scholarship, and years of discussion, that went into the making of the edition. This was conducted over more than a decade and — to paraphrase the famous statement in the Whistler trial — reflected the knowledge of lifetimes. Fortunately, the correspondence between the three writers, and those they consulted, are now in public collections. The Barke papers are a discrete, and substantial, collection in the Mitchell Library in Glasgow, and include correspondence from and to DeLancey Ferguson. Smith's papers are in separate collections. The National Library of Scotland holds his personal copy of the American edition, with extensive annotations. Edinburgh University Library has the related correspondence between Smith and Gershon Legman, which shows that Legman wished to be involved in the edition prior to his publication of *The Merry Muses* with Cunningham's inclusions. He shared information fairly freely with Smith in the early stages of their correspondence but, as the 1959 *Merry Muses* moved to publication, became somewhat more cagey. There is also correspondence between Smith and the scholar and bibliophile W.N.H. Harding, and the folklorist Hamish Henderson, who responded openly to Smith's queries about parallels between Burns's work and 1950s Scottish folk culture. Henderson, for instance, in a letter of September 1955, offered to arrange 'a listening session some time this winter', so that Smith could hear 'a number of the *The Merry Muses* songs which are still in folksay circulation', inviting Barke to join them on that occasion.[67]

---

[67] The Barke Papers, Box 1D; Box 2D.

Because the letters show how the edition evolved and the editors' respective responsibilities — not much of this is reflected in the published edition — it is worth mentioning at least a few of the highlights here, both between Barke and Ferguson, and Smith and Barke. According to those involved, as noted by Smith in *Lines Review* and mentioned by Barke in his correspondence with Ferguson, the 1959 edition seems to have come about largely due to a chance meeting in a bar in 1955, by which time the project was already quite advanced, between Sydney Goodsir Smith and James Barke. While Smith's memory of the meeting is fairly convivial,[68] Barke evidently took some time to consider his offer of working on the book collaboratively, rather than competing, as is evident from his letter to Ferguson of 10 March 1955:

> Sydney Goodsir Smith, a youngish Edinburgh poet, was about to issue a private edition of *The Merry Muses* based on M'Naught. I met him the other day and told him he was wasting his time and that you had the proper texts for most of Burns's own efforts in this line.
>
> He now wants me to collaborate. I'm tempted. But I've just told him (in a letter) that I can do nothing without your consent. And, to quote: 'if there is to be any recompense going he's (you are) entitled to a share.'
>
> I shall not divulge or use your texts as given to me without your consent; you must be paid *pro rata*: you should be acknowledged.[69]

Barke hopes that Ferguson will 'come in' as an editor and, relatively quickly, the three did agree to collaborate. Their

[68] Sydney Goodsir Smith, obituary of James Barke, *Lines Review* (14) Spring 1958. See, too, The Barke Papers, Box 2B.

[69] The Barke Papers. Box 7A.

correspondence shows very different dynamics at work. Barke played the central role: writing regularly to Ferguson and Smith; the latter two corresponded less regularly – remembering, too, that while Barke and Ferguson corresponded for over 10 years, the relationship between Ferguson and Smith was rather newer. However, they wrote fairly frequently too, as might be expected, once Barke had passed away. Barke and Ferguson had a close, but respectful relationship; Barke was keenly aware that Ferguson was the senior scholar, and Ferguson treats Barke with affection but more as a student than as a peer. Barke and Smith have an open and spirited correspondence, showing that they enjoyed a social, as well as scholarly, friendship. Smith, while acknowledging Ferguson's seniority, and the *gravitas* which his name added to the project, seems sometimes to have been irritated by the senior scholar (largely by suggestions, for instance, that Smith pay occasional visits to Abbotsford, or Dunfermline, being unaware of the distance and difficulty in such trips from Edinburgh in the 1950s). It is evident that there were editorial clashes, at least by 1955, with Barke taking Smith's side, on occasion, when Ferguson wanted to apply stringent scholarly standards, which Smith sometimes thought to be inappropriate to their audience. Between December 1955 and January 1956, in particular, relations grew fraught and frosty as Barke and Smith got on with their work, and Smith began to feel cut off from Ferguson. It was only Barke's diplomatic skills that salvaged the project. On other occasions, and particularly towards the end of Barke's life, when his energy was understandably waning, Smith played peace-maker. The idea of discrete sections, for instance, to avoid Ferguson pulling out of the project towards the end, was Smith's.

It is evident, too, from the papers that, while Ferguson had contributed a great deal in terms of locating manuscripts in the earliest stages of the project, that Smith was increasingly responsible, latterly, for chasing up loose ends, and for much of the irritating checks, including the proof reading, that come towards the end of any scholarly project. Smith also played a useful role at an earlier stage in tracking down, for instance, the 1799 edition, bringing in the assistance of his contacts, and especially Maurice Lindsay, as his foreword acknowledges, to locate the Rosebery copy. Smith also seems to have been the first to raise the idea of including music, which Barke thought should only accompany Burns's own texts. Unfortunately, Barke's extensive notes — many made through the correspondence with Ferguson, of which he made sure his secretary took copies — do not feature strongly in the published edition, and it is for this reason, that I would like to discuss them here.

By the point that Smith started working with them, Barke and DeLancey Ferguson were already fairly far advanced in their planning of the edition and had built a strong scholarly partnership. They had corresponded since 1946 and often; usually more than once a month. They engaged in a great deal of discussion about the details of Burns's life, and were open in their sharing of their ongoing interpretations of his work, correspondence, and acquaintances. As well as discussions of their own work, they shared materials: Ferguson sent Barke articles on more than one occasion, and Barke sent copies of his books, dedicating *The Wonder of All the Gay World* to Ferguson.[70] They discussed other writers on Burns, too. Catherine Carswell, for instance, is considered in detail and with some ambivalence. The *Burns Chronicle* comes in for hostile scrutiny. In a letter of 17 December 1946, for instance, Ferguson introduces what will be a repeated theme in the correspondence: his lasting dislike of J.C. Ewing who, he believed − he refers to this belief throughout the correspondence − blocked the publication of some of his work in the *Chronicle,* as well as speaking out against him in different contexts.[71] He suggests, too, that the early 20th century editors of the *Burns Chronicle* were, at times, malicious, alleging for instance on 7 September 1947 that Ewing had asked Lachlan M'Lean Watt 'to annihilate [Robert] Fitzhugh' because, 'they were so afraid that they might advertise Fitz's book that they ommitted all specific reference to it'.[72] Most of the correspondence, however, is more amiable.

The very first letter in the papers from Barke to Ferguson is dated 1 June 1946. Here, he sends Ferguson an inscribed copy of *The Wind that Shakes the Barley* and expresses his debt to Ferguson's work. He opens the way, too, for future discussions, hoping, 'you would be favourably disposed to helping me to gain access to sources of information at present closed to me.'[73] Ferguson replied on 30 September 1946, thanking Barke for his compliment, and expressing admiration for the novelist: 'you have made

[70] James Barke *The Wonder of All the Gay World* (London: Collins, 1949).

[71] The Barke Papers, Box 9C and copy in Box 7A.

[72] The Barke Papers, Box 9C and copy in Box 7A.

[73] The Barke Papers, Box 7A.

young Robin alive and credible, which is more than the avowed biographers are able to do.' However, he could not help Barke with sources in Scotland, as his two closest friends, 'who never failed me in assisting my researches', George Shirley and Davidson Cook, were by then deceased.[74]

The friendship developed rapidly and, by late 1946, the two men were exchanging views about *The Merry Muses*. A letter of 16 November shows that, by then, Barke had heard of the Dunfermline volume and was considering a new edition of *The Merry Muses*; he enters the debate, too, regarding the 1800 edition: 'I seem to have been working along the same lines as you with regard to the so-called *Merry Muses*. And I think I can establish the fact that the 1800 edition (if there ever was such an edition) was not printed from Burns's manuscript'. Barke also draws Ferguson's attention to sources he had recently discovered, 'including a holograph volume by that Holy Willie of Burnsiana — J.C. Ewing, dated 1912 — prior to the M'Naught! I have yet to examine the documents. When I have done I will write to you more fully'. Barke's respect for Ferguson is evident, as he hopes he will be worthy of the 'honour' Ferguson has done him by corresponding, as 'the greatest Burns scholar who has so far appeared on the scene, and whose work in Burns will live as long as Burns lives.'[75]

Ferguson was frank with Barke at all times. On 17 December 1946, for instance, he surprises Barke by introducing his discovery of Currie's interpolation (mentioned in his

---

[74] The Barke Papers, Box 9C and copy in Box 7A.

[75] The Barke Papers, Box 7A.

essay here) putting into Burns's mouth the statement 'a very few of them are my own'. At this stage, Ferguson had the notion of publishing *The Merry Muses*, but few publishers were interested (later, Gershon Legman would try to persuade him to publish in France). Ferguson evidently was not familiar yet with the Ewing manuscript, and is intrigued by Barke's reference to it. It is worth quoting Ferguson's letter, as a typical example of the openness and sharing of scholarly information that took place between these two very different writers:

> What you say about *The Merry Muses* comes most appositely. A few weeks ago, I discovered, right here in New York, the holograph of Burns's letter to John McMurdo (# 604 in my edition). No editor since Currie has seen it. Currie's text is complete, except for the formal conclusion — or rather, it's more than complete. It's the letter, you remember, in which Burns refers to his collection of bawdy songs; I, along with a lot of other people, have quoted from it the sentence, I now discover, was interpolated by Currie; it isn't in the MS at all. No doubt a good many of the verses in Burns's collection were folksongs that he had taken down, but he made no effort to minimize his own contribution.

> I have chuckled several times over the idea that J.C. Ewing was responsible for a holograph collection of suppressed Burnsiana. If you ever get a sight of the volume, I hope you'll tell me all about it. I've long thought of preparing an honest edition of the suppressed poems, and to secure the involuntary aid of Ewing in such a project would be the perfect revenge. So far, unfortunately, I've not been able to find a publisher interested in the project, and I have no desire to print privately and clandestinely.[76]

---

[76] The Barke Papers, Box 9C and copy in Box 7A.

In his reply, of 1 March 1947, Barke is grateful for the information about the Currie interpolation and introduces the idea of a new four to six volume 'complete edition' of Burns's work, to be published by Collins (who was producing Barke's novels on Burns): 'I would handle the poems and songs. We might agree to check back on each other's works'. The negotiations for this project would take up a great deal of energy from both authors and is discussed at length in their correspondence. Unfortunately, despite meeting with Ferguson in America, and considering the project at length, Collins pulled out at the last moment, leaving Barke to complete his own anthology of Burns's work, which he refers to here as a 'Best of Burns – Poetry, Prose, and Music' instead.[77]

It is in the spring of 1947, too, that the notion of collaboration on the bawdy work or, as Ferguson refers to it, the 'suppressed poems', is first raised, still as part of their proposed complete edition. Ferguson asks: 'What are you planning to do with the suppressed poems? I have one or two which are wholly unpublished, and the complete texts of several others which are garbled or incomplete in *The Merry Muses*'. He thinks publishing these would be timely: 'In view of the sort of language which nowadays gets printed in novels, it seems fairly silly to continue to draw veils over Burns's fairly innocent bawdry'.

In the draft of his response, of April 1947, as well as stressing the need to include music with the complete works, Barke asked Ferguson specifically for opinions on

---

[77] The Barke Papers, Box 7A. See James Barke, ed, *Poems and Songs of Robert Burns* (London: Collins, 1955).

The Merry Muses: 'What am I going to do about *The Merry Muses*? (I prefer to call this The Crochallan Song Book). I will press for the publication of the authentic Burns bawdy poems in the definitive edition. I may not win the fight; but your influence will be valuable'. In terms of copy text, he had considered the various possibilities; while he had not yet examined the Ewing transcript, 'like you, I have come to the conclusion that the 1800 edition (supposed to be repeated in the 1911 edition) was never printed from Burns's manuscript'. Barke asks Ferguson if he knows of John S. Farmer's *Merry Songs and Ballads* (1895) and, more-over, if he could, 'let me have transcriptions of the unpublished bawdy poems you have?' thanking Ferguson for sending information from the *Modern Philology* of August 1932: 'none of these verses can be ignored. They may offer internal evidence of the most valuable kind and this apart altogether from their erotic content'. Ultimately, Barke observed, 'if we cannot get the Crochallan verses into our projected edition we must do one ourselves. Eventually (otherwise) I will do one myself. I have plenty to say on the subject'. Barke, too, had a specific query for Ferguson about the Crochallan Fencibles, and Robert Cleghorn's involvement with it, wondering if Cleghorn had been, a 'regular attender'; personally, he suspected this was not the case, nor that he made, 'anything like a habit' of bawdy singing sessions.[78]

By the spring of 1947, the two writers were intending to publish the 'suppressed poems' within the complete (later they refer to it as 'definitive') edition. On 28 May, Barke wrote to Ferguson again, showing that, by then, he had

[78] The Barke Papers, Box 7A.

consulted the Ewing transcript in Dunfermline papers, and familiarised himself with the history of Burns editing:

> Yesterday I sat in Dunfermline Toon reading James C. Ewing's manuscript copy of *The Merry Muses of Caledonia*. In the absence of good red wine, to say nothing of the lack of honest whisky, this was a stimulating experience. There is no question — this is in Ewing's handwriting; and his introduction, which I attach herewith, settles any doubt.
>
> Added piquancy is given to the entire 'Holy Willie' set-up when we consider the manuscript was made with the intention of having a new edition edited by William Ernest Henley!!!
>
> I have a feeling that Ewing does not know where this copy now lies; and the fear that he may somehow get to know about it and manage to have it removed or destroyed rather perturbs me. I will see what can be done to have a transcript made of it; but I have very little time at the moment.

Barke, in fact, identified a '"Merry Muses" gold-mine' in Dunfermline, consulting eight editions of the text there: 'One or two appear to be valuable. All of them are in first-class condition and have been privately bound in "the most elegant style"'. He was impressed with the significance of the Ewing transcript, although he had only managed a 'cursory examination' of its contents; comparing this with M'Naught's version, 'It seems to me that Ewing's manuscript is much more complete and authentic. One of the other editions contains some of the most amazing examples of Victorian pornography (in prose and verse) I have ever seen'. Barke enclosed a transcript of the preface, noting the rivalry between M'Naught and Ewing: 'obviously M'Naught "stole a march" on him when he published his Burn's Federation edition'. He adds, 'the one and only time I discussed this with Ewing, he was at great pains to point out that M'Naught was entirely unjustified in using the Burns Federation imprint'.[79] On 25 June, Ferguson expressed his excitement at Barke's discovery of the Dunfermline collection: 'I neglected to visit Dunfermline while I was working on the letters, after being assured by the librarian there that they had no MSS'. He suggests microfilming the Ewing manuscript, 'as a precaution against the old boy's attempting to destroy it'.[80] On 12 August 1947, Barke informed Ferguson that he had made 'tentative arrangements' to microfilm the Ewing manuscript in Dumfermline.[81]

They had originally intended to include *The Merry Muses* within their projected definitive edition, perhaps in a supplementary volume. However, when Ferguson met with W.A.R. Collins, recalling this meeting in a letter to Barke of 24 September, this idea had been dismissed: 'if they are to be included at all, we'd probably have to put them in with the rest, and say as little about them as possible.'[82] Collins wanted a listing of 'the letters and other documents which have not been collected in correct or complete texts, together with the small group of suppressed poems which I have copied from MS'. Ferguson promises to send this to Barke. Ferguson notes some of the decisions they will have to make regarding 'the scope and nature of the editorial material'; whether they should 'emulate Henley and Henderson in collating, and recording all the variant readings in, all the MSS and first

---

[79] The Barke papers, Box 7A.

[80] The Barke Papers, Box 9C and copy Box 7A.

[81] The Barke Papers, Box 7A.

[82] The Barke Papers, Box 7A.

editions', for instance, or to make, 'a simple text edition, with a minimum of annotation?' In particular, he wonders what to do with the bawdy materials.

By 7 October 1947, things had moved on; Barke informed Ferguson 'with great regret' that they would have to omit 'the suppressed poems' from the complete works; he, however, would 'fight to the last ditch to get them in.'[83] Writing a day later, so sadly unaware of this change, Ferguson, bringing Barke up to date on the 25 letter manuscripts which had appeared since his own edition, noted particularly, regarding *The Merry Muses*, that he had manuscript copies, 'in addition to those of which I gave the full text in the Letters' for several additional poems: '"Come, rede me, dame", "Come cowe me, minnie", "In Edinbro' town they've made a law", from 'authentic MS' and 'Epistle to Alex. Findlater, with a gift of eggs', "I'll tell ye a tale of wife", "There was two wives, an' twa witty wives" and 'The Fornicator'; the latter set were, 'completed from MSS which give fuller texts than appear in any edition I have seen', along with 'While Prose-work and rhymes are hunted as crimes' which, to the best of his knowledge, was 'wholly unpublished'. Although this was not used, then, in the abortive complete, or definitive edition, Ferguson had produced the beginning of a textual listing which would form the basis for decisions regarding the holograph copies used for the 1959 *Merry Muses*.[84] From now on, the correspondence between Barke and Ferguson becomes very detailed, focussing on textual decision-making as well as the fascinating *minutiae* of Burns's biography. While this is

---

[83] The Barke Papers, Box 7A.

[84] The Barke Papers, Box 9C and copy in Box 7A.

fascinating reading it is, unfortunately, too comprehensive and lengthy to be discussed here.

Ferguson trusted Barke. On 15 October 1947 he shows his respect for his correspondent's judgement and makes suggestions for how to frame the pieces in their still-planned joint edition; overall, though, he was happy to leave Barke in charge: 'I'd be perfectly willing to leave the interpretative comment to you, and to confine my own editorial contributions to the elucidation of the prose. In that way – unless of course you should decide to defend George Thomson – I think we could avoid contradicting each other'.[85]

Barke, on the other hand, often seems somewhat in awe when writing to Ferguson. With Smith, however, he writes as an equal. In the Barke–Smith correspondence, incidentally, Ferguson is often referred to, affectionately, as 'Fergy' – a term Barke never used to Ferguson directly. A letter to Smith of 23 February 1956[86] shows Barke involved in a hands-on way with the final textual preparations, and considerations for his own introductory essay. He promised to send the music for sections I and, at this point, also for II, for which he had primarily used the James C. Dick collection of Burns *Songs* as his source.[87] This letter indicates that Smith was responsible for the final listing of contents, with the other editors commenting on his selection. Barke encloses his personal copy

---

[85] The Barke Papers, Box 9C.

[86] EUL Gen 1773.

[87] James C. Dick *The Songs of Robert Burns, Now First Printed with The Melodies For Which They were Written: A Study in Tone-Poetry With Bibliography, Historical Notes, And Glossary* (London: Henry Frowde, 1903)

of M'Naught's 1911 edition for Smith's use; at this point, they were still looking at the Ewing manuscript from Dunfermline, and Barke urges Smith to arrange for a copy to be made.

Ferguson wrote to Smith too, on 28 February 1956[88], saying he would send his preface, and transcripts, in due course and when they were needed. The tone of his letter is curt, showing that compromises had been made, and that Ferguson was disappointed with some of the final decisions. He wanted it to be clear that 'I am responsible for the MS-based material only', although he was less worried about how the material was classified, as long as the verses from holograph were identified. The letter shows, too, that he was conscious of a rift having developed between himself and the Scottish-based editors; he had become cast, even affectionately, as the 'highbrow' versus the more down-to-earth writers:

> From my highbrow angle, the weakness of the volume is going to be its tacit acceptance of the '1800' edition as still having authority. We give its whole contents, whether B's work or not. But the logical approach would be from the *Scots Musical Museum*, Thomson's Select Collection, and the Poems, not from the MMC at all. When we know that B composed decent words for a bawdy song, then give the bawdy version in the earliest text we can find. If B alludes to bawdy items which weren't the sources of purified versions, the same procedure is in order. But each item not taken from a holograph source should be documented with specific references to prove B's knowledge and use of it. If it can't be documented, it should be thrown out, whether it's in the MM or not.

---

[88] The Barke Papers, Box 9C.

> I realize, though, that the volume has to be some sort of compromise between scholarship and commercialism. Most customers would be annoyed to learn that earlier editions include items which we omit, however good our reasons for ommitting them. Hence all that I insist on is arrangement and annotation which will leave no doubts about the nature of B's connection with each item.

While there were differences of opinion, the editors still worked together, as they needed to, as a team. Ferguson added that he had written to the Morgan library, to find out if the 'Henley Archive' includes 'any of the H & H worksheets'.

Smith's own corrections from the final stages of the project — by which time, sadly, Barke had passed away — are in the University of Delaware's Department of Special Collections,[89] as mentioned above, and shows fairly major changes were being made, too, including changes to the title pages. In the first proofs, which are in the Barke papers in the Mitchell library, and also in the second proofs, the title is *Robert Burns's The Merry Muses of Caledonia. The Crochallan Song Book*. This subtitle was not used on the finished copy. The proofs confirm that Ferguson pulled back on his attachment to the project, as his doubts in corresponding with Barke and Smith suggest. In the original second proof, Ferguson's name comes first: 'Edited by J. DeLancey Ferguson James Barke Sydney Goodsir Smith'. This is altered, following Ferguson's request, in the finished version, where the credits read: 'James Barke and Sydney Goodsir Smith. With a Prefatory

---

[89] 'Sydney Goodsir Smith Papers', University of Delaware Manuscript Collection 226, item F24.

Note and some authentic Burns Texts contributed by J. DeLancey Ferguson'. Similarly, the publication details are altered, from the proofs' 'M. Macdonald. Edinburgh. For the Auk Society', to the finished version's 'Edinburgh: M. Macdonald', where the Auk Society is not mentioned explicitly.

Quite substantial decisions were being taken even at this late stage of play, for instance as to how the texts were to be presented in terms of their spelling consistency. In the foreword, for instance, Smith's changes and amendments are particularly visible. Some are relatively minor; other changes are more significant. One introductory paragraph, for instance, is deleted, regarding Barke's role with the music:

> His work on the identification of the tunes of the songs was unfortunately in a fragmentary state, and these notes were kindly taken over by Mr Robin Richardson as an act of friendship and a tribute to James Barke's memory. We called in the aid of three eminent musicians, Mr Iain Whyte, Conductor of the BBC Scottish Orchestra, Mr Cedric Davie, Master of Musick at St Andrews University, and Mr Frances Collinson, composer and musicologue. To all these gentlemen we are most grateful for their unselfish labours.

Presumably, this work was not completed and, perhaps, the involvement of several other authorities explains why Barke's musical notes are missing. As a sad aside, there is an insert in typescript, which replaced this paragraph in the final issue of the 1959 edition, with the exception of the phrase 'and not for want of seeking': 'and so far we have not run to earth an editor capable of completing this task — and not for want of seeking. To satisfy the natural impatience of subscribers we are now issuing the texts by themselves'. The Delaware papers, too, include Smith's manuscript notes for the announcement of the text, revealing that the first print run was of 1,000 copies.

REVIEWS

Reviews of the 1959 edition were, as might be expected, mixed although the Scottish press, in general, admired its intentions. The *Glasgow Herald*,[90] in a piece titled 'Editing Burns's Bawdry' noted: 'no doubt it is appropriate — cocking a learned snook at the unco' guid — that the most considerable new work of Burns scholarship arriving in time for the bicentenary should be a collection of Burns's bawdry.' It found the 1959 edition, 'a new, if not a pioneering work', noting the text was based on the Rosebery edition, and praising 'scrupulous editorship'. The *Herald* considered this edition to be, 'the nearest approximation to the lost notebook that the poet once lent to John McMurdo of Drumlanrig containing, it is presumed, all the prizes of his "violent propensity to Bawdry"'. The *Daily Express*[91] was impressed by the novelty of finding Burns's 'earthy' poems, like 'Comin' thro' the Rye,' 'John Anderson, my Jo' and 'Green Grow the Rashes O' in forms which were 'startlingly different from those sung on concert platforms today'.

Notices of the American editions were more cursory. *Time*[92] drew attention to Burns in the context of other 'great writers, who were also pornographers' from Mark Twain

---

[90] *Glasgow Herald* Thursday 22 January 1959.

[91] *Daily Express* 9 January 1959.

[92] 'The Bawdy Scot', *Time* 8 May 1964.

to Benjamin Franklin, Swift, Byron, Swinburne and Thackery. In this company, 'Perhaps the most famous smutmaster is Robert Burns [...] The collection as now published is as close to the original as scholarship is likely to achieve, barring the rediscovery of Burns's own notebook.' *Time,* however, thought only the 'hard-core enthusiast' for Burns would enjoy the American edition by Barke, Smith and Ferguson: 'the scholarly apparatus smothers the poems. What is worse for the prurient reader, Burns's Scottish dialect [...] is here often incomprehensible — even the dirty words.' *Inside Books*,[93] similarly, found it difficult to comprehend: 'Hoot mon! Nae mair than a wee wurrd on THE MERRY MUSES OF CALEDONIA, bawdy folk songs, ancient or modern, all of them either written or collected by Robert Burns'. Douglas Parker, in 'Parker's Bookshelf',[94] came back to Smith's conclusion, noting, 'one can make some attempt at seeing the poet whole'. Like Smith, he admired the qualities of Burns's, and Scotland's, bawdry for being neither 'childish' nor 'immature'; instead, 'it is a highly witty approach to the most earthy associations of the greatest source of humor for humans'.

To conclude, it is hoped this Introduction has given at least a flavour of the development of *The Merry Muses* into the 1959 edition. It is complex textually, it is complicated as a song collection, and the relationship with Burns complicates things further. In spite of all of this, or because of it, *The Merry Muses of Caledonia* is ripe for scholarly and critical reassessment: as a set of songs which need to

---

93 *Inside Books*, May 1964.
94 'Parker's Bookshelf', copy in NLS ACC 10397/4.

be viewed as songs rather than as poems; as a set of books which needs to be rigorously collated (perhaps minus the misleading 1827 texts) and as a set which richly deserves to be republished. In terms of Burns, it should perhaps be viewed as much as poetic posturing — in a private context for his gentlemanly friends — as is should be seen as representative of an arguably neglected aspect of his work. Reissuing this 1959 edition is a step, I hope, in a process which Barke, Smith and Ferguson played a major role in beginning. *The Merry Muses of Caledonia* richly deserves to be treated as a serious book even if it is still, in many ways, highly elusive.

Valentina Bold
Dumfries, January 2009

FOREWORD

IT IS A matter of deepeſt regret to Professor Ferguson and myself that James Barke, who had been ailing for some time, did not live to see the completion of this book to which he had devoted so much time, research and 'honeſt Scotch enthusiasm.' He died aged 52 in March 1958, mourned by lovers of Burns the world over. His Introduction was left in the form of a rough draft, which I have only touched here and there in the way of punctuation and arrangement. His work on the identification of the tunes of the songs was unfortunately in a fragmentary ſtate and so far we have not been able to find an edîtor capable of completing this task. To satisfy the natural impatience of subscribers we are now issuing the texts by themselves.

It was a chance remark of my friend and fellow Burnsian, Mr Maurice Lindsay. that led me to Lord Rosebery's unique copy of the original c.1800 edîtion of *The Merry Muses* that forms the basis of the present edîtion. To Lord Rosebery's great kindness in giving me access to this precious opusculum I have referred in the course of my Introduction; to Mr Lindsay also I would tender the gratîtude of both edîtors and subscribers.

Before this happy chance occurred we had laboured long wîth the baffling myſtery of sometimes as many as six different versions of a particular song – all declaredly taken from the c.1800 edîtion, from this particular and unique copy of Lord Rosebery's that had belonged to William Scott Douglas. It was Miss Rodger of the Dunfermline Public Library who unlocked for me the doors of the innermoſt secret chambers of the Murison Burns Collection and firſt displayed to my aſtonishment the Ewing transcript of this edition that proved to differ so alarmingly from Duncan M'Naught's Burns Federation edition of 1911 and that ſtarted off the inveſtigations the fruîts of which lie before you now.

Another bouquet muſt go to Mr W.N.H. Harding of Chicago, USA, whose collection of old songbooks muſt be one of the fineſt in the world and who kindly transcribed for me many songs from his – also unique – copy of *The Giblet Pye* (*c*.1806). Until we discovered the 1800 edition of the *Muses* these were some of the oldeſt texts we had.

For other courtesies I muſt thank Mr D.M. Lloyd of the National Library of Scotland, Mr M.C. Pottinger of the Scottish Central Library and Mr Basil Megaw of the School of Scottish Studies, Edinburgh Univerſîty.

S.G.S.
Edinburgh, November 1958

NOTE

Punctuation and ſtyle in Sections I and VI follow Burns's holograph. Elsewhere, punctuation as a rule follows the text, but where this was very erratic ît has sometimes been emended. Inconſiſtencies in spelling are lîteral.

SOURCES AND TEXTS OF THE
SUPPRESSED POEMS

By J. DeLANCEY FERGUSON

THAT Burns collected bawdy folksongs, and added to them, is a fact not questioned even by the bardolators who strive to ignore it. He devoted a special notebook to the collection; his most detailed, and most often quoted, allusion to it occurs in a letter to John M'Murdo of Drumlanrig which was probably written in February, 1792:

> I think I once mentioned something to you of a Collection of Scots Songs I have for some years been making: I send you a perusal of what I have gathered.—I could not conveniently spare them above five or six days, and five or six glances of them will probably more than suffice you.—When you are tired of them please leave them with Mr Clint of the King's Arms.—There is not another copy of the Collection in the world, & I should be sorry that any unfortunate negligence should deprive me of what has cost me a good deal of pains.—

More than two years earlier, on sending a copy of 'I'll Tell You a Tale of a Wife' to Provost Maxwell of Lochmaben, the poet had added. 'You see, Sir, I have fulfilled my promise: I wish you would think of fulfilling yours, and come & see the rest of my Collection.—' He had tried his hand at original composition of such verses at least as early as 1784, when he copied 'My Girl She's Airy' into his Commonplace Book: he had begun recording folk bawdry at least as early as 1786 — in other words before he had met James Johnson and become actively concerned with the *Scots Musical Museum*. His transcript of 'Brose an' Butter' was taken down on the reverse of a draft letter to

Margaret Kennedy of Daljarrock. That letter was probably written in late autumn, 1785; the song, on the clear evidence of his handwriting, must have been copied down within the next 12 months or so.

As to what happened to the collection after Burns's death, the earliest version is Robert Chambers's:

> Unluckily, Burns's collection of these facetiae (including his own essays in the same walk) fell… into the hands of one of those publishers who would sacrifice the highest interests of humanity to put an additional penny into their own purses; and, to the lasting grief of all the friends of our Poet, they were allowed the honours of the press. The mean-looking volume which resulted should be a warning to all honourable men of letters against the slightest connection with clandestine literature, much more the degradation of contributing to it…

Duncan M'Naught, quoting this passage in his preface to the Burns Federation reprint of *The Merry Muses*, added in a footnote that the collection 'was obtained on loan from Mrs Burns on false pretences, and never returned.' He did not document this statement, any more than he documented 'the authority of Professor Wilson' for an assertion that Burns, on his deathbed, was offered 50 pounds for the collection and repelled the offer with horror. However, it is always hard to document what never happened, and the real history of Burns's papers was a matter of record long before Robert Chambers's day.

Late in 1796 Dr James Currie agreed to write a life of Burns, and to edit his works, for the benefit of the poet's widow and children. John Syme, one of Burns's closest friends in Dumfries, undertook to collect documents — all the letters he could induce their recipients to release (that to John M'Murdo, just quoted, was one of them), together with everything hand-written he could find in the poet's home. What he had accumulated he forwarded to Currie in February 1797. 'I received,' the Doctor recalled, 'the complete sweepings of his drawers and of his desk – as it appeared to me – even to the copy-book on which his little boy had been practising his writing.'

Those complete sweepings included whatever notebooks and journals Burns had kept, as well as his loose papers. The Glenriddell MSS, both the Commonplace Books, the journals of the Border and Highland tours, the notebook which began as farming memoranda and ended as a poetical miscellany – all these are known to have been in Currie's custody. There is no reason to doubt that *The Merry Muses* (call it that for convenience, though there is no proof that the title is Burns's) was included in the consignment. One bit of evidence, indeed, is almost proof-positive that Currie had the collection.

When he printed the much-quoted letter to John M'Murdo, Currie interpolated a sentence which Burns had failed to write: 'A very few of them are my own' – a sentence italicized by every apologist from Currie's day to ours. Unless he had seen Burns's manuscript, the editor would have no motive for the forgery. In the letter Burns does not claim *any* of the collection as his own.

These facts cannot be controverted, but they can be ignored. They have been, by all the apologists who cling to the tale that the verses reached print through some scoundrel who fraudulently obtained the manuscript from Jean Burns. These same apologists allege that *The Merry Muses* was printed in, or near, Dumfries about 1800. The paper is watermarked '1800,' which provides a *terminus a quo*; if there is any evidence that Dumfries was the place it has not been divulged. But in 1800 the manuscript, unless he had already destroyed it, was still in Currie's hands, in Liverpool, and it is inconceivable that anyone so prudish can have been a party to the publication. He published his edition in that year, but returned none of the papers in his custody. He intended a comprehensive revision and enlargement of his work.

That intent was frustrated by his death in 1805, but still the papers were not returned. Some were given away — the farming memoranda book, and other documents as well, were in William Roscoe's library in the 1820's — some may have been lost or destroyed. Many remained in the hands of Currie's descendants until 1865, when they were sold at auction. The one certainty is that none of them was ever at Jean Burns's disposal after February, 1797. Hence, if *The Merry Muses* was really printed at Dumfries about 1800, it was printed from some other source than Burns's holograph collection.

I once believed that most of the documents which Currie's successors have failed to locate were destroyed by the Doctor or his heirs. I no longer think so. Though some doubtless perished through carelessness, the slow reappearance in recent years of 'lost' manuscripts absolves the Curries from charges of wholesale or deliberate destruction. Currie *may* have felt *The Merry Muses* scandalous enough to demand purification by fire. On the other hand, he may merely have kept the volume under lock and key, as Burns himself did. M'Naught asserted that 'what appear to be stray leaves still find their way occasionally into the manuscript market.' As usual, he offered no supporting evidence. Bawdy verses by Burns certainly exist in separate holographs as well as in letters, but none that I have seen bears any clear indication, such as page numbers, of deriving from a manuscript volume. The collection *may* have been broken up or destroyed. Equally well, it may still be hidden in the cache where a Victorian owner concealed it from his family. One guess is as good as another.

But if Currie had the original, what was the source of the '1800' volume? One can only conjecture. Before conjecturing, though, one must make certain postulates about the nature and scope of Burns's collection. First, in the case of folksongs, it would obviously contain texts differing little, if at all, from his jottings from oral recitation and from the copies he transcribed for friends. Next, in the case of his own compositions in the *genre*, the texts would be final ones, not rough drafts; he would be unlikely to enter the verses in the book until they were in a form which satisfied him. Finally, one would expect the volume to include all, or almost all, his own compositions which he viewed as unfit for general circulation. But the '1800' edition conforms to none of these three standards.

Not many of Burns's jottings survive, but the two or three available for comparison all show numerous divergencies from the *Merry Muses* text. Thus his version of 'Brose an' Butter,' set down not later than 1786, consists, like that in the *Muses*, of five stanzas and a chorus. But the last two lines of the chorus are different; the stanza-order differs; Burns's text lacks the *Muses*' closing stanza but includes a stanza lacking in the *Muses*.

'Cumnock Psalms' was most certainly in Burns's collection: he copied it out, for George Thomson's edification, in 1794. Presumably he had his book in front of him. Yet his version has a different refrain and three lines widely variant from the *Muses*. We know, moreover, that Burns had songs not in the *Muses* at all. In March, 1795, for instance, he quoted to Patrick Miller Jr. 'an old Scottish stanza' beginning 'There cam a soger here to stay.' Obviously it came from his collection. But it is missing in the '1800' *Muses*, only to appear, garbled, as stanza two of 'The Reels o' Bogie' in the even less authentic edition of 1827. The first editor missed it entirely; the second got it wrong. *Ergo*, neither printed from Burns's holograph.

What applied to the folksongs applies *a fortiori* to Burns's own compositions. Since he often copied from memory, minor textual differences are to be expected; changes of form, and omissions of whole stanzas, are not, if the printer worked from holographs. Yet the *Muses* version of 'The Fornicator' has only four stanzas, whereas the one known manuscript has six. The version of 'I'll Tell You a Tale of a Wife' which Burns sent to Provost Maxwell on December 20, 1789, has 11 stanzas. The *Muses* text has only eight, and the three that are missing include the best travesty of Calvinistic logic. We have the poet's own word that the song was part of his collection. A printer working from that collection could hardly manage to overlook four whole stanzas.

Equally convincing is the text of 'When Princes and Prelates.' Of that song two holographs survive, written more than 18 months apart. Burns composed the song at Sanquhar on December 12, 1792, and sent it off at once to Robert Cleghorn. In July 1794, he copied it out for

George Thomson. This second manuscript differs in only one half-line from the Cleghorn text. But the *Muses* version includes two additional stanzas — one repetitious, the other incompletely rhymed — and has different line-structure throughout. Obviously what Burns had written in 1792 still satisfied him in 1794. When, then, is he likely to have reworked the song in a wholly different form?

This argument might be followed through all the verses which survive in holograph, for few of the manuscripts agree *verbatim* and *literatim* with the *Muses*. But equally significant is the absence from the *Muses* of verses which Burns is known to have written or collected. That volume includes three lyrics from 'The Jolly Beggars,' but none of them is the closing chorus, 'A fig for those by law protected.' Yet in September, 1793, Burns told George Thomson, 'I have forgot the Cantata you allude to, as I kept no copy, & indeed did not know that it was in existence; however, I remember that none of the songs pleased myself, except the last — something about
"Courts for cowards were erected,
"Churches built to please the priest".'

Even if we assume that the poet, for some obscure reason, was mystifying Thomson, the dilemma remains. If Burns had a copy, and *The Merry Muses* was really printed from his collection, the whole of the 'Beggars' should be there. If he told Thomson the truth, the nameless editor must have obtained his texts elsewhere.

Still stranger is the absence of 'Holy Willie's Prayer.' It never occurred to Burns that the great soliloquy would one day stand among his collected masterpieces, but he knew it was a masterpiece. So did his friends, who were always pestering him for copies. Though it had been printed in a Stewart and Meikle pamphlet in 1799, it was not openly included in his works until 1810; hence it should have rated top billing in the *Muses*. However, 'Holy Willie,' like 'Grizzel Grimme,' is not a song; therefore it might not have been in the same notebook with the lyrics. But 'My Girl She's Airy,' 'When Prose-work and Rhymes,' and 'There was Twa Wives' are most definitely songs, and the two last were composed in the same years as 'Act Sederunt' and 'When Princes and Prelates.' If the one pair were copied into the collection, it is hard to understand why the others were not also.

It has taken far too many words to reach a simple conclusion. If *The Merry Muses* was printed in Dumfries or, more likely, Edinburgh in 1800, it could not have been taken from a holograph in Dr Currie's home in Liverpool. Even if it was printed elsewhere, at another date, it still could not have been taken from the holograph, for the texts are both inaccurate and incomplete. The obvious — and only — alternative is that the *Muses* was compiled from versions set down from memory, or from hasty transcriptions by hands other than the poet's. Plenty of cronies, in Dumfries and elsewhere, could have brought together the collection on those terms, but it is easier to say who probably did not do it than to say who probably did.

The title page dedicates the verses to the Crochallan Fencibles, which suggests an Edinburgh rather than a Dumfries provenance. Traditionally, Robert Cleghorn was the intermediary in transmitting Burns's cloaciniads to the club. But if Cleghorn had had any part at all in the printing, the *Muses* would — to cite only two examples — have

included 'There was Twa Wives' and the Cleghorn text of
'When Princes and Prelates.' Cleghorn, therefore, is ruled
out. Had John Syme or Alexander Cunningham been
involved, one would expect some hint of the fact in their
extant correspondence. It is easy enough to guess at others
who *might* have done it: in Dumfries, for instance, Colonel
dePeyster or John M'Murdo; in Edinburgh, Charles Hay
(later Lord Newton), or the poet's 'facetious little friend,'
William Dunbar, or even Peter Hill. But without clues
guessing is useless.

In sum, then, the '1800' edition ceases to have any unique
authority. Whatever the source of its contents, it was not
printed from Burns's own manuscript collection of bawdy
verse. We may have to accept its versions in default of better;
we must never trust them.

Our present edition can make no sweeping claim to
accuracy or completeness. For about a score of pieces,
however, it offers texts directly based on Burns's own
manuscripts. That is more than can be said of any of its
predecessors.

Falls Village, Connecticut,
May 1956

NOTE

The contents of the present volume represent a variety of sources and
a diversity of editorial opinion. My share in the work consists of this
preface and of the texts on which the headnotes bear my initials. — DLF

PORNOGRAPHY AND BAWDRY IN LITERATURE AND SOCIETY

By JAMES BARKE

THE NATURE of pornography and obscenîty in lîterature is complex. Its origin dates back to the origin of lîterature and to the essential lîterature concerning sexual characterîstics of man and woman. The aesthetic and sociological aspects of bawdry are worth some consideration. What, for instance, is meant exactly by the words pornography and obscenîty in relation to lîterature in general and poetry and folk-song in particular? The Oxford Dictionary defines pornography as 'licentious wrîting (Greek porné, harlot)' and obscenîty as '... indecent, bawdy,' but these definîtions are subject to the law of change. Also, they do not *define*. Is *The Song of Songs* pornographic? What about Dunbar's 'Twa Mairrît Wemen and the Wedow' or John Cleland's *Fanny Hill*? Officially, to-day, Lawrence's *Lady Chatterly's Lover* is pornographic but James Joyce's *Ulysses* is not. It all seems to be very much a matter of fashion, of taste, of opinion. I saw Joyce's *Ulysses* denounced in Britain and America as outrageous pornography. I have lived to see ît openly sold and displayed in Brîtish bookshops, and I have read that ît is regarded as essential or even compulsory reading in certain universîties in the USA.

All of which is very interesting but not very helpful in attempting to arrive at an understanding of what constîtutes pornography or obscenîty. Aesthetic values change, social values change; bawdry is subject to the same laws as any other human activîty. There never has and never can be ideal freedom in writing or speech or action. All activity is subject to what human society at any given time and place permits, and, in consequence, many artists, frustrated by the ban on freedom to deal with sexual experience, have had recourse to secret or semi-secret bawdry. Most forms of society have ruthlessly suppressed bawdry while at the same time tolerating a black market in pornography. Against, for example, the non-sexual nature of the Victorian novel stood the underground trade in pornography — much of it of the crudest nature, much of it nauseatingly vile.

Crudity in organising, in art forms, sexual awareness and sensitivity, has long been with man. In Britain to-day it finds its most violent expression on the walls of public conveniences. In village, town or city, wherever a convenience affords a blank wall, there will be found, either in word or drawing, the violence, hatred, disgust, nausea, loathing, joy, ecstasy, longing for and ridicule of — sex. And not only in male conveniences; some female conveniences outdo the male in verbal and pictorial sexual expression. The study of this aspect of sexual awareness has not been adequately undertaken in Britain. But the pattern in Scotland, Wales and England seems fairly uniform.

Alongside what might be called urinal art flourishes the art of the smoke-room, tap-room story, the smutty tale or joke, the blue story. The appeal of this form of sexual safety valve is common to all sections of society in Britain. I am assured by authorities in America, France, Germany, Poland and Russia that it is equally common with them. There are social nuances of course. There are men who 'draw the line' at telling certain types of story in the presence of their wives, or in the company of other women, but who in the company of men know no limits. This is true of women also. The teller of the most crude bawdy stories I ever had the misfortune to know was a Kirk of Scotland elder whose wife, an avid listener, was equally prominent in Kirk work. I have also heard Roman Catholic priests, Kirk of Scotland clergymen, notable lay preachers (Fundamentalist type), learned savants, venerable artists, and other respectable men indulge in the verbal equivalent of urinal art at its crudest.

The creative artist cannot look on all this with equanimity. Bawdy art is bad art in so far as it debases and corrupts the instinct to procreation. Urinal art is bad art. Until very recently the word fuck carried with it, in literature, all the hypnotic power of a verbal atom bomb. In English literature, Lawrence, Joyce, and Henry Miller (to mention a few) have eliminated the hysteria and shock from it. Conversationally, of course, it has always been with us.

'Fuck' I take to be an onomatopoeic word equivalent of the sound made by the penis in the vagina. Here I differ from Mr Eric Partridge who considers that it denotes violence. It was once an honest enough word and has an honourable history. But early enough in literature it became a taboo word. To-day it may be regarded either as the most tender or the most disturbing word in our language.

What applies to fuck is equally relevant to the word cunt — except that it is, poetically, a much harsher word, deriving as it does from the hardening of the Latin *cunus*. But this word, too, had an honest use and has an honourable history. To-day, fuck and cunt, and their cognates, are largely used as debased expletives. Their public use, though

general in Britain, constitutes an indictable offence —
though arrest seldom occurs unless they are bawled out in
a public place by a person — not uncommonly a teenage girl
— usually under the influence of alcohol.

But though literary scholars, like medical scholars, must
acquire a neutral attitude to the literary and medical
aspects of sexual phenomena, the literary scholars must not
in any way minimise the effect of words on the untrained
ear. The evocative power of a word spoken or printed, like
a pictorial image or photograph, can be devastating. I have
witnessed a full-grown and responsible adult male become
almost insane and undergo profound physical disturbance
at being called a bastard. Once in a Highland lochside
hotel bar I witnessed a scene that almost amounted to
verbal rape. A young red-haired Highland girl was bar-
maid. A number of middle-class customers were in the
bar. Presently a drunken lout entered and demanded a
drink. Apparently he had been refused just previously. He
looked, in drink, an evil and debauched character. The
barmaid politely and firmly refused him a drink. With a
viciousness that cannot be conveyed in print he said: 'Then
gie me a hair frae your dirty big red cunt!' The effect on the
girl was pitiful. Her facial blood vessels seemed as if they
would burst on the instant. She clutched the bar and
trembled; the expression in her eyes was agonising. The
lout swayed for a moment and then lurched out of the bar
as the barmaid, covering her face and sobbing hysterically,
ran out from behind the bar into the hotel corridor. I
knew the hotel manageress and she told me afterwards that
the girl was quite ill for several days.

Certainly the State, the executive power in human society,
must exercise the power of censorship to a certain extent,

and the more enlightened the State, the more enlightened the censorship. Intellectuals may protest about all forms of control – as I hope they always will – but the fact remains that artistic freedom can never be absolute but must always remain relative and, consequently, ever-changing. We, of this generation, know only too painfully what blood lust could be brought to boiling point, torture and bestial mania, by the mere incantations of such slogans as Heil Hitler! Perish Judea! and Fuck the Pope! Even the word Peace, as Giles the English cartoonist once brilliantly depicted, can in certain circumstances become a dirty and unclean word.

The foregoing observations are necessary before an evaluation of, or even an approach to, Burns's bawdry can be made. This bawdry, of which Burns was legitimately proud, cannot yet be brought into the full light of day. Burns, who would have welcomed this edition, would have understood without any argumentation why it has to be 'private and not for sale to the public.' But I am proud to be associated with this edition since it establishes to a satisfactory degree just what constitutes Burns's contribution to Scottish bawdry. Scottish bawdry has many peculiar characteristics. It is extremely frank – and it is fundamentally humorous and hence humanistic. It is extremely vigorous and, if it can be said to smell, it smells on the whole like the not unpleasant smell of horse droppings. It reeks of the stable rather than the urinal. To certain olfactory organs it gives the effect of new-mown hay.

To my generation of Scots, Burns, popularly, was the author of two pieces of bawdy doggerel – of which, poetically, he was incapable. On innumerable occasions in the Scottish variety theatre, and sometimes in pantomime, it only required the comedian to give such lines as 'The cuddy rins aboot the braes' or 'As I stood on the pier o' Leith' to convulse the major part of the audience — especially the married women. One comedian assured me that he had used the 'Cuddy' line for 30 years all over Scotland and it had never once failed to bring the house down. Thus, and in other ways, suppression of what Burns actually wrote has resulted in the damnedest obscene trash being ascribed to his pen.

I was brought up in West Fife until I was 13 years old, in a pleasant household alien to bawdry — or at least inside the four domestic walls. But outside the house, in school and with friends of my own age and upwards to senility, bawdry was general and commonplace: no one gave it much conscious thought. In the school playground, long before puberty, the boys, and sometimes the girls, chanted such bawdy songs as 'Mary Ann' (to the tune of 'The girl I left behind me').

> O Mary Ann had a leg like a man
> And a great big hole in her stockin';
> A chest like a drum
> And a big fat bum
> And a hole to shove your cock in!

To the tune of 'Cock o' the North' we chanted:

> My Aunt Mary had a canary
> Up the leg o' her drawers,
> For oors and oors
> It cursed the Boers
> And won the Victoria Cross.

And to the tune of 'Two lovely black eyes':
  Oor Mary's white drawers,
  Oor Mary's white drawers,
  A hole in the middle
  To let Mary piddle,
  Oor Mary's white drawers,

To 'Pop goes the Weasel':
  Long and thin goes too far in
  And doesn't please the ladies;
  Short and thick does the trick
  And brings out proper babies.

There were many similar bairns' bawdy rhymes, songs and chants common to West Fife in the first two decades of the 20th century. Comparing notes with a pious Episcopalian approaching his 80s, I found that the identical bairns' bawdry was common to the city of Perth in the 1880s. I must add, however, that the word fuck was so little used as to be almost unknown among school children; and adults rarely or ever used it in the presence of children. Cunt, strangely enough, was commonplace in its legitimate and cognitive use. Sexual intercourse and mutual masturbation was by no means uncommon in the 10—14 age groups. Certain girls were almost nymphomaniacally aggressive. Sexual exhibitionism in classrooms from boys to girls from the age of eight was not uncommon.

The point I wish to stress here is that in Edwardian Scotland there was a universal and firmly established bawdy folk-culture in existence, coupled with much seemingly precocious and promiscuous sexual experience. Visual experience of the sexual mating of all animals was debarred to no one of whatever age or sex, except the mating of ftallion and mare, which was taboo to all women and children (other than surreptitiously). If, as I have been assured on unimpeachable teftimony, the effect on certain otherwise ftaid and respectable women (married and spinfters) of witnessing the mating of mare and ftallion was to induce an almoft inftantaneous fainting away (orgasm) and an inability to resift the sexual advances of any male who might be on the spot, regardless of age or social condition, then it muft be admitted that licentious literature, or any other licentious art form, conftitutes highly inflammable and socially dangerous material.

But, socially, I doubt if this problem can be solved by suppression. Pornography and obscenity exift in many art and pseudo-art forms and have a widespread diftribution. It obviously caters for a genuine human need. Where art forms are frankeft and leaft suppressed or inhibited, the less the debased or licentious art forms attract. If our educational syftem were franker and less inhibited, there would be less need for such manifeftations as urinal art.

I come back to urinal art. It is universal-in whatever form: *ergo*, it represents a basic human urge: it organises, after a fashion, something fundamental in the human make-up. Urinal art in Britain exifts in its primary, almoft primal, condition and in many slightly sublimated or relatively respectable, hence permitted, forms.

Permitted forms today exift in 'the living theatre,' ice shows, variety shows, illuftrated magazines, ftrip cartoons, and so forth. The pictorial representation of the female buft is a case in point. Even the moft decorous and respectable of family newspapers, magazines and journals give prominence to the moſt exaggerated forms of female breaſts. A television walker-on achieved ſtardom by merely displaying her abnormally developed bosom. She was not permītted to open her mouth — her buſt presumably spoke volumes.

It is noteworthy that Burns's bawdry has līttle or nothing to say in celebration of this part of the female anatomy. Burns could celebrate a 'hairy cunt' but he ignored the female breaſts. To-day, photographers concentrate on these and on the hips and *mons veneris* in bikini or other abbreviated 'bathing' dress: Burns's bawdry mainly concentrates on the male and female pudenda. It is remarkably free from any suggeſtion of perversīty, though there is the exaggeration and caricature common to all bawdry. The male tendency to exaggerate the physical aspect of the penis is everywhere in evidence, and he seems to extend to the female the common male belief in the sexual efficacy of an oversized penis. Women are much wiser than this. But the male has ever had the tendency to boaſt not only of the size of the penis but also of the number of ejaculations achievable in a single bout of intercourse. All this, of course, is normal and quīte innocuous: no one other than extreme youth is deceived.

There seems līttle doubt but that Burns was 'well hung' and was probably what is called over-sexed. But sexologists are rightly becoming doubtful as to what conſtitutes the term over-sexed. Some men are capable of regular and repeated acts of vigorous intercourse into their 80s; ſtrong, robuſt men in their prime border on seeming impotence — wīthout being impotent. There is not yet sufficient data available to establish a norm: probably there never will be. Women, too, represent all states from the frigid to the nymphomaniac. On balance, however, there does seem to be enough evidence to show that sexual desire is stronger in the female than in the male. If the sexual urge were limited to the act of procreation things would be very different, but the crux of the matter is that the sexual urge is primary, insatiable, irresistible, all-powerful and ruthlessly selfish. Since the processes of defloration and birth are in themselves both unpleasant and dangerous, Nature had to make the sexual urge so powerful as to overcome all obstacles of whatever kind or extent. And since man's sexual activity is not governed by seasonal heat, the surplus of sexual energy over and above the procreative need is enormous and ever present; and neither starvation nor overwork can kill it. As an appetite, however, sex must be controlled in some fashion for social reasons.

A civilisation demands a degree of cleanliness. The need to keep the body clean is based on hygienic and aesthetic considerations. There is an equal need to keep the mind clean – if only for reasons of mental health – but cleanliness has nothing to do with pruriency – or puritanism. The sexual act may be the consummation of love between the sexes, and where the intention is procreative it may be regarded as fulfilling its highest function. Any activity that tends to degrade this supreme function must be regarded as retrogressive and anti-social and essentially pornographic. But it cannot be denied that in modern man sexual activity is also an end in itself – an appetite demanding satisfaction. Nine-tenths of sexual activity is of this order.

Against the all-powerful drive to make sex irresistible stand the sanctions of society that limit and suppress free sexual indulgence. Herein lies the social value and significance of bawdry: it provides a safety-valve against intellectual and emotional sexual pressure and stress. The Scots peasant in singing his bawdy song freed himself from inhibitory pressures and tended to ease sexual tensions — especially through laughter.

It cannot be denied that a society in which urinal art flourishes is in an unhealthy condition: it may even be said, without exaggeration, to be in a dangerously diseased condition. Urinal art and healthy laughing bawdry are two opposite expressions of the primary sexual urge. English bawdry is ever inclined to 'snirtle in its sleeve': the prurient snigger is seldom far away. In the main, Scots bawdry is frank, ribald, robustly Rabelaisian, rich in erotic imagery and extraordinarily fanciful in invention.

The flowering of this Scottish art-form reached perfection in 'The Ball o' Kirriemuir.' This ballad-song developed from a 20 verse work celebrating an actual event to its present-day form in which there are hundreds of verses and innumerable variants. Some 30 years ago a local historian, in the Kirriemuir district, gave me this story of its origin. Around the 1880s a barn dance (harvest-home or kirn dance) was held in the barn of a neighbouring farm. On this occasion the young fellows gathered rose hips and removed the tiny yellow hirsute seeds. These were scattered on the earthen floor of the barn. The girls danced bare-footed. Female drawers were not in general use but, where worn, were of the open crutch or 'free trade' pattern. In the ſtour of the dance the small hip seeds lodged around the pudendal hair and set up a pubic and vaginal îtch. In other words they conſtîtuted a powerful external aphrodisiac. In addîtion to this, some wag had added a modicum of Spanish fly to the punch bowl. A final touch was the placing of a divot, or sod of grass, in the well of the hanging paraffin lamp. This shortened the life of the illumination to coincide roughly wîth the time the internal and external aphro-disiacs became effective.

The upshot was an orgy of major proportions and it was this orgy that was celebrated in the original 'Ball o' Kirriemuir.' Generations of bothy lads embroidered on the original until ît was soon impossible to tell where the original began or ended. Two world wars spread ît among the personnel of the services and they added and subtracted and amended until to-day the thing is wîthout beginning or end — and few there are who know anything of îts origin.

The original chorus seems to have been:
    Wi' a fa'll dae ît this time
        Fa'll dae it noo?
    The yin that did ît laſt time
        Canna dae ît noo.

Typical of the original seems to be the verse:
    They were fuckin' in the barn;
    They were fuckin' in the ricks;
    An' ye couldna hear the music
    For the swishin' o' the pricks.

Possibly a contemporary allusion is evinced in

    The minifter's wife was there as weel
    A' buckled to the front;
    Wi' a wreath o' roses roun' her airse
    An' thrissels roun' her cunt.

Her daughter was not so protected by this ingenious belt of chaftity:

    The minifter's dochter tae was there
    An' she gat roarin' fu';
    Sae they doubled her owre the midden wa'
    An' bulled her like a coo.

But if the harveft had been home ît would not have been possible for the farmer to bewail this loss:

    Big Rab the fermer cursed and swore
    An' then he roared and grat;
    For his forty acre corn field
    Was nearly fuckît flat.

It is typical of the Scots that when the Highland Division entered Tripoli after the success of the North African campaign, they paraded before Winfton Churchill singing verses from 'The Ball o' Kirriemuir' in their luftieft voice. The broadcaft recording of this hiftoric event had, subsequently, to be scrapped. It is reported that, at firft, Churchill was slightly puzzled by the song but soon broke into 'a broad grin.'

This indeed is the great leaven that works through almoft all Scottish bawdry. It is never sneering or sly or prurient or sexy or tîtillating. It is almost always blunt and broad and extremely coarse, but seldom vulgar in the music-hall sense; ît is never filthy in the sense of the traditîonal 'feelthy poftcards.' It is seldom refined and, when ît is, ît is refined in the sense that 'The Yellow Yellow Yorlin'' is refined; ît is luſty like a good broad bare female buttock.

Burns's bawdry is always coarse, seldom wîtty, never salacious and not often of a high level. It is unashamedly masculine. There is some evidence of a scatological or coprophilous intereſt, as in 'There was twa wives' and the ballad of 'Grizzel Grimme,' and in abnormal sexual physiology, as in 'Come Cowe me, Minnie.' I confess that when I firſt read this song, as a youth, ît ſtruck me as particularly pointless and coarse. I considered Mary's pudendal peculiarîty as altogether imaginary, but when I came to ſtudy the physiology and psychology of sex I discovered that Mary's condîtion was unusual but in no wise unique. Havelock Ellis quotes at leaſt one case where the female pudendal hair was of such a nature as to preclude any attempt at penetration. Again, regarding peculiarîties of the male organ, while members of 10, 12, 14 or even 18 inches are not common, they do exiſt, if infrequently. So that when 'The deevil's dizzen Donald drew,' i.e. 13 inches ('Put butter in my Donald's brose'), we cannot accuse the poet of downright lying. Indeed the more we know about sex in all îts aspects the more we find that bawdry — at leaſt Scottish folk-song bawdry — is guilty of under-ſtatement.

On the basis of much experience and long ſtudy, I think that in Britain to-day (and possibly in America, since Brîtain generally is dominated by American commercial culture) our sexual *mores* represent a profound degeneration of spirîtual values and that this is a product of a basely materialiſtic and commercial civilisation. We are living in an age that is hag-ridden by sex — in a degenerate sense. All commercial art tends to exploit and exacerbate the sexual impulse at its most animal level. Pornography and obscenity in its crudest and vilest forms now fail to bring the most tentative blush to the most innocent teenager – especially the female. This, of course, where there is adequate strength of character, need not be considered an evil. But when it leads to the physical, mental and spiritual weakening of the individual, then society and the race is correspondingly weakened.

The overall tasks facing society, if society is to endure, demand a high totality of human competence. Hotted-up sex, alcoholism and the need for distraction at animal level (near-nude shows and Marciano-type boxing and so on) spell social decay and the ultimate ruination of civilised society. Sex must be self-disciplined, as eating and drinking must be self-disciplined. And where self-discipline is not effective then there must be some form of social discipline.

On the other hand, sex must be brought out of the dirty bed sheets and fetid darkness of outmoded inhibitions and taboos. An attitude and approach to sex at once hygienic and social must be deliberately cultivated. We must recognise that the sexual, basically procreative, urge is perhaps the most dominant in our life. We must recognise that it is primarily procreative but that the sexual desire and procreative need became divorced many thousands of years ago, that talk of the sublimation of the sex urge into higher forms of activity is largely wishful thinking, that unless the female is to be reduced to a round of successive pregnancies and the male to be a slave to a succession of helpless infants, then sex-in-itself must be given a suitable social outlook other than the foul antisocial outlet of the brothel and the street prostitute.

Contraceptive techniques have removed the fear of the unwanted child and the female need no longer fear the consequences of sexual indulgence. The separation of sex and procreation without recourse to perversion has become absolute. Society is much the healthier for this. Unwanted, unprovided-for children are the tragedy of the earth. There are too many souls in a restricted and ever-shrinking world condemning their parents and ultimately themselves to a treadmill of industrial-commercial slavery and to an ever-intensifying struggle against starvation. But no amount of sociology of this or that 'ism' is going to produce the un-sexed individual. The sexual interpretation of history proves that the sex impulse will wreck whatever barriers are erected against it.

Until such time as man achieves a civilisation based, among other things, on the integration and maximum gratification of the sex impulse, bawdry will provide an invaluable safety-valve. There may come a day (and I am still Utopian enough to believe this may be possible) when men and women will live wisely and cleanly and healthily in mind and body and spirit. In that day there will be no need for bawdry as there was no need for it in the Garden of Eden. Even the most sanguine Utopian at his most optimistic realises that this much-to-be-wished-for day will be a long time a-coming and that it will have to be resolutely, consciously, even desperately striven for. Not so to strive or believe in the validity of the struggle is to turn the face to the wall of life and die.

The old Scots proverb that 'a standing cock has nae

conscience' is profoundly true, but if civilisation is not to relapse, as it has so often relapsed in the past, it must acquire a conscience. Burns, who knew the terrible strength of a standing cock, did much to supply it with such a conscience. Hence his bawdry is never wholly amoral. There is always some moral in it, implicit or explicit. Hence its strength and its glory and its importance for us to-day. It was not idly that he wrote to Robert Cleghorn: 'If that species of Composition be the Sin against the Haly Ghaist 'I am the most offending soul alive.' And indeed he was – and for the most valid reasons. Certain it is that without an understanding of Burns's bawdry there can be no full understanding of his contribution to history and particularly to the history of the struggle for a society that will ensure the maximum of human happiness.

It may be objected that bawdry has little or nothing to do with sociology. But I do not think that any human activity can be completely divorced from sociological considerations. In any case, I make no apology for raising the issue. Burns himself continually raised it. His personal and social ethic he summed up very neatly in the lines:

> In wars at home I'll shed my blood –
> Life giving wars o' Venus;
> The deities that I adore
> Are social peace and plenty.
> I'm better pleased to mak' one more
> Than be the death o' twenty.

We are his debtors for so much that he has given to the world, and not least for what he did in freeing sex from any taint of sin or shame or guilt or pruriency. In his day perhaps his bawdy verses were indeed, as he said, 'not quite ladies' reading' but since then, intellectually at least, women have advanced and they are now as free of the field of bawdry as the men. Maybe they always were. Only today there is little false modesty and a more frank acceptance of equality in this as in so many other fields of activity.

MERRY MUSES INTRODUCTORY
By SYDNEY GOODSIR SMITH

A S PROFESSOR DELANCEY FERGUSON says, this edition of *The Merry Muses* 'can make no sweeping claim to accuracy or completeness;' this will only be possible when Burns's original notebook is discovered. It is an attempt to gather together what has survived of Burns's activities in the field of bawdy song, as author, editor or collector.

In Section I, Professor Ferguson has provided texts from authentic holograph manuscripts of the Bard; the bulk of the rest of the book is taken from the sole surviving copy known of the original *Muses*, now in the possession of the Rt. Hon. the Earl of Rosebery, K.T., and it is due to his lordship's kindness and generosity that we are able to present at last the authentic text of that much debated volume. The world of Burns scholarship is in his debt, for until now they have seen only garbled 19th and early 20th century versions of this unique collection of Scottish folksong as it existed in Burns's day.

In 1911 Duncan M'Naught produced his famous (or infamous) Burns Federation edition which he stated to have been reproduced from the very volume that now reposes in Lord Rosebery's library (hereinafter called MMC or the 1800 edition – the paper is watermarked 1799 twice and 1800 eight times). A comparison of the two texts will show how far this statement was correct. Not even the contents are the same and the truly enormous number of textual variations are merely 'improvements' made by M'Naught or by William Scott Douglas, editor of Burns's *Works* (6 vols., 1877–1879), who once owned this unique copy and who has defaced the pages with numerous alternative readings which M'Naught in his edition has often preferred to the printed text. In this connection it is important to remember that both M'Naught and Scott Douglas were amateur versifiers. An example of Scott Douglas's carryings-on will be seen in Plate 2 ('Elibanks')[1]; he has obviously just been playing himself.

In the Murison Burns Collection in Dunfermline Public Library there is a transcript of the 1800 edition made by J.C. Ewing 'about the year 1893' (according to his note) for an intended edition by W.E. Henley, a project that never matured. Fifty copies of another transcript were made in 1904 for J.S. Farmer, Editor of *Merrie Songs and Ballads Prior to 1800* (1897) – for sale at 10 guineas a throw! Both Ewing's and Farmer's transcripts, of the identical Scott Douglas-Rosebery copy, are inaccurate and vary one from another to a considerable degree; both quote Scott Douglas's holograph emendations as 'variants.' The next stage is for M'Naught in his edition of 1911 to prefer these 'variants' to the printed text and to incorporate them silently. Sometimes they correspond to the corrupt versions in the 1827 edition which it was M'Naught's laudable intention to expose as fraudulent. This present edition is the first to reproduce the 1800 texts *verbatim et literatim*. On the only occasion ('The Fornicator') where we have a Burns holograph of verses printed in MMC 1800 and there amended by Scott Douglas, we find the printed text – of the stanzas common to both – corresponds to Burns's and differs from Douglas's.

---

[1]   This plate is omitted from the Luath edition. VB

Here, I muſt gently and wíth respect differ from Professor
Ferguson when he says 'In the case of folksongs [Burns's
notebook] would obviously contain texts differing líttle, if
at all, from his jottings from oral recítation and from the
copies he transcribed for friends. In the case of his own
compoſitions in the *genre*, the texts would be final ones,
not rough drafts; he would be unlikely to enter verses in
the book until they were in a form which satisfied him.' I
am afraid poets are not always like that; some are aye
tinkering with 'final' versions; Burns's own texts vary
between the Kilmarnock and Edinburgh edítions. In
modern times, W.B. Yeats rewrote many of his early
poems when publishing his *Collected Works*, and, more
recently, Mr W.H. Auden has done the same. In the case
of folksong Burns might easily improve or alter a line here
and there when transcribing them for friends; he was not
a 20th century scholar or even an unimaginative and
earneſt collector like David Herd; he was a poet. However,
this is not an important point.

One day, maybe, Burns's notebook will come to light and
we shall know all. In the meantime, we offer you this
approximation. The contents of the present edítion
might be described as an 'ideal' *Merry Muses* — what might or
conceivably could be found if Burns's notebook were
discovered. To make room for 16 new ítems we have
jettisoned 10 songs from the 1800 edítion which are
available in the ordinary edítions, *viz.*, those from 'The
Jolly Beggars' ('I am a Bard,' 'Let me ryke up,' 'I once was
a Maid') and 'The Rantin' Dog the Daddie o't,' 'Anna,'
'My wife's a wanton wee thing,' 'Beneath a green shade,'
'Wha is at my Bower Door?' 'My Auntie Jean,' and 'The
Cooper o' Cuddy.' The new songs are taken eíther from

Burns's own MSS, as in Section I, or from printed sources such as the 1827 edition of the *Muses*, *The Giblet Pye* (c.1806) and David Herd's collections. They are all connected with Burns; either his own work or ascribed to him (Section II) or songs from which he rewrote polite versions. This latter category (Section III) is an important one and central to the collection.

In 1787 in Edinburgh, Burns met James Johnson, an engraver, who 'from an honest Scotch enthusiasm [has] set about collecting all our native Songs and setting them to music' (20.10.1787). He invited Burns to help him and the Bard entered into the collaboration with enthusiasm — 'I have been absolutely crazed about it.' He had become a folksong collector — and a folksong writer. From this point on, for the last 10 years of his life, this was his chief occupation. Wherever he went, his tours in the Highlands and Borders, doing his rounds as Exciseman in Galloway, he jotted down songs and fragments that he heard, to be worked up later into presentable shape for Johnson's *Scots Musical Museum* (6 vols., 1787–1803), and later George Thomson's *Select Collection of Original Scottish Airs* (5 vols., 1793–1826). Many of these, if not most, would be bawdy and many would find a place in his Notebook.

> With a strange contradiction to the grave and religious character of the Scottish people, they possessed a wonderful quantity of indecorous traditionary verse, not of an inflammatory nature, but simply expressive of a profound sense of the ludicrous in connection with the sexual affections. Such things, usually kept from public view, oozed out in the merry companies such as Burns loved to frequent.

Thus Robert Chambers in his *Life and Works of Robert Burns*
(1851–52). One such merry company where the non-
inflammatory verse 'oozed out' were the Crochallan
Fencibles, a drinking club of which Burns was a member,
who met at Dawney Douglas's tavern in the Anchor Close
off the High Street of Edinburgh. It was for them the *Muses*
were oftensibly put together.

In Section III there are nearly 30 such songs which Burns
transmuted into polîte versions and which in their new
form have travelled the world over. In Section IV there are
another 30 odd tîtles which, had he lived longer, might
likewise have found their way into decorous society. The
polîte muft never contemn their indecorous beginnings;
all our beginnings are, to Holy Willie, 'indecorous.'
Enough of that. Apart from collecting, Burns occasionally
tried his own hand at the game and what we know of these
will be found in Sections I and II. By and large, as Henley
has pointed out, they are not much superior to the
genuine folk examples – if such a category can be defined,
for we are all folk. To this the rider should be added that
in copying into his notebook a folksong received from,
say, a ploughman, Burns has often, demonftrably, tidied
ît up a bît. In a few cases we can compare his version wîth
that of a contemporary collector who was not a poet,
David Herd (*viz.*, 'Jockey was a bonnie lad'). In one or two
cases he wrote a bawdy version of his own as well as
producing a purified one for the drawing-rooms ('Had I
the wyte?').

In Section II we have perhaps been over generous in our
ascriptions. Where there is real evidence that these are
Burns's own work we have said so; in other cases the

ascriptions are merely the opinions of different editors such as Henley and Henderson, Hecht, Scott Douglas or ourselves. Scott Douglas may have been an irresponsible editor in some ways, but he had a flair for Burns and on occasions his unsubstantiated notions have subsequently been proved documentarily — as in 'Nine Inch will please a Lady' — so we decided to cite his attributions when we have agreed with him. I should point out here that when I say 'we' I mean James Barke and myself; Professor Ferguson is a scholar such as we are not and is rightly suspicious of all such ascriptions unbacked by documentary evidence. For this reason, his contribution to the present volume is by his own request limited to Section I and 'The Libel Summons.'

As to the poetic value of these songs, apart from their importance in literary history, folk lore and sociology — or even maybe anthropology and psychology — opinions must differ. Their biographical value is indubitable; we cannot know Burns completely without them. The Burns who wrote that masterpiece of sentiment 'John Anderson, my jo, John,' was the same Burns who collected and transcribed the 'John Anderson' in this book; the Burns who wrote 'Had I the wyte?' in the *Collected Poems* is the same Burns who wrote the version in these pages. We are none of us all pure or all impure, but few are honest or indiscreet enough to let our right hand know what our left hand doeth; maybe we are all of us merely, in Tallulah Bankhead's deathless words, 'pure as driven slush.' Byron, on reading some of these songs in Burns's then unpublished letters, commented in his journal (13.12.1813), 'What an antithetical mind! — tenderness, roughness — delicacy, coarseness — sentiment, sensuality — soaring and grovelling, dirt and deîty − all mixed up in that one compound of inspired clay!' A true observe and one that could well be applied to the Scots genius as a whole.

Certainly, as a wrîter, Burns is one of the frankeſt − or moſt indiscreet, depending how you look on ît − in hiſtory. This grandiosîty of indiscretion he shares wîth Byron and Dunbar, in our own lîterature, and wîth Villon and Catullus, Belli and (in a sentimental way) Whîtman, in others. To these names we might add Donne, Shakespeare and Rabelais − in their very different but all very human ways. In this regard I would quote Whîtman's reference to the *Merry Muses* (for which I am indebted to another *grand indiscret*, Mr Hugh MacDiarmid):

> In these composîtions ... there is much indelicacy ... but the composer reigns alone, wîth handling free and broad and true, and is an artiſt ... Though so much is to be said in the way of fault-finding, drawing black marks, and doubtless severe lîterary crîticism, after full retrospect of his works and life, the aforesaid 'odd kind chiel' remains to my heart and brain as almoſt the tendereſt, manlieſt, and (even if contradictory) deareſt flesh−and−blood figure in all the ſtreams and cluſters of by-gone poets. (*Nonesuch* edn., ed. E. Holloway, 825−833).

'Deareſt flesh−and−blood figure' − that is a right word, I think, and ît is probably this qualîty that has given Burns his peculiarly affectionate fame among the Scots and, for all I know, elsewhere. His undisguised enjoyment of bawdry, which we all share but not always admît, is part of this open humanîty that endears him to us. As James Barke says, there is nothing prurient or sniggering in these songs, nothing eîther, in Chambers's words, 'of an inflammatory character' − they are hearty uninhibîted belly laughs. It is a mercy they have survived; they are a unique relic of their period, far superior to their somewhat mawkish English; Anglo-Scottish and Anglo-Irish contemporaries ('Una's Lock' in this volume is typical of these latter); and we should be poorer without them. As Burns wrote to James Hoy in 1787 (enclosing 'one or two poetic bagatelles which the world have not seen, or, perhaps, for obvious reasons, cannot see') 'they may make you laugh a little, which, on the whole, is no bad way of spending one's precious hours and still more precious breath.' And who could disagree with that?

ABBREVIATIONS

Ald   *Poetical Works of Robert Burns* (ed. George A. Aîtken),
           Aldine Edîtion, Wm. Pickering, London 1839
           and 1893.

Archiv   *Archiv für das Studium der neucren Sprachen und Lîteraturen*,
           cxxix, 363–374; cxxx, 57–72.

B.Chr.   *Robert Burns Chronicle*, Burns Federation,
           Kilmarnock.

DH   David Herd, *The Ancient and Modern Scots Songs*, *Heroic
           Ballads &c*, Edinburgh 1769 and 1776.

DLF   J. DeLancey Ferguson.

DLF.*L*   J. DeLancey Ferguson, *The Letters of Robert Burns*,
           edîted from the original manuscripts, Oxford
           1931.

Giblet   *The Giblet Pye*, / being the / Heads, Tails, Legs and
           Wings, / of the Anacreontic songs of the celebrated
           / R. Burns, G.A. Stevens, Rochester, T. L–tle, /
           and others. / Some of which are taken from the
           Original Manus/cripts of R. Burns, never before
           published / ... Shamborough: / Printed by John
           Nox / ... (*c*.1806).

HH   W.E. Henley and T.F. Henderson, *The Poetry of
           Robert Burns*, Edinburgh 1896 (Centenary Edîtion).

Ht.Hd.   Hans Hecht, *Songs from David Herd's MSS*, Edinburgh
           1904.

JB   James Barke.

JCD.*N*   J.C. Dick *Notes of Scottish Song* by Robert Burns,
           wrîtten in an Interleaved Copy of *The Scots Musical
           Museum*, London, 1908.

JCD.*S*   J.C. Dick, *The Songs of Robert Burns*, with the
           Melodies for which they were written, London
           1903.

JCE   J.C. Ewing's transcript of *The Merry Muses of
           Caledonia* 'Dumfries *c*.1800,' in the Murison
           Burns Collection, Dunfermline.

JSF   J.S. Farmer, *Merrie Songs and Ballads Prior to 1800*,
           Privately Printed 1897.

MM27   *The Merry Muses*, a Choice Collection of Favourite
           Songs from many Sources by Robert Burns,
           [predated] 1827.

MMC   *Merry Muses of Caledonia*; A Collection of Favourite
           Scots Songs, Ancient and Modern: Selected for
           use of the Crochallan Fencibles. Undated
           (*c*.1800).

M'N   *The Merry Muses of Caledonia*; (Original Edition) A
           Collection of Favourite Scots Songs Ancient and
           Modern; Selected for use of the Crochallan
           Fencibles ... A Vindication of Robert Burns in
           connection with the above publication and the
           spurious editions which succeeded it. Printed and
           Published under the Auspices of the Burns
           Federation. For Subscribers Only. Not for Sale.
           1911. 'Introductory and Corrective' by Vindex
           [Duncan M'Naught].

MP   *Modern Philology* xxx.i, August 1932. (New York,
           USA).

PMLA   *Publications of the Modern Language Association of America*
           LI, 4, December 1936 (New York, USA).

SD   W. Scott Douglas, annotator of MMC (*q.v.*).

SGS   Sydney Goodsir Smith.

SMM   James Johnson, *The Scots Musical Museum*, Consisting of Six Hundred Scots Songs. (Edinburgh 1787). New Edition ed. Wm. Stenhouse, Edinburgh 1853.

TTM   *The Tea-Table Miscellany*, Edinburgh: Printed by Mr Thomas Ruddiman for Allan Ramsay ... 1724. Also Dublin 1729, and Tenth Edition, London 1740.

IN BURNS'S HOLOGRAPH

I
A. BY BURNS

The Notes in this section are by
Professor DeLANCEY FERGUSON (DLF)
unless otherwise initialled.

I'LL TELL YOU A TALE OF A WIFE

TUNE: *Auld Sir Symon*

MS formerly in collection of Mr Lucius Wilmerding, New York. Burns sent this song to Provost Robert Maxwell of Lochmaben, 20 December 1789, with this prefatory note:

> ... I shall betake myself to a subject ever fertile of themes, a Subject, the turtle-feast of the Sons of Satan, and the delicious, secret Sugar-plumb of the Babes of Grace; a Subject, sparkling with all the jewels that Wit can find in the mines of Genius, and pregnant with all the stores of Learning, from Moses & Confucius to Franklin & Priestly – in short, may it please Your Lordship, I intend to write BAUDY!

At the end of the song, he added:

> You see, Sir, I have fulfilled my promise: I wish you would think of fulfilling yours, and come & see the rest of my Collection.– [DLF, *L* I, 377].

Among the accessible extant MSS, this is the only one which Burns definitely describes as part of his 'Collection.' It is therefore highly significant that the text in *The Merry Muses*, where it is entitled 'The Case of Conscience,' lacks stanzas 3, 6 and 7 – fairly conclusive evidence in itself that the printed text could not have been taken from the poet's own notebook. [DLF]. Catherine Carswell considers this 'infamous and ludicrous' song to have been inspired by Clarinda. [SGS].

I'll tell you a tale of a Wife,
    And she was a Whig and a Saunt;
She liv'd a most sanctify'd life,
    But whyles she was fash'd wi' her —.—

    Fal lal &c.

2   Poor woman! she gaed to the Priest,
        And till him she made her complaint;
    'There's naething that troubles my breast
        'Sae sair as the sins o' my —.—

3   'Sin that I was herdin at hame,
        'Till now I'm three score & ayont,
    'I own it wi' sin & wi' shame
        'I've led a sad life wi' my —.—'

4   He bade her to clear up her brow,
        And no be discourag'd upon 't;
    For holy gude women enow
        Were mony times waur't wi' their —.—

5   It's naught but Beelzebub's art,
        But that's the mair sign of a saunt,
    He kens that ye're pure at the heart,
        Sae levels his darts at your —.—

6   What signifies Morals & Works,
        Our works are no wordy a runt!
    It's Faith that is sound, orthodox
        That covers the fauts o' your —.—

7   Were ye o' the Reprobate race
        Created to sin & be brunt,
    O then it would alter the case
        If ye should gae wrang wi' your —.—

8   But you that is Called & Free
      Elekît & chosen a saunt,
  Will't break the Eternal Decree
      Whatever ye do wi' your — ? —

9   And now with a sanctify'd kiss
      Let's kneel & renew covenant:
  It's this — and ît's this — and ît's this —
      That settles the pride o' your —.—

10 Devotion blew up to a flame;
      No words can do justice upon't;
  The honest auld woman gaed hame
      Rejoicing and clawin her —.—

11 Then high to her memory charge;
      And may he who takes ît affront,
  Still ride in Love's channel at large,
      And never make port in a — ! ! ! *

* In a letter to Robert Ainslie, 29 July 1787 (PMLA, LI, 4),
  Burns quotes what appears to be an alternative final stanza:
    Then, hey, for a merry good fellow;
      And hey, for a glass of good strunt;
    May never we SONS OF APOLLO
      E'er want a good friend and a —.

St 4	LINE 3	MMC	For haly gude …
St 5	LINE 1	*Ibid*.	It's nocht …
St 5	LINE 4	*Ibid*.	Sae he levels …
St 10	LINE 3	*Ibid*.	… auld carlin …
St 11	LINE 2	*Ibid*.	And may he wha taks ît …

[SGS]

BONIE MARY

TUNE: *Minnie's ay glowering o'er me* –

MS formerly in Bixby Collection, St Louis. On 25 October 1793 (?), Burns sent this song, and 'Act Sederunt of the Session,' to Robert Cleghorn 'in all the sincerity of a brace of honeſt Port.' (DLF, *L* ii, 212). His preface is well known:

> There is, there muſt be, some truth in original sin. – My violent propensity to B——dy convinces me of it. – Lack a day! if that species of Composition be the Sin againſt 'the Haly Ghaiſt,' 'I am the moſt offending soul alive.' – Mair for taiken, A fine chiel, a hand-wail'd friend & crony o' my am, gat o'er the lugs in loove wi' a braw, bonie, fodgel hizzie frae the English-side, weel-ken'd i' the brugh of Annan by the name o', Bonie Mary, & I tauld the tale as follows. – NB The chorus is auld –

Since Burns alleges a personal basis for the song, a conjectural identification of 'Wattie' is Walter Auld, saddler in Dumfries, who occasionally took charge of parcels for the poet in his Ellisland days. The *Scots Magazine* for December 1793, liſts Auld as having been declared bankrupt on 17 December. Published in MMC. [DLF]

Chorus
Come cowe me, minnie, come cowe me;
Come cowe me, minnie, come cowe me;
The hair o' my a— is grown into my c—t,
And they canna win too [*sic*], to m—we me.

1   When Mary cam over the Border,
     When Mary cam over the Border;
     As eîth 'twas approachin the C—t of a hurchin,
     Her a— was in sic a disorder. —

2   But wanton Wattie cam weſt on't,
     But wanton Wattie cam weſt on't,
     He did ît sae tickle, he left nae as meikle
     'S a spider wad bigget a neſt on't. —

3   And was nae Wattie a Clinker,
     He m—w'd frae the Queen to the tinkler
     Then sat down, in grief, like the Macedon chief
     For want o' mae warlds to conquer. —

4   And O, what a jewel was Mary!
     And O, what a jewel was Mary!
     Her face ît was fine, & her bosom divine,
     And her c—nt ît was theekît wi' glory.

Come cowe &c.

Chorus	line 4	MMC	… win in for to…
St 3	line 1	*Ibid.*	… a blinker.

                                 [SGS]

ACT SEDERUNT OF THE SESSION

TUNE: *O'er the muir among the heather*

MS formerly in Bixby Collection, St Louis. This song was
sent to Robert Cleghorn, 25 October 1793, in the same
letter * with 'Come cowe me, minnie.' (DLF, L ii 212). It
was printed, with some transpositions, in MMC. [DLF]

A Scots Ballad —

In Edinburgh town they've made a law,
    In Edinburgh at the Court o' Session,
That standing pr—cks are fauteors a',
    And guilty of a high transgression. —

Chorus

Act Sederunt o' the Session,
    Decreet o' the Court o' Session,
That standing pr—cks are fauteors a',
    And guilty of a high transgression.

2   And they've provided dungeons deep.
        Ilk lass has ane in her possession;
    Untill the wretches wail and weep,
        They there shall lie for their transgression.

Chorus

Act Sederunt o' the Session,
    Decreet o' the Court o' Session,
The rogues in pouring tears shall weep,
    By act Sederunt o' the Session. —

* '... From my late hours last night, & the dripping fogs & damn'd
cast wind of this stupid day, I have left me as little soul as an oyster.
– 'Sir John, you are so fretful, you cannot live long.' – 'Why, there
is it! Come, sing me a BAUDY-SONG to make me merry!!! '–"

[Song follows]

WHEN PRINCES AND PRELATES

TUNE: *The Campbells are Coming*

Burns composed this song at Sanquhar — after, to judge
by the handwriting, a convivial evening — and despatched
it immediately to Robert Cleghorn. The MS is now in the
Huntington Library, and is dated 12 December 1792. In
July 1794, Burns sent a copy to George Thomson,
eliciting from that usually prim and proper editor the
comment, 'What a pity this is not publishable.' (DLF, L ii,
250). Both versions consist of six stanzas; apart from
variations in spelling, their only important differences
are that the Cleghorn text has 'people' instead of 'folk'
and is worded differently in the final stanza, here given
in a footnote.

The *Merry Muses* has two additional stanzas, inserted
between stanzas 3 and 4, and 4 and 5, respectively, of the
present text. In the absence of manuscript authority,
these may be considered interpolations. Dumouriez had
defeated the Austrians at Jemmappes about a month
before Burns wrote the Cleghorn version; the Duke of
York stanza could not have been composed before 1793.
But both could have been completed long before July
1794, and if Burns had meant them as part of his final
version he would have included them in the Thomson
copy. [DLF]

When princes & prelates & het-headed zealots
    All Europe hae set in a lowe,
The poor man lies down, nor envies a crown,
    And comforts himself with a mowe. —

Chorus —

And why shouldna poor folk mowe, mowe, mowe,
    And why shouldna poor folk mowe:
The great folk hae siller, & houses & lands,
    Poor bodies hae naething but mowe. —

2   When Br—nsw—ck's great Prince cam a cruising to
          Fr—nce,
    Republican billies to cowe,
Bauld Br—nsw—ck's great Prince wad hae shawn
        better sense,
    At hame with his Princess to mowe. —

And why should na &c.

3   Out over the Rhine proud Pr—ss—a wad shine,
    To *spend* his best blood he did vow;
But Frederic had better ne'er forded the water,
    But spent as he docht in a mowe. —

And why &c.

4   By sea & by shore! the Emp—r—r swore,
    In Paris he'd kick up a row;
But Paris sae ready just leugh at the laddie
    And bade him gae tak him a mowe. —

And why &c.

5   Auld Kate laid her claws on poor Stanislaus,
        And Poland has bent like a bow:
    May the deil in her a— ram a huge pr—ck o' brass!
        And damn her in h—ll with a mowe!

And why &c.

6   But truce with commotions & new-fangled notions,
        A bumper I trust you'll allow:
    Here's George our gude king & Charlotte his queen
        And lang may they tak a gude mowe! *

---

* In the Cleghorn copy, this stanza reads:

But truth with commotions & new-fangled notions,
  A bumper [I'll fill it I vow (deleted)] I trust you'll allow:
Here's George our good king, & lang may he ring,
  And Charlotte & he tak a mow. —

And why should na &c.

Interpolated stanzas in MMC read:

When the brave Duke of York
  The Rhine first did pass,
Republican armies to cow, cow, cow.
  They bade him gae hame,
To his P—ss—n dame,
  An' gie her a kiss an' m—w, a m—w.

An why, &c.

The black-headed eagle.
  As keen as a beagle,
He hunted o'er height an' o'er howe, howe, howe.
  In the braes of Gemap,
He fell in a trap,
  E'en let him come out as he dow, dow, dow.

An' why, &c.

WHILE PROSE-WORK AND RHYMES
TUNE: *The Campbells are Coming*

Hitherto unpublished. From an original holograph, formerly in the possession of Mr Owen D. Young, and now in the Berg Collection, New York Public Library. Theme and meter are identical with 'When Princes and Prelates.' [DLF]

A Ballad

While Prose-work & rhymes
    Are hunted for crimes,
And things are — the devil knows how;
    Aware o' my rhymes,
    In these kittle times,
The subject I chuse is a —

Some cry, Constitution!
    Some cry, Revolution!
And Politics kick up a rowe;
    But Prince & Republic,
    Agree on the Subject,
No treason is in a good —

Th' Episcopal lawn,
    And Presbyter band,
Hae lang been to ither a cowe;
    But still the proud Prelate,
    And Presbyter zealot
Agree in an orthodox —

Poor Justice, 'tis hinted —
    Ill natur'dly squinted,
The Process — but mum — we'll allow —
    Poor Justice has ever
    For C—t had a favor,
While Justice could tak a gude —

Now fill to the brim —
    To her, & to him,
Wha willingly do what they dow;
    And ne'er a poor wench
    Want a friend at a pinch,
Whase failing is only a —

NINE INCH WILL PLEASE A LADY

To its ain tune —

Printed in MMC. M'Naught describes it as 'anonymous,
but evidently old; perhaps brushed up a little.' Never-
theless, in its present form it is probably Burns's own
work. Three lines of stanza I survive in a fragmentary
letter from Ellisland, perhaps addressed to Alexander
Dalziel (DLF, L i, 295), which is now in the Watson
Collection, Scottish National Portrait Gallery. The
present text is taken from a photostat of a holograph in
the Esty Collection, Ardmore, Pennsylvania. [DLF]. In
MMC the tune is given as 'The Quaker's Wife.' [SGS].

1   'Come rede me, dame, come tell me, dame,
      'My dame come tell me truly,
  'What length o' graith, when weel ca'd hame,
      'Will sair a woman duly?'
  The carlin clew her wanton tail,
      Her wanton tail sae ready —
  I learn'd a sang in Annandale,
      Nine inch will please a lady. —

2   But for a koontrie c—nt like mine,
      In sooth, we're nae sae gentle;
  We'll tak tway thumb-bread to the nine,
      And that's a sonsy p—ntle:
  O Leeze me on my Charlie lad,
      I'll ne'er forget my Charlie!
  Tway roarin handfu's and a daud,
      He nidge't it in fu' rarely. —

3   But weary fa' the laîthron doup,
        And may ît ne'er be thrivin!
    It's no the length that maks me loup,
        But ît's the double drivin. —
    Come nidge me, Tam, come nudge me, Tam,
        Come nidge me o'er the nyvel!
    Come lowse & lug your battering ram,
        And thrash him at my gyvel!

ODE TO SPRING

TUNE: *The tither morn*

MS, Morgan Library, New York. In January 1795, Burns
wrote to George Thomson (DLF, L ii, 283):

'... Give me leave to squeeze in a clever anecdote of my
Spring originality: —

'Some years ago, when I was young, & by no means the
saint I am now, I was looking over, in company with a belle
lettre friend, a Magazine Ode to Spring, when my friend
fell foul of the recurrence of the same thoughts, & offered
me a bet that it was impossible to produce an Ode to
Spring on an original plan. — I accepted it, & pledged
myself to bring in the verdant fields, — the budding
flowers, — the chryftal ftreams, — the melody of the groves,
— & a love-ftory into the bargain, & yet be original. Here
follows the piece, & wrote for music too!'

The Ode was included in MMC; the present text is from
Burns's letter to Thomson. [DLF]

When maukin bucks, at early f—s,
　　In dewy grass are seen, Sir;
And birds, on boughs, take off their m—s,
　　Amang the leaves sae green, Sir;
Latona's son looks liquorish on
　　Dame Nature's grand impètus,
Till his p—go rise, then weftward flies
　　To r—ger Madame Thetis.

Yon wandering rill that marks the hill,
    And glances o'er the brae, Sir,
Glides by a bower where many a flower
    Sheds fragrance on the day, Sir;
There Damon lay, with Sylvia gay,
    To love they thought no crime, Sir;
The wild-birds sang, the echoes rang,
    While Damon's a—se beat time, Sir. —

First, wi' the thrush, his thrust & push
    Had compass large & long, Sir;
The blackbird next, his tuneful text,
    Was bolder, clear & strong, Sir;
The linnet's lay came then in play,
    And the lark that soar'd aboon, Sir;
Till Damon, fierce, mistim'd his a—,
    And f—'d quite out of tune, Sir. —

O SAW YE MY MAGGIE?

TUNE: *O Saw ye na my Peggy?*

From holograph MS in the Library of Abbotsford, bound in with Sir Walter Scott's copy of Burns's *The Fornicator's Court*, the fly-leaf of which is inscribed anonymously (presumably by the printer or publisher): 'Thick paper — only 10 copies printed. To Sir Walter Scott, Bart., June 1823.' There is no imprint or colophon. Printed in MMC and there described in a pencilled note by Scott Douglas as 'Old.' Also appeared MM27. Burns's Note on the song 'Saw Ye Nae My Peggie' in the Interleaved SMM (JCD.*N* 4) reads: 'This charming song is much older, and indeed much superior to Ramsay's verses, 'The Toast' [TTM 1724, 47], as he calls them. There is another set of the words, much older still, and which I take to be the original one, but though it has a very great deal of merit it is not quite ladies' reading.' There is another version in Herd (DH 1769, 175). Although Burns claims this as his own (see Footnote) he can only mean 'in part.' [SGS]

1   Saw ye my Maggie?
    Saw ye my Maggie?
    Saw ye my Maggie?
        Comin oer the lea?

2   What mark has your Maggie,
    What mark has your Maggie,
    What mark has your Maggie,
        That ane may ken her be?

[2a]   [Wry-c—d is she,
 Wry-c—d is she,
  Wry-c—d is she,
   And pishes gain' her thie.]

3 My Maggie has a mark,
 Ye'll find it in the dark,
 It's in below her sark,
   A little aboon her knee.

4 What wealth has your Maggie,
 What wealth has your Maggie,
 What wealth has your Maggie,
   In tocher, gear, or fee?

5 My Maggie has a treasure,
 A hidden mine o' pleasure,
 I'll howk it at my leisure,
   It's alane for me.

8 How meet you your Maggie,
 How meet you your Maggie,
 How meet you your Maggie,
   When nane's to hear or see?

7 Ein that tell our wishes,
 Eager glowing kisses,
 Then diviner blisses,
   In holy ecstacy!—

6   How be ye your Maggy,
     How be [ye] your Maggy,
     How be ye your Maggy,
          An loe nane but she?

9   Heavenly joys before me,
     Rapture trembling o'er me,
     Maggie I adore thee,
          On my bended knee!!!

[st. 2a]. This stanza occurs in MMC but not in the MS or in MM27;
it might well have been added by Burns when copying the song into
his notebook, just as, in the MS, stanzas 6 and 7 are obviously
afterthoughts, written in the margin in a different ink, with a
different pen, and all stanzas numbered subsequently. The song is
here printed in the stanza order in MMC; the numbering is as
numbered by Burns in the MS at Abbotsford.

The song is followed by this note in Burns's holograph:

'In the name of Venus, Amen! — Know all men by these
Presents, that I, the Author of the foregoing Verses make over
and convey from me and my heirs whatever the Copy Right
and Property of & in the said Verses to & in favor of, Mr
Alexr. Findlater, for his behoof & especially that He, in the
hour of Concupiscence, & the power of the Flesh, by giving
vent in the channel of Poesy & Song, may keep the said
Propensities from hurrying him into the actual momentum
of the horrid sin of Uncleanness. — The Author.' [SGS]

TO ALEXANDER FINDLATER

Here firſt printed in full, from a transcript of the original holograph in the Rosebery Collection. The two closing ſtanzas, and the firſt four lines of ſtanza 1, were printed in the Chambers-Wallace *Life and Works of Burns* (Edinburgh, 1896), iii, 261–2. *Cf.* DLF, *Letters*, ii, 13–14. There seems no reason for assuming, as Wallace did, that these verses and the prose note accompanied the same gift of eggs. [DLF]

Ellisland Saturday morning

Dear Sir,

our Lucky humbly begs
Ye'll prie her caller, new-laid eggs:
L—d grant the Cock may keep his legs,
 Aboon the Chuckies;
And wi' his kittle, forket clegs,
 Claw weel their dockies!

Had Fate that curſt me in her ledger.
A Poet poor, & poorer Gager,
Created me that feather'd Sodger,
 A generous Cock,
How I wad craw & ſtrut and r—ger
 My kecklin Flock!

Buskît wi' mony a bien, braw feather.
I wad defied the warſt o' weather:
When corn or bear I could na gather
 To gie my burdies;
I'd treated them wi' caller heather,
 And weel-knooz'd hurdies.

Nae cursed CLERICAL EXCISE
On honeſt Nature's laws & ties;
Free as the vernal breeze that flies
    At early day,
We'd taſted Nature's richeſt joys,
    But ſtint or ſtay. —

But as this subject's something kittle,
Our wiseſt way's to say but little;
And while my Muse is at her mettle.
    I am, moſt fervent.
Or may I die upon a whittle!
    Your Friend & Servant —

                      ROBt BURNS

THE FORNICATOR

TUNE: *Clout the Cauldron*

This song commemorates Burns's amour with Betty
Paton, for which he did public penance in the kirk. The
present text is from a transcript, by the late Davidson
Cook, of a MS in the Honresfield collection. The printed
version in MMC gives only the first four stanzas. [DLF]

A new Song

Ye jovial boys who love the joys,
    The blissful joys of Lovers,
Yet dare avow, with dauntless brow,
    When the bony lass discovers,
I pray draw near, and lend an ear,
    And welcome in a Frater,
For I've lately been on quarantine,
    A proven Fornicator.

Before the Congregation wide,
    I passed the muster fairly,
My handsome Betsy by my side,
    We gat our ditty rarely;
But my downcast eye did chance to spy
    What made my lips to water,
Those limbs so clean when I between
    Commenc'd a Fornicator.

With rueful face and signs of grace
    I pay'd the buttock-hire,
But the night was dark and thro' the park
    I could not but convoy her;
A parting kiss, I could not less,
    My vows began to scatter,
My Betsy fell — lal de dal lal lal,
    I am a Fornicator.

But for her sake this vow I make,
    And solemnly I swear it,
That while I own a single crown
    She's welcome for to share it;
And my roguish boy his Mother's joy
    And the darling of his Pater,
For him I boast my pains and cost,
    Although a Fornicator.

Ye wenching blades whose hireling jades
    Have tipt you off blue-joram,
I tell you plain, I do disdain
    To rank you in the Quorum;
But a bony lass upon the grass
    To teach her esse Mater,
And no reward but fond regard,
    O that's a Fornicator.

Your warlike Kings and Heros bold,
    Great Captains and Commanders;
Your mighty Caesars fam'd of old,
    And conquering Alexanders;
In fields they fought and laurels bought,
    And bulwarks strong did batter,
But still they grac'd our noble list,
    And ranked Fornicator!!!

MY GIRL SHE'S AIRY

TUNE: *Black Joke*

MS, from a transcript of the original holograph, sold at Sotheby's, 13 November 1934. These verses, unknown to any edition of *The Merry Muses*, were composed during Burns's amour with Betty Paton, and were copied into his Commonplace Book in September 1784. The following version was sent to Robert Ainslie, 29 July 1787. [DLF]

> My Girl she's airy, she's buxom and gay,
> Her breath is as sweet as the blossoms in May;
> A touch of her lips it ravishes quîte;
> She's always good natur'd, good humor'd and free:
> She dances, she glances, she smiles wîth a glee;
> Her eyes are the lightenings of joy and delight:
> Her slender neck, her handsome waiſt
> Her hair well buckl'd, her ſtays well lac'd,
> Her taper whîte leg, wîth an et, and a, c,
> For her a, b, e, d, and her c, u, n, t,
> And Oh, for the joys of a long winter night! ! !

THERE WAS TWA WIVES

Not in any edition of *The Merry Muses*. Scott Douglas printed a garbled version of part of the first stanza. Burns sent the song to Robert Cleghorn, probably in January 1792 (DLF, L ii, 103), with the following introduction:

> ... I make you [a] present of the following new Edition of an old Cloaciniad song, [a] species of composition which I have heard you admire, and a kind of song which I know you wanted much. − It is sung to an old tune, something like Tak your auld cloak about you −.

This text is from a transcript, by the late Davidson Cook, of a MS in the Honresfield collection. [DLF]

There was twa wives, and twa witty wives,
    As e'er play'd houghmagandie,
And they coost out, upon a time,
    Out o'er a drink o' brandy;
Up Maggy rose, and forth she goes,
    And she leaves auld Mary flytin,
And she f—rted by the byre-en'
    For she was gaun a sh—ten.

She f—rted by the byre-en'
    She f—rted by the stable;
And thick and nimble were her steps
    As fast as she was able:
Till at yon dyke-back the hurly brak,
    But raxin for some dockins,
The beans and pease cam down her thighs,
    And she cackit a' her stockins.

1 B. COLLECTED BY BURNS

BROSE AN' BUTTER

This is the earliest surviving specimen of Burns's work as
a collector of folksongs. The text is written on the reverse
of his draft of a letter to Margaret Kennedy of Daljarrock
(formerly in the Adam Collection, New York). That
letter was composed either in 1786 or in the autumn of
1785, and the handwriting of the song proves that it is
approximately contemporary with the letter. The second
stanza of Burns's version does not appear in MMC, which
has, however, a final stanza not in Burns's MS. The order
of his stanzas differs also. [DLF]

Gie my Love brose, brose,
    Gie my Love brose an' butter;
An' gie my Love brose, brose,
    Yestreen he wanted his supper.

Jenny sits up i' the laft,
    Jocky wad fain a been at her;
There cam a win' out o' the wast
    Made a' the windows to clatter.

    Gie my Love brose &c.

A dow's a dainty dish;
    A goose is hollow within:
A sight wad mak you blush,
    But a' the fun's to fin'.

    Gie my &c.

My Dadie sent me to the hill,
  To pow my minnie some heather;
An' drive it in your fill,
  Ye're welcome to the leather.

  Gie my &c.

A mouse is a merry wee beast;
  A modewurck wants the een;
An' O for the touch o' the thing
  I had i' my nieve yestreen.

  Gie my Love &c.

The lark she loves the grass;
  The hen she loves the stibble;
An' hey for the Gar'ner lad,
  To gully awa wi' his dibble.

Extra final stanza from MMC:

 We a' were fou yestreen,
   The nicht shall be its brither;
 And hey, for a roaring pin
   To nail twa wames thegither!

In MMC lines 3 and 4 of the chorus read:

 For nane in Carrick wi him
   Can gie a c—t its supper.

           [SGS]

CUMNOCK PSALMS

MS, Morgan Library, New York. In September 1794, Burns wrote to George Thomson (DLF, L ii, 257):

> Do you know a droll Scots song more famous for its humor than delicacy, called, The grey goose & the gled? — Mr Clarke took down the notes, such as they are, at my request, which I shall give with some decenter verses to Johnson. — Mr Clarke says that the tune is positively an old Chant of the ROMISH CHURCH; which corroborates the old tradition, that at the Reformation, the Reformers burlesqued much of the old Church Music with setting them to bawdy verses. As a further proof, the common name for this song is Cumnock Psalms. — As there can be no harm in transcribing a stanza of a Psalm, I shall give you two or three: possibly the song is new to you.

Printed in MMC. [DLF]

As I looked o'er yon castle wa',
 I spied a grey goose & a gled;
They had a fecht between them twa,
 And O, as their twa hurdies gade. —

Chorus

With a hey ding it in, & a how ding it in,
 And a hey ding it in, it's lang to day:
Tal larietal, tallarietal
 Tal larietal, tal lane thy.

2 She strack up & he strack down.
 Between them twa they made a mowe,
And ilka fart that the carlin gae,
 It's four o' them wad fill a bowe.

  With a hey ding it in &c.

3   Temper your tail, Carlin, he cried,
        Temper your tail by Venus' law;
    Double your dunts, the dame replied,
        Wha the deil can hinder the wind to blaw!

        With a hey &c.

4   For were ye in my saddle set,
        And were ye weel girt in my gear,
    If the wind o' my arse blaw you out o' my cunt,
        Ye'll never be reckoned a man o' weir. —

        With a hey &c.

5   He placed his Jacob whare she did piss,
        And his ballocks whare the wind did blaw,
    And he grippet her faſt by the goosset o' the arse
        And he gae her cunt the common law.

        With a hey &c.

Burns to Thomson: 'So much for the Psalmody of Cumnock.'
Thomson's appended comment: 'Delicate psalmody indeed. G.T.'
(DLF, L ii, 257).

Stanzas 2 and 3 occur slightly changed as ſtanza 2 of 'Wha the Deil
can Hinder the Wind to blaw' (see Section IV). Burns's 'decenter
verses' are 'As I ſtood by yon rooflesſ tower' (HH iii, 144). [SGS]

GREEN GROW THE RASHES O [A]

This recension of an old Scots song was sent by Burns to John Richmond, 3 September 1786, with the note in which he announced that Jean Armour had just borne him twins. (DLF, L I, 41). The MS was included in the Armour sale at the American Art Association-Anderson Galleries, New York, 22 April 1937; the present text is from the holograph, examined by courtesy of Mr David A. Randall of Charles Scribner's Sons. [DLF]

A Fragment —

Chorus —

Green grow the rashes O,
Green grow the rashes O,
The lasses they hae wimble bores,
The widows they hae gashes O.

1   In sober hours I am a priest;
        A hero when I'm tipsey, O;
    But I'm a king and ev'ry thing,
        When wi' a wanton Gipsey, O.

        Green grow &c.

2   'Twas late yestreen I met wi' ane.
        An' wow, but she was gentle, O!
    Ae han' she pat roun' my cravat,
        The tither to my p— O.

        Green grow &c.

3   I dought na speak — yet was na fley'd—.
        My heart play'd duntie, duntie, O;
   An' ceremony laid aside,
       I fairly fun' her c—ntie, O.—

       Green grow &c.

                       — Multa desunt —

MMC has two versions. One (see Section II), which Scott Douglas in a pencilled note attributes to Burns, is entirely different, in its stanzas but has the chorus as above. The other which MMC describes as 'An Older Edition' (i.e. version), consists of stanzas 2 and 3 as above, with lines 3 and 4 of the chorus as:

   The sweetest bed that e'er I got
   Was the bellies o' the lassies, O.

One or other or all of these versions inspired Burns's famous song of the same name (HH I, 25). [SGS]

MUIRLAND MEG

TUNE: *Saw ye my Eppie McNab*

Published in MMC, where ît has a chorus:
> And for a sheep-cloot she'll do't, she'll do't,
> And for a sheep-cloot she'll do't;
> And for a toop-horn she'll do't to the morn,
> And merrily turn and do't, and do't.

M'Naught calls ît 'An old song.' The following text, in Burns's later hand, is copied, by permission, from a holograph which in February 1949, was in the possession of the Rosenbach Company, New York. It lacks the chorus. [DLF]

> Among our young lassies there's Muirland Meg,
> She'll beg or she work, & she'll play or she beg,
> At threteen her maidenhead flew to the gate,
> And the door o' her cage ſtands open yet. —
>
> Her kîttle black een they wad thirl you thro',
> Her rose-bud lips cry, kiss me now;
> The curls & links o' her bonie black hair, —
> Wad put you in mind that the lassie has mair. —
>
> An armfu' o' love is her bosom sae plump,
> A span o' delight is her middle sae jimp;
> A taper, whîte leg, & a thumpin thie,
> And a fiddle near by, an ye play a wee! —
>
> Love's her delight, & kissin's her treasure;
> She'll ſtick at nae price, & ye gie her gude measure.
> As lang's a sheep-fît, & as girt's a goose-egg,
> And that's the measure o' Muirland Meg.

TODLEN HAME

(By David McCulloch of Ardwell, Galloway)

MS formerly in the Bixby Collection, St Louis. Printed in DLF, *L* ii, 309. Not in any edition of *The Merry Muses*. Burns wrote from Dumfries, 21 August 1795, to his Crochallan crony Robert Cleghorn of Saughton Mills, Edinburgh, enclosing another bawdy song, which we have been unable to trace [SGS]:

> … Inclosed you have Clarke's Gaffer Gray. – I have not time [to make a] copy of it, so, when you have taken a copy for yourself, please return me the Original. – I need not caution you against giving copies to any other person. – 'Peggy Ramsay,' I shall expect to find in Gaffer Gray's company, when he returns to Dumfries. – … PS Did you ever meet with the following, Todlin hame – By the late Mr McCulloch, of Ardwell – Galloway –

When wise Solomon was a young man o' might,
He was canty, & liked a lass ilka night;
But when he grew auld that he was na in trim,
He cried out, 'In faith, Sirs! I doubt it's a sin!'
    Todlen hame, todlen hame,
    Sae round as a neep we gang todlen hame. –

But we're no come to that time o' life yet, ye ken;
The bottle's half-out – but we'll fill it again:
As for Solomon's doubts, wha the devil cares for't!
He's a damn'd churlish fallow that likes to spill
  sport.
Todlen &c.

A bicker that's gizzen'd, it's nae worth a doit;
Keep it wat, it will haud in — it winna let out:
A chiel that's ay sober, is damn'd ill to ken;
Keep him wat wi' gude drink — & ye'll find him out
    then. —
Todlen &c.

May our house be weel theekit, our pantry ay fu'.
Wi' rowth in our cellar for weetin' our mou';
Wi a tight, caller hizzie, as keen as oursels,
Ay ready to souple *the whistle & bells*!!!
Todlen hame &c"

WAP AND ROW

This song was printed as No. 457 in Vol. V of *The Scots Musical Museum* to the tune of 'The Reel o' Stumpie,' and under that title was included in MMC, where it has three stanzas. The present text is taken from a holograph formerly in the Gribbel Collection, Philadelphia, where it was accompanied by the two prose memoranda which follow. [DLF]

Chorus – (Note, the song begins with the Chorus)
Wap & row, wap & row,
    Wap & row the feetie o't
I thought I was a maiden fair,
    Till I heard the greetie o't. –

My daddie was a fiddler fine,
    My minnie she made mantie, O,
And I myself a thumpin quine,
    And try'd the rantie-tantie O.

      Wap and row &c.

Tibbie Nairn's exclamation, coming in one Sunday evening from hearing Mr Whitefield–

'G—d's mercy! no a c—ndum in this house for the gentlemen! God help me, what'll come o' this house when I'm in the arms o' the blessed Jesus!' –

Observation of a beggar woman in the Merse on a sturdy herdlad giving her a –

'God's blessin on you, my bairn! I hae haen mair flesh in my pot, but I canna say I had ever mair kail.' –

The two other ſtanzas printed in MMC are interpolated between the chorus and ſtanza above:

> Lang kail, pease and leeks,
>   They were at the kirſt'nin' o't,
> Lang lads wanton [i.e. wanting] breeks,
>   They were at the getting o't.

> The Bailie he gaed fartheſt ben,
>   Mess John was ripe and ready o't;
> But the Sherra had a wanton fling,
>   The Sherra was the daddie o't.

[SGS]

THERE CAM A SOGER

MS, National Portrait Gallery, Edinburgh. On 8 March 1795, Burns wrote to Patrick Miller, Jr., of Dalswinton (DLF, L ii, 291):

'When you return to the country, you will find us all *Sogers*. This a propos, brings to my mind an old Scotish ſtanza —' which he quotes as follows.

The verse is not in MMC, but an obviously garbled version of ît forms ſtanza 3 of 'The Reels of Bogie' (see Section IV) as printed in the 1827 edîtion. [DLF]

> There cam a soger here to ſtay,
>   He swore he wadna ſteer me;
> But, lang before the break o' day,
>   He cuddl'd, muddl'd near me:
> He set a ſtiff thing to my wame,
>   I docht na bide the bends o't;
> But lang before the grey morn cam,
>   I soupl'd baîth the ends o't. —

SING, UP WI'T, ALLY

MS, from a transcript of the original holograph sold at Sotheby's, 13 November 1934. (PMLA, L i, 4). This fragment, probably traditional, is included in a letter from Burns to Robert Ainslie, 29 July 1787. It is not in any edition of *The Merry Muses*. [DLF]

> Sing, Up wi't, Aily, Aily;
>> Down wi' kimmerland jock;
> Deil ram their lugs, quo' Willie,
>> But I hae scour'd her dock!
>
>> Encore!

GREEN SLEEVES

Probably traditional. The text is from a holograph in the
Huntington Library, which has on its recto the song,
'And I'll kiss thee yet, yet, … My bonie Peggy Alison.'
The lines are not in any edition of *The Merry Muses*; the
music is not in Dick. A Jacobite version of the words was
taken down by Boswell from Flora MacDonald's dicta-
tion. Its chorus is as the first stanza below. (*Tour of the
Hebrides*, 26 September 1773). [DLF]

> Green sleeves and tartan ties
> Mark my true love whare she lies:
> I'll be at her or she rise,
> > My fiddle and I thegither.

> Be it by the chrystal burn,
> Be it by the milkwhite thorn;
> I shall rouse her in the morn,
> > My fiddle and I thegither.

See also Ht. Hd. 177.

Green sleeves and pudden-pyes,
Come tell me where my true love lyes.
And I'll be wi' her ere she rise:
> Fidle a' the gither!

Hey ho! and about she goes,
She's milk in her breasts, she's none in her toes.
She's a hole in her a—, you may put in your nose.
> Sing: hey, boys, up go we!

Green sleeves and yellow lace,
Maids, maids, come, marry apace!
The batchelors are in a pitiful case
> To fidle a' the gither.

[SGS]

FROM PRINTED SOURCES

II

BY OR ATTRIBUTED TO BURNS

Notes in this section are by
SYDNEY GOODSIR SMITH
unless otherwise initialled

THE PATRIARCH

TUNE (in MMC): *The Auld Cripple Dow*

From MMC. A note by W. Scott Douglas in JCE reads:
'Original MS [which we have been unable to trace — SGS]
possessed by Mr Roberts, Town-Clerk of Forfar. It is
headed:

> 'A Wicked Song.
> 'Author's name unknown.
> 'Tune — The Waukin' o' a winter's night.

'The Publisher to the Reader,
'Courteous Reader,

'The following is certainly the production of one of
those licentious, ungodly (too-much-abounding in this
our day) wretches who take it as a compliment to be called
wicked, providing you allow them to be witty. Pity it is
that while so many tar-barrels in the country are empty,
and so many gibbets untenanted, some example is not
made of these profligates.'"

To which M'Naught (in M'N) adds: 'Burns pursues this
satirical-humorous vein in his mock manifesto as 'Poet-
Laureat and Bard in Chief ... of Kyle, Cuningham and
Carrick,' addressed ['in the name of the NINE'] to
William Chalmers and John M'Adam, 'Students and
Practitioners in the ancient and mysterious Science of
Confounding Right and Wrong.''

'RIGHT TRUSTY [it runs]: Be it known, that ... We
have discovered a certain [bawdy], nefarious, abominable
and wicked Song or Ballad, a copy whereof We have here
inclosed; Our Will therefore is ... the said copy ... be

consumed by fire [at the Cross of Ayr] ... in the presence of all Beholders, in abhorrence of, and terrorem to, all such Compoſitions and Composers ... Given at Mauch-line this twentieth day of November, Anno Domini one thousand seven hundred and eighty-six. GOD SAVE THE BARD.' (DLF, L i, 52).

As honeſt Jacob on a night,
    Wi' his beloved beauty,
Was duly laid on wedlock's bed.
    And noddin' at his duty.

    Tal de dal &c.

'How lang, she says, ye fumblin' wretch,
    'Will ye be f—g at ît?
'My eldeſt wean might die of age,
    'Before that ye could get ît.

'Ye pegh and grane, and groazle there,
    'And mak an unco splutter,
'And I maun ly and thole you here,
    'And fient a hair the better.'

Then he, in wrath, put up his graîth,
    'The deevil's in the hizzie!
'I m—w you as I m—w the lave,
    'And night and day I'm bisy.

'I've bairn'd the servant gypsies baîth,
    'Forbye your tîtty Leah;
'Ye barren jad, ye put me mad,
    'What mair can I do wi you.

'There's ne'er a m—w I've gi'en the lave,
    'But ye ha'e got a dizzen;
'And d—n'd a ane ye'se get again,
     'Although your c—t should gizzen.'

Then Rachel calm, as ony lamb,
    She claps him on the waulies;
Quo' she, 'ne'er fash a woman's clash.
    'In trowth ye m—w me braulies.

'My dear 'tis true, for mony a m—w,
    'I'm your ungratefu' debtor,
'But ance again, I dinna ken,
    'We'll aiblens happen better.'

Then honest man! Wi' little wark,
    He soon forgat his ire;
The patriarch, he coost the sark,
    And up and till't like fire!

THE BONNIEST LASS

From MM27, reprinted in M'N. Not in MMC. 'Much in
the vein of 'The Patriarch',' says M'Naught. There is little
room for doubt that this is by Burns. [JB, SGS]

The bonniest lass that ye meet neist
    Gie her a kiss an' a' that,
In spite o' ilka parish priest,
    Repentin' stool, an' a' that.

    For a' that an' a' that,
        Their mim-mou'd sangs an' a' that,
    In time and place convenient,
        They'll do't themselves for a' that.

Your patriarchs in days o' yore,
    Had their handmaids an' a' that;
O' bastard gets, some had a score
    An' some had mair than a' that.

    For a' that an' a' that,
        Your langsyne saunts, an' a' that,
    Were fonder o' a bonie lass,
        Than you or I, for a' that.

King Davie, when he waxed auld,
    An's bluid ran thin, an' a' that,
An' fand his cods were growin' cauld,
    Could not refrain, for a' that.

For a' that an' a' that,
    To keep him warm an' a' that,
The daughters o' Jerusalem
    Were waled for him, an' a' that.

Wha wadna pity thae sweet dames
    He fumbled at, an' a' that,
An' raised their bluid up into flames
    He couldna drown, for a' that.

    For a' that an' a' that,
        He wanted pith, an' a' that;
    For, as to what we shall not name,
        What could he do but claw that.

King Solomon, prince o' divines,
    Wha proverbs made, an' a' that,
Baith mistresses an' concubines
    In hundreds had, for a' that.

    For a' that an' a' that,
        Tho' a preacher wise an' a' that,
    The smuttiest sang that e'er was sung
        His Sang o' Sangs is a' that.

Then still I swear, a clever chiel
    Should kiss a lass, an' a' that,
Tho' priests consign him to the deil,
    As reprobate, an' a' that.

    For a' that an' a' that,
        Their canting stuff, an' a' that,
    They ken nae mair wha's reprobate
        Than you or I, for a' that.

GODLY GIRZIE

TUNE: *Wat ye wha I met yestreen*

From MMC. Ascribed to Burns by Scott Douglas. M'Naught says 'Anonymous, but quite in Burns's style.' DLF in MP (xxx, i) writes:

A holograph of 'Godly Girzie' is described in the *Burns Chronicle*, iii (1894), 142. It bears the caption, 'A new song – from an old story:' the quoted [first] stanza varies in a couple of readings from the *Muses* text. M'Naught is silent about this MS, which appears to confirm Burns's authorship.' According to the *Burns Chronicle's* description, the song is written on the back of a page containing 'Yestreen I had a pint o' wine.' In i, 3 'Kilmarnock' has been written in above 'The winnocks' [deleted].

The night it was a haly night,
  The day had been a haly day;
Kilmarnock gleamed wi' candle light,
  As Girzie hameward took her way.
A man o' sin, ill may he thrive!
  And never haly-meeting see!
Wi' godly Girzie met belyve,
  Amang the Cragie hills sae hie.

The chiel' was wight, the chiel' was stark,
  He wad na wait to chap nor ca',
And she was faint wi haly wark,
  She had na pith to say him na.
But ay she glowr'd up to the moon,
  And ay she sigh'd most piouslie;
'I trust my heart's in heaven aboon,
  'Whare'er your sinfu' p—e be.'

WHA'LL MOW ME NOW?

TUNE: *Comin' thro' the rye*

From MMC. Attributed to Burns by Hecht (*Archiv*); by DLF
(MP, xxx, i, Aug. 1932); by Aîtken, who prints in part
ſtanzas i, ii, v, vi, in *Ald* 1893 (iii, 75); and by Scott Douglas
in a pencilled note in MMC. 'An old song,' says M'Naught.

O, I hae tint my rosy cheek,
 Likewise my waſte sae sma';
O wae gae by the sodger lown,
 The sodger did ît a'.

 O wha'll m—w me now, my jo,
  An' wha'll m—w me now:
 A sodger wi' his bandileers
  Has bang'd my belly fu'.

Now I maun thole the scornfu' sneer
 O' mony a saucy quine;
When, curse upon her godly face!
 Her c—t's as merry's mine.

Our dame hauds up her wanton tail,
 As due as she gaes lie;
An' yet misca's [a] young thing.
 The trade if she but try.

Our dame can lae her ain gudeman,
 An' m—w for glutton greed;
An' yet misca' a poor thing,
 That's m—n' for îts bread.

Alake! sae sweet a tree as love,
Sic bitter fruit should bear!
Alake, that e'er a merry a—e,
Should draw a sa'tty tear.

But deevil damn the lousy loon,
Denies the bairn he got!
Or lea's the merry a—e he lo'ed,
To wear a ragged coat!

On the last stanza, DLF (*op.cit.*) writes, and JB and SGS concur, that 'One is bound to agree with Professor Hecht and other critics in holding that Burns never wrote a more characteristic stanza than the closing one.'

HAD I THE WYTE SHE BADE ME [A]

From MMC. 'The inference is irresistible,' say Henley
and Henderson (iii, 411), 'that the fragment in the Herd
MS [see Section iii] suggested two songs to Burns: one for
publication [HH, iii, 149], the other — *not*.' Hecht (*op.cit.*)
considers this 'variant in the *Merry Muses* probably
composed by Burns,' and later, in comparing the Herd
and *Muses* versions, says 'There is no doubt whatever that
Burns himself was the author of the changes,' and with
this verdict JB and SGS entirely agree. Scott Douglas in a
pencilled note in MMC says 'Old with retouching' and
M'Naught 'An old song.'

> Had I the wyte, had I the wyte,
>> Had I the wyte she bad me;
> For she was steward in the house,
>> And I was fit-man laddie;
> And when I wadna do't again,
>> A silly cow she ca'd me;
> She straik't my head, and clapt my cheeks,
>> And lous'd my breeks and bad me.
>
> Could I for shame, could I for shame,
>> Could I for shame deny['d] her,
> Or in the bed was I to blame,
>> She bad me lye beside her:
> I pat six inches in her wame,
>> A quarter wadna fly'd her;
> For ay the mair I ca'd it hame,
>> Her ports they grew the wider.

My tartan plaid, when it was dark.
    Could I refuse to share it;
She lifted up her holland-sark,
    And bad me fin' the gair o't:
Or how could I amang the garse,
    But gie her hilt and hair o't;
She clasped her houghs about my a—e,
    And ay she glowr'd for mair o't.

DAINTY DAVIE [A]

From MMC. Considered by Hecht (*op.cit.*) to be Burns's own version of the old song (see Section iii and footnote).

Being pursu'd by the dragoons,
    Within my bed he was laid down
And weel I wat he was worth his room,
    My ain dear dainty Davie.

    O leeze me on his curly pow,
    Bonie Davie, dainty Davie;
    Leeze me on his curly pow,
    He was my dainty Davie.

My minnie laid him at my back,
    I trow he lay na lang at that,
But turn'd, and in a verra crack
    Produc'd a dainty Davie.

Then in the field amang the pease,
    Behin' the house o' Cherrytrees,
Again he wan atweesh my thies,
    And, splash! gaed out his gravy.

But had I goud, or had I land,
    It should be a' at his command;
I'll ne'er forget what he pat i' my hand,
    It was a dainty Davie.

JB and SGS share Hecht's opinion when he writes in *Archiv*: 'Herd's first verse [see Section iii] is missing in MMC. The third is enlarged to two verses which for reaons of gradation and development of the episode are transferred to the beginning of the poem. The rhyme 'gravy' inſtead of Herd's regularly repeated 'Davie' [in this regard, see also 'The Tailor cam to clout the claes' in Section iii may be taken as an indication that the verse was not in the original version. Noteworthy also is the desire to make clearer the allusion to the proper name Cherrytrees (also in the third verse) which is hardly recognisable in Herd's version. The fourth verse with the ſtrong beginning of lines I and 2 is missing in Herd. The comparison makes ît clear that the version of Dainty Davie in MMC was derived from the version given by Herd wîth express artiſtic intentions. There is no doubt whatever that Burns himself was the author of these changes. This supports our conjecture that even in the cases in which we have no other versions apart from those in MMC the giſt of the song may be old but very frequently ît underwent the poet's encroachment to heighten the artiſtic effect.'

THE TROGGER

TUNE: *Gillicrankie*

From MMC. 'May very well be from Burns' (HH iii, 415)
— it has our vote (JB, SGS). Attributed to Burns 'certainly'
by Scott Douglas in a pencilled note in MMC. Described
by M'Naught as 'anonymous — probably not older than
Burns's time.'

As I cam down by Annan side,
  Intending for the border,
Amang the Scroggie banks and braes
  Wha met I but a trogger.
He laid me down upon my back,
  I thought he was but jokin',
Till he was in me to the hilts,
  O the deevil tak sic troggin!

What could I say, what could I do,
  I bann'd and sair misca'd him,
But whiltie-whaltie gaed his a—e,
  The mair that I forbade him:
He stell'd his foot against a stane,
  And doubl'd ilka stroke in,
Till I gaed daft amang his hands,
  O the deevil tak sic troggin!

Then up we raise, and took the road,
  And in by Ecclefechan,
Where the brandy-stoup we gart it clink,
  And the strang-beer ream the quech in.
Bedown the bents o' Bonshaw braes,
  We took the partin' yokin';
But I've claw'd a sairy c—t sinsyne,
  O the deevil tak sic troggin!

PUT BUTTER IN MY DONALD'S BROSE

From MMC, where it is entitled 'For a' that and a' that.'
Attributed to Burns by Henley and Henderson (HH ii,
304). Burns used the first two lines of the refrain for the
Bard's Song and the Sailor's Song in 'The Jolly Beggars'
(HH ii, 1) and in 'Is there for Honest Poverty' (HH iii,
271). He wrote to Thomson, 3 August 1795 (DLF, L ii,
307): 'I inclose you a 'For a' that & a' that' which was
never in print: it is a much superiour song to mine — I
have been told that it was composed by a lady —.'

> Put butter in my Donald's brose,
>> For weel does Donald fa' that;
> I be my Donald's tartans weel
>> His naked a—e and a' that.
>
>> For a' that, and a' that,
>>> And twice as meikle's a' that,
>> The lassie gat a skelpit doup,
>>> But wan the day for a' that.
>
> For Donald swore a solemn aith,
>> By his first hairy gravat!
> That he wad fight the battle there,
>> And stick the lass, and a' that.
>
> His hairy b—s, side and wide,
>> Hang like a beggar's wallet;
> A p—e like a roaring-pin,
>> She nicher'd when she saw that!!!

Then she turn'd up her hairy c—t,
    And she bade Donald claw that;
The deevil's dizzen Donald drew,
    And Donald gied her a' that.

HERE'S HIS HEALTH IN WATER

TUNE: *The job o' journey wark* (says SD)

From MMC. Composed by Burns in 1786. Stanza i appeared in SMM 1796 (V. 494) and most editions subsequently.

Altho' my back be at the wa,
　　An' tho' he be the fau'tor;
Altho' my back be at the wa',
　　I'll drink his health in water.
O wae gae by his wanton sides,
　　Sae brawly's he cou'd flatter.
I for his sake am slighted sair,
　　An' dree the kintra clatter;
But let them say whate'er they like,
　　Yet, here's his health in water.

He follow'd me baith out an' in,
　　Thro' a' the nooks a' Killie;
He follow'd me baith out an' in,
　　Wi' a stiff stanin' p—llie.
But when he gat atween my legs,
　　We made an unco splatter;
An' haith, I trow, I soupled it,
　　Tho' bauldly he did blatter;
But now my back is at the wa',
　　Yet here's his health in water.

i.　7　MMC misprints　I for his sake I'm ...
i.　8　MMC misprints　An' drees ...

THE JOLLY GAUGER

TUNE: *We'll gang nae mair a rovin'*

From MMC. Parody, 'claimed for a fellow-exciseman'
(HH ii, 297), of *The Jolly Beggar*, traditionally attributed to
King James v. DLF considers it might be by Burns: 'If not
... original with Burns ... probably touched up by him'
(MP xxx, i). Attributed to Burns by Scott Douglas in a
pencilled note in MMC. It has obviously been written
round the 'Observation of a beggar woman in the Merse'
which Burns took the trouble to preserve in the MS of
'Wap and Row' (Section i).

> There was a jolly gauger, a gauging he did ride,
> And he has met a beggar down by yon river side.
>
>> An weel gang nae mair a rovin' wi' ladies to the
>> wine,
>> When a beggar wi' her meal-pocks can fidge
>> her tail sae fine.
>
> Amang the broom he laid her; amang the broom
> sae green,
> And he's fa'n to the beggar, as she had been a
> queen.
>
>> And we'll gang &c.
>
> My blessings on thee, laddie, thou's done my turn
> sae weel,
> Wilt thou accept, dear laddie, my pock and pickle
> meal?
>
>> And weel, &c.

Sae blyth the beggar took the bent, like ony bird in
    spring,
Sae blyth the beggar took the bent, and merrily did
    sing.

    And weel, &c.

My blessings on the gauger, o' gaugers he's the
    chief,
Sic kail ne'er croſt my kettle, nor sic a joint o beef.

    And weel, &c.

O GAT YE ME WI NAETHING?

TUNE: *Jacky Latin*

From MMC. Origin of Burns's song 'The Lass o' Ecclefechan' (HH iii, 156). Attributed to Burns by Henley and Henderson (iii, 415); by Scott Douglas in a pencilled note in MMC; and in MM27. Might quite well be by Burns on the basis of an old fragment, probably the first two lines.

Gat ye me, O gat ye me,
  An' gat ye me wi' naething?
A rock, a reel, a spinning wheel,
  A gude black c—t was ae thing.
A tocher fine, o'er muckle far,
  When sic a scullion gat it;
Indeed, o'er muckle far, gudewife,
  For that was ay the fau't o't.

But had your tongue now, Luckie Lang,
  O had your tongue and jander,
I held the gate till you I met,
  Syne I began to wander;
I tint my whistle an' my sang,
  I tint my peace an' pleasure,
But your green grave now, Luckie Lang,
  Wad airt me to my treasure.

GIE THE LASS HER FAIRIN'

TUNE: *Cauld kail in Aberdeen*

From MMC. Attributed to Burns in MM27 and by Scott
Douglas in a pencilled note in MMC. Quite likely too; the
tune was one of his favourites.

O gie the lass her fairin' lad,
        O gie the lass her fairin',
An' something else she'll gie to you,
        That's waly worth the wearin';
Syne coup her o'er amang the creels,
        When ye hae taen your brandy,
The mair she bangs the less she squeels,
        An' hey for houghmagandie.

Then gie the lass a fairin', lad,
        O gie the lass her fairin',
And she'll gie you a hairy thing,
        An' of it be na sparin';
But coup her o'er amang the creels,
        An' bar the door wi' baith your heels,
The mair she bangs the less she squeels,
        An' hey for houghmagandie.

GREEN GROW THE RASHES [B]

From MMC, where ît is ascribed to Burns by Scott
Douglas in a pencilled note. Burns wrote to George
Thomson in April 1793: 'At any rate, my other Song
'Green grow the Rashes' will never suît. — That Song is
current in Scotld under the old tîtle, & sung to the merry
old tune of that name; which of course would mar the
progress of your Song to celebrîty.' (DLF, L ii, 162). See
also Section i.

> O wat ye ought o' fisher Meg,
>   And how she trow'd the webster, O,
> She loot me see her carrot c—t,
>   And sell'd ît for a labster, O.

> Green grow the rashes, O,
>   Green grow the rashes, O,
> The lassies they hae wimble-bores,
>   The widows they hae gashes, O.

> Mistress Mary cow'd her thing,
>   Because she wad be gentle, O,
> And span the fleece upon a rock,
>   To waft a Highland mantle, O.

> An' heard ye o' the coat o' arms,
>   The Lyon brought our lady, O,
> The crest was, couchant, sable c—t,
>   The motto — 'ready, ready,' O.

> An' ken ye Leezie Lundie, O,
>   The godly Leezie Lundie, O,
> She m—s like reek thro' a' the week,
>   But finger f—s on Sunday, O.

TAIL TODLE

TUNE: *Chevalier's Muster-Roll* (says SD)

From MMC, where it is attributed to Burns by Scott Douglas in a pencilled note. There are versions of this still extant. Burns might have tidied it up a bit when he came to write it down, but probably not much more than that.

Our gudewife held o'er to Fife,
    For to buy a coal-riddle;
Lang or she came back again,
    Tammie gart my tail todle.

    Tail todle, tail todle;
    Tammie gart my tail todle;
    At my a—e wi' diddle doddle,
    Tammie gart my tail todle.

When I'm dead I'm out o' date;
    When I'm sick I'm fu' o' trouble;
When I'm weel I step about,
    An' Tammie gars my tail todle.

Jenny Jack she gae a plack,
    Helen Wallace gae a boddle,
Quo' the bride, it's o'er little
    For to mend a broken doddle.

I REDE YOU BEWARE O'
THE RIPPLES

TUNE: *The Taylor's faun thro the bed*

From MMC. Original of Burns's song 'The Bonnie Moor Hen' (HH iv, 20) which Clarinda advised him not to publish 'for your sake and mine,' in a letter dated 30 January 1788. In MMC, Scott Douglas, in a pencilled note, attributes this version to Burns, as do Henley and Henderson (HH iv, 89).

I rede you beware o' the ripples, young man,
I rede you beware o' the ripples, young man;
Tho' the saddle be saft, ye needna ride aft,
For fear that the girdin' beguile ye, young man.

I rede you beware o' the ripples, young man,
I rede you beware o' the ripples, young man;
Tho' music be pleasure, tak' music in measure,
Or ye may want win' i' your whistle, young man.

I rede you beware o' the ripples, young man,
I rede you beware o' the ripples, young man;
Whate'er ye bestow, do less than ye dow,
The mair will be thought o' your kindness, young man.

I rede you beware o' the ripples, young man,
I rede you beware o' the ripples, young man;
Gif you wad be strang, and wish to live lang,
Dance less wi' you're a—e to the kipples, young man.

OUR JOHN'S BRAK YESTREEN

TUNE: *Gramachree*

From MMC, where it is attributed to Burns by Scott
Douglas in a pencilled note.

Twa neebor wives sat i' the sun,
    A twynin' at their rocks,
An' they an argument began,
    An' a' the plea was c—ks.

'Twas whether they were sinnens strang,
    Or whether they were bane?
An' how they row'd about your thumb,
    An how they stan't themlane?

First, Raichie gae her rock a rug,
    An' syne she claw'd her tail;
'When our Tam draws on his breeks,
    'It waigles like a flail.'

Says Bess, 'they're bane I will maintain,
    'And proof in han' I'll gie;
'For our John's it brak yestreen,
    'And the margh ran down my thie.'

GRIZZEL GRIMME

By Burns. From HH (ii, 459): '... Inscribed by Burns in a volume of the *Glenriddell Collections*... The epitaph is thus prefaced: 'Passing lately through Dunblane, while I stopped to refresh my horse, the following ludicrous epitaph, which I picked up from an old tombstone among the ruins of the ancient Abbey, struck me particularly, being myself a native of Dumfriesshire.' The common version of the last two lines is this: 'O Death, thou surely art not nice To lie with sic a bitch'.'

> Grim Grizzel was a mighty Dame
> Weel kend on Cluden-side:
> Grim Grizzel was a mighty Dame
> O' meikle fame and pride.

> When gentles met in gentle bowers
> And nobles in the ha',
> Grim Grizzel was a mighty Dame,
> The loudest o' them a'.

> Where lawless Riot rag'd the night
> And Beauty durst na gang,
> Grim Grizzel was a mighty Dame
> Wham nae man e'er wad wrang.

> Nor had Grim Grizzel skill alane
> What bower and ha' require;
> But she had skill, and meikle skill,
> In barn and eke in byre.

Ae day Grim Grizzel walkèd forth,
　　As she was wont to do,
Alang the banks o' Cluden fair,
　　Her cattle for to view.

The cattle sh— o'er hill and dale
　　As cattle will incline,
And sair ît grieved Grim Grizzel's heart
　　Sae muckle muck tae tine.

And she has ca'd on John o' Clods,
　　Of her herdsmén the chief,
And she has ca'd on John o' Clods.
　　And tell'd him a' her grief: —

"Now wae betide thee, John o' Clods!
　　I gie thee meal and fee,
And yet sae meickle muck ye tine
　　Might a' be gear to me!

"Ye claut my byre, ye sweep my byre,
　　The like was never seen;
The very chamber I lie in
　　Was never half sae clean.

"Ye ca' my kye adown the loan
　　And there they a' discharge:
My Tammie's hat, wig, head and a'
　　Was never half sae large!

'But mind my words now, John o' Clods,
  And tent me what I say:
My kye shall sh— ere they gae out,
  That shall they ilka day.

'And mind my words now, John o' Clods,
  And tent now wha ye serve;
Or back ye'se to the Colonel gang,
  Either to steal or starve.'

Then John o' Clods he looked up
  And syne he looked down;
He lookèd east, he lookèd west,
  He lookèd roun' and roun'.

His bonnet and his rowantree club
  Frae either hand did fa';
Wi' lifted een and open mouth
  He naething said at a'.

At length he found his trembling tongue,
  Within his mouth was fauld: —
"Ae silly word frae me, mádam,
  Gin I daur be sae bauld.

'Your kye will at nae bidding sh—,
  Let me do what I can;
Your kye will at nae bidding sh—
  Of onie earthly man.

'Tho' ye are great Lady Glaur-hole,
 For a' your power and art
Tho' ye are great Lady Glaur-hole,
 They winna let a fart.'

'Now wae betide thee, John o' Clods!
 An ill death may ye die!
My kye shall at my bidding sh—,
 And that ye soon shall see.'

Then she's ta'en Hawkie by the tail,
 And wrung wi' might and main,
Till Hawkie rowted through the woods
 Wi' agonising pain.

'Sh—, sh—, ye bîtch,' Grim Grizzel roar'd,
 Till hill and valley rang;
'And sh—, ye bîtch,' the echoes roar'd
 Lincluden wa's amang.

TWO EPITAPHS

From *The Court of Equity*, An Episode in the Life of Burns, Printed for Private Circulation, Edinburgh 1910. See also *B.Chr.* 1902 (109).

JOHANNES FUSCUS [JOHN BROWN]

HIC JACET

QUONDAM HOROLOGIORUM FABER IN M[AUCHLINE]

Lament him, M[auchline] husbands a',
  He aften did assist ye!
Tho ye had bidden years awa
  Your wives [wad] ne'er hae miss't ye.

Ye M[auchline] bairns, as bye ye pass
  To school in bands thegither,
O tread but lightly on the grass,
  Perhaps he was your father!

EPITAPH FOR

H[UGH] L[OGAN], ESQ., OF L[AIGHT]

Here lyes Squire Hugh — ye harlot crew,
  Come mak' your water on him,
I'm sure that he weel pleas'd would be
  To think ye pish'd upon him.

III

OLD SONGS USED BY BURNS

FOR POLITE VERSIONS

Notes in this section are by
SYDNEY GOODSIR SMITH
unless otherwise initialled

HAD I THE WYTE [B]

From Ht.Hd (117). Hecht writes: 'The fragment sugg-
ested Burns's 'Had I the Wyte' [HH iii, 149] and a less
delicate piece in *The Merry Muses*' (see Section ii).

Had I the wyte? had I the wyte?
Had I the wyte? She bad me,
And ay she gied me cheese and bread
To kiss her when she bad me,
For she was stewart in the house,
And I was footman-ladie,
And ay she gied me cheese and bread *
To kiss her, when she bad me.

* Sir Walter Scott's marginal note in Herd's MS:

'For the two last lines read
    And when I could na do't again:
    Silly loon she ca'd me.'

Scott had borrowed Herd's MSS while compiling his *Minstrelsy of the
Scottish Border*, as he acknowledges in his Introduction.

DAINTY DAVIE [B]

From Ht.Hd (140) and DH 1776 (ii, 215). Herd's note
reads: 'The following song was made upon Mess David
Williamson on his getting with child the Lady Cherrytree's
daughter, while the soldiers were searching the house to
apprehend him for a rebel.' This is the older version; the
other, attributed to Burns, will be found in Section II
together with Hecht's comparison of the two. The chorus
gave rise to Burns's song 'Now rosy May' (HH iii, 245).
Burns's note in the Interleaved Copy of SMM reads: 'The
original verses of Dainty Davie and the anecdote which gave
rise to them, are still extant, and were their delicacy equal to
their humour, they would merit a place in any collection.'
(JCD, N 12). Not in any edition of *The Merry Muses*.

It was in and through the window broads,
And all the tirliewirlies o'd:
The sweetest kiss that e'er I got
Was from my Dainty Davie.

O leeze me on your curly pow,
Dainty Davie, dainty Davie,
Leeze me on your curly pow,
Mine ain dainty Davie.

It was down amang my daddy's pease,
And underneath the cherry-trees:
O there he kist me as he pleas'd,
For he was mine ain dear Davie.

When he was chased by a dragoon,
Into my bed he was laid down,
I thought him wordy o' his room,
And he's ay my dainty Davie.

LET ME IN THIS AE NIGHT

From Ht.Hd (149); also in DH 1776 (ii, 167). Original of
Burns's song of same name (HH iii, 274). Not printed
in any edition of *The Merry Muses*.

'O lassie, art thou sleeping yet,
Or are you waking, I wou'd wit?
For love has bound me hand and foot,
And I wou'd fain be in, jo.

O let me in this ae night, this ae, ae, ae night,
O let me in this ae night, and I'll ne'er come back
again, jo.

The morn it is the term-day,
I maun away, I canna stay:
O pity me, before I gae,
And rise and let me in, jo.

O let me in this ae night, this ae, ae, ae night,
O let me in this ae night, and I'll ne'er come back
again, jo.

The night it is baith cauld and weet,
The morn it will be snaw and sleet,
My shoen are frozen to my feet
Wi' standing on the plain, jo.

O let me in this ae night, this ae, ae, ae night,
O let me in this ae night, and I'll ne'er come back
again, jo.

I am the laird of windy-wa's,
I come na here without a cause,
And I hae gotten mony fa's
Upon a naked wame o!'

O let me in this ae night, this ae, ae, ae night,
O let me in this ae night, and I'll ne'er come back
again, jo.

'My father's wa'king on the ſtreet,
My mither the chamber-keys does keep,
My chamber-door does chirp and cheep,
And I dare nae let you in, jo!'

O gae your way this ae night, this ae, ae, ae night,
O gae your way this ae night, for I dare nae let you
in, jo!

'But I'll come ſtealing saftly in
And cannily make little dinn,
And then the gate to you I'll find,
If you'l but direct me in, jo!'

O let me in this ae night, this ae, ae, ae night,
O let me in this ae night, and I'll ne'er come back
again, jo.

'Caſt aff the shoen frae aff your feet,
Caſt back the door up to the weet,
Syne into my bed you may creep
And do the thing you ken, jo.'

O well's on me this ae night, this ae, ae, ae night,
O well's on me this ae night, that ere I let you in, jo!

    She let him in sae cannily,
    She let him in sae privily,
    She let him in sae cannily,
    To do the thing ye ken, jo.

O well's on me this ae night, this ae, ae, ae night,
O well's on me this ae night, that ere I let you in, jo!

    But ere a'was done and a' was said,
    Out fell the bottom of the bed,
    The lassie lost her maidenhead,
    And her mither heard the din, jo.

O the devil take this ae night, this ae, ae, ae night,
O the devil take this ae night, that ere I let ye in, jo!

In Herd's MS the choruses for ii, iii, iv, and vi, are merely indicated
by 'O let &c,'

Chorus 5   DH 1776   ... ways ...
Chorus 7   *Ibid.*   O well's me on ...

THE TAILOR

From DH 1769 (318) and MM27. Not in MMC. Suggested Burns's song 'The Tailor he cam here to sew' (HH iii, 179, 432). This text is Herd's except for each line 5 in stanzas iv–ix which are taken from MM27; in Herd's text line 5 repeats line 3 throughout.

The tailor came to clout the claise,
  Sic a braw fellow,
He filled the house a' fou o' fleas,
  Daffin down, and daffin down,
He filled the house a' fou o' fleas,
  Daffin down and dilly.

The lassie slept ayont the fire,
  Sic a braw hissey!
Oh! she was a' his heart's desire,
  Daffin down, and daffin down,
Oh! she was a' his heart's desire,
  Daffin down and dilly.

The lassie she fell fast asleep,
  Sic a braw hissey!
The tailor close to her did creep,
  Daffin down, and daffin down,
The tailor close to her did creep,
  Daffin down and dilly.

The lassie waken'd in a fright,
  Sic a braw hissey!
Her maidenhead had taen the flight,
  Daffin down, and daffin down,
A tailor's bodkin caused the flight,
  Daffin down and dilly.

She sought it butt, she sought it ben,
  Sic a braw hissey!
And in beneath the clocken-hen,
  Daffin down, and daffin down,
It wasna but, it wasna ben,
  Daffin down and dilly.

She sought it in the owsen-ſtaw,
  Sic a braw hissey
Na, faith, quo' she, it's quite awa',
  Daffin down, and daffin down,
That tailor loon has ſtown't awa',
  Daffin down and dilly.

She sought it 'yont the knocking-ſtane,
  Sic a braw hissey!
Some day, quo' she, 'twill gang its lane,
  Daffin down, and daffin down,
For my tirly-wirly mak's its mane.
  Daffin down and dilly.

She ca'd the tailor to the court,
    Sic a braw hissey!
And a' the young men round about,
    Daffin down, and daffin down,
To gar the tailor mend her clout,
    Daffin down and dilly.

She gart the tailor pay a fine,
    Sic a braw hissey!
Gi'e me my maidenhead agen;
    Daffin down, and daffin down,
I'll hae my maidenhead again,
    Daffin down and dilly.

O what way wad ye hae't agen?
    Sic a braw hissey!
Oh! just the way that it was taen,
    Daffin down, and daffin down,
Come, just the way that it was ta'en,
    Daffin down and dilly.

EPPIE McNAB

From *The Giblet Pye* (*c*.1806). Not in any edition of the *Merry Muses*. Origin of Burns's song of same name (HH iii, 101). Another version in Ht. Hd. (113). Burns's note in the Interleaved Copy of SMM: 'The old song with this title, has more wit than decency' (JCD.*N* 58).

O saw ye my Eppie McNab, McNab?
O saw ye my Eppie McNab, McNab?
She's down i' the yeard, she's kissen the laird,
As whilom's wi' honest Jock Rob, Jock Rob.

My blessings upo' thee, Jock Rob, Jock Rob,
My blessings upo' thee, Jock Rob, Jock Rob,
For in my gavel ye drive sic a dool,
Gard a' my buttocks play bab, bab, bab.

When first I met wi' thee, Jock Rob, Jock Rob,
When first I met wi' thee, Jock Rob, Jock Rob!
Thy breeks they were hol'd, and thy – hung out,
And thy – play'd ay did dod, did dod.

When first I met Eppie McNab, McNab,
I met wi' Eppie McNab, McNab;
Thy wee bit dud sark it play'd dod o' thy dab,
And thy – was as black as a crab, a crab.

DUNCAN GRAY

From MMC. Another version in Ht.Hd (208). Basis of
two of Burns's songs in Scots of same name (HH iii, 23,
215), and one in English entitled 'Let not women e'er
complain' (HH iii, 219). Of this last one Burns wrote
significantly to Thomson on 19 October 1794:

> These English songs gravel me to death.—! have not that
> command of the language that I have of my native tongue.
> — In fact, I think my ideas are more barren in English
> than in Scottish. — I have been at 'Duncan Gray' to dress
> it in English, but all I can do is deplorably stupid. (DLF,
> L ii, 268).

Henley & Henderson (iii, 452) and also Hecht (Ht.Hd
319) consider Burns used Herd's MSS when collecting
material for the *Scots Musical Museum* and that this version of
'Duncan Gray' has been touched up by the Bard in
transcribing. The variations in Herd are given in the
footnotes below. Examination of these will show that a
literary hand (and whose but Burns's?) has been tidying
up the cruder parts of the original. Herd has an extra
final stanza.

    Can ye play me Duncan Gray,
        Ha, ha, the girdin' o't;
    O'er the hills an' far awa,
        Ha, ha, ha, the girdin' o't,
    Duncan came our Meg to woo,
    Meg was nice an' wadna do,
    But like an ither puff'd an' blew
        At offer o' the girdin' o't.

Duncan, he cam here again,
   Ha, ha, the girdin' o't,
A' was out, an' Meg her lane,
   Ha, ha, ha, the girdin' o't;
He kiss'd her butt, he kiss'd her ben,
He bang'd a thing against her wame;
But, troth, I now forget its name,
   But, I trow, she gat the girdin' o't.

She took him to the cellar then,
   Ha, ha, the girdin' o't,
To see gif he could do't again,
   Ha, ha, ha, the girdin' o't;
He kiss'd her ance, he kiss'd her twice,
An' by the bye he kiss'd her thrice
Till deil a mair the thing wad rise
   To gie her the long girdin' o't.

But Duncan took her to his wife,
   Ha, ha, the girdin' o't,
To be the comfort o' his life,
   Ha, ha, ha, the girdin' o't;
An' now she scauls baith night an' day,
Except when Duncan's at the play;
An' that's as seldom as he may,
   He's weary o' the girdin' o't.

i, 2, 4 Ht.Hd	The refrain is 'High, hey the girdin' o't' throughout.
i, 5—8 *Ibid*	Duncan he came here to woo On a day when we were fou' And Meg she swore that she wou'd spew, If he gaed her the girdin o't.
i, 7	An ither = an ether, adder.
ii, I *Ibid*	But Duncan he came here again
ii, 3 *Ibid*	And a' was out, but Meg her lane.
ii, 7 *Ibid*	But trouth I now forgot its name.
iii. 5—8 *Ibid*	He kiss'd her twice, he kiss'd her thrice, Till deil amair the thing wou'd rise Although she cried out baith her eyes To get the lang girdin o't.
iv, 5—8 *Ibid*	But she scolds away both night and day Without that Duncan still wou'd play, And ay she cries: 'Fy, Duncan Gray. Come gae me the girdin o't.'

Extra fifth stanza from Ht.Hd (208):

> He bought his wife a peck of malt,
> High, hey the girdin o't,
> And bade her brew good swats o' that.
> High, hey the girdin o't,
> She brew'd it thick, she mask'd it thin,
> She threw the tap, but nane wou'd run.
> Till Duncan he slipt in his pin,
> And then she got the girdin o't.

LOGAN WATER

From MMC. Origin of Burns's song of same name (HH iii, 262). He wrote to Thomson on 7 April, 1793, 'I remember two ending lines of a verse in some of the old Songs of 'Logan Water' (for I know a good many different ones) which I think pretty —

> 'Now my dear lad maun face his faes,
>   'Far far frae me & Logan braes!'

Also in DH 1776 (ii, 230) and Ht.Hd (116); the variations here are most probably improvements made by Burns in transcribing.

> The Logan burn, the Logan braes,
> I helped a bonie lassie on wi' her claes;
> First wi' her stockings an' syne wi' her shoon,
> But she gied me the glaiks when a' was done.

> But an I had kend, what I ken now,
> I wad a bang'd her belly fu';
> Her belly fu' and her apron up,
> An' shew'd her the road to the Logan kirk.

i, 1	DH	Logan water and Logan braes
i, 2	*Ibid*	... claiths; Ht. Hd. . . . claes
i, 3	DH	... and then ...
i, 4	*Ibid.*	And she gave me...
ii, 1	*Ibid.*	Omits 'an'
ii, 2	*Ibid.*	I should have bang'd ... fou
ii, 4	*Ibid.*	And hae shew'd her the way to Logan-kirk.

THE MILL MILL-O

From MMC. Origin of 'The Soldier's Return' (HH iii, 212), by way of Allan Ramsay's 'Beneath a green shade …' (TTM 1724, 153). Herd has a version (Ht.Hd 115) but this is much superior poetically and has obviously felt the touch of Burns's hand. Burns wrote to Thomson, 7 April 1793: 'The original song, 'The Mill mill O' though excellent, is, on account of decency, inadmissable.'

> As I came down yon water side
>> And by yon Shillin hill, O;
> There I spied a bonny lass,
>> A lass that I loed right weel, O.
>
>> The mill, mill, O, and the kill, kill, O,
>> An' the coggin' o' Peggy's wheel, O,
>> The sack an' the sieve, a' she did leave,
>> An' danc'd the millars reel, O.
>
> I spier'd at her, gin she cou'd play,
>> But the lassie had nae skill, O;
> An' yet she was nae a' to blame,
>> She pat it in my will, O.
>
> Then she fell o'er, an' sae did I,
>> An' danc'd the millars reel, O,
> Whene'er that bonny lassie comes again,
>> She shall hae her ma't ground weel, O.

i, 1   Ht.Hd.   … came up yon…
i, 2   *Ibid*   And down yon…;

i, 3	*Ibid*	There I did spy ...
i, 4	*Ibid*	A lass I loo'd ...
ii. 1	*Ibid*	I asked her if she could play
ii, 4	*Ibid*	She put ît ...
iii. 2	*Ibid*	An' so we made a reel O
iii. 3	*Ibid*	... bony lass ...
iii, 4	*Ibid*	... malt ...

Chorus Only first line given in Herd's MS.

MY AIN KIND DEARIE

TUNE: *The Lea Rig*

From MMC. Basis of Burns's song 'The Lea Rig' (HH iii, 284). The first stanza (identical, except for the refrain 'My ain kind deary O,' and 'I'll rowe thee' for 'I'll lay thee') is quoted by Burns in the Interleaved SMM (JCD. *N* 17) as 'the old words of this song ... which were mostly composed by poor [Robert] Ferguson, in one of his merry humours.'

I'll lay thee o'er the lee-rig,
    Lovely Mary, deary, O;
I'll lay thee o'er the lee-rig,
    My lovely Mary, deary, O.
Altho' the night were ne'er so wet,
    An' I were ne'er so weary O;
I'd lay thee o'er the lee-rig,
    My lovely Mary, deary, O.

Look down ye gods from yonder sky,
    An' see how blest a man am I;
No envy my fond heart alarms,
    Encircled in my Mary's arms.
Lyin' across the lee-rig,
    Wi' lovely Mary, deary, O;
Lyin' across the lee-rig,
    Wi' my ain kind deary, O.

SHE ROSE AND LOOT ME IN

From MMC. Origin of Burns's song 'Tho' cruel fate should bid us part' (HH iii, 12), often attributed to Francis Semple of Beltrees. A version in TTM (Dublin 1729, 128) purified by Ramsay who, says Burns in the Interleaved SMM, 'I believe it was ... took it into his head to clear it of some seeming indelicacies, and made it at once more chaste and more dull.' (JCD. *N* 20. 'The original song ... with the music,' says Dick (JCD. *N* 89), 'is in Playford's *Choyce Ayres* 1685.'

> The night her silent sable wore,
>   An' gloomin' was the skies;
> O' glitt'rin' stars appear'd no more
>   Than those in Nelly's eyes:
> When at her father's gate I knock'd,
>   Where I had often been;
> Shrouded only in her smock,
>   She rose an' loot me in.
>
> Fast lock'd within my fond embrace,
>   She tremblin' stood asham'd;
> Her glowin' lips an' heavin' breasts,
>   At every touch enflam'd;
> My eager passion I obey'd,
>   Resolv'd the fort to win;
> An' she, at last, gave her consent
>   To yeild an' let me in.

O then! what bliss beyond compare,
    I knew no greater joy;
Enroll'd in heavenly happiness,
    So bless'd a man was I;
An' she, all ravish'd wîth delight,
    Bad me aft come again,
An' kindly vow'd that ev'ry night
    She'd rise an' let me in.

But ah! at laſt, she prov'd wi' bairn,
    An' sat baîth sad an' dull;
An' I wha was as much concern'd,
    Look'd e'en juſt like a fool;
Her lovely eyes wi' tears ran o'er,
    Repentin' her rash sin;
An' ay she curs'd the fatal hour
    That e'er she loot me in.

But, who cou'd from such beauty go,
    Or yet from Nelly part;
I lov'd her dear, an' couldna leave
    The charmer of my heart,
We wedded and conceal'd our crime,
    Then all was weel again,
An' now she blesses the happy night
    She rose an' loot me in.

i, 3   MMC misprints   'no more appear'd'
iii, 1   MMC misprints   'bless'

THE COOPER O' DUNDEE

TUNE: *Bonny Dundee*

From MMC. An old version of 'Whare gat ye that happed mealbannock?' (HH iii, 2).

Ye coopers and hoopers attend to my dîtty,
  I sing o' a cooper wha dwelt in Dundee;
This young man he was baîth am'rous and wîtty,
  He pleas'd the fair maids wi' the blink o' his e'e.

He was nae a cooper, a common tub-hooper,
  The moſt o' his trade lay in pleasin' the fair;
He hoopt them, he coopt them, he bort them, he
  plugt them.
   An' a' sent for Sandie when out o' repair.

For a twelvemonth or sae this youth was respected,
  An' he was as bisie, as weel he could be,
But bis'ness increas'd so, that some were neglected,
  Which ruin'd trade in the town o' Dundee.

A baillie's fair daughter had wanted a coopin',
  An' Sandie was sent for, as oft time was he,
He yerkt her sae hard that she sprung an end-hoopin',
  Which banish'd poor Sandie frae bonny Dundee.

YE HAE LIEN WRANG, LASSIE

TUNE: *Up and waur them a', Willie*

From MMC. Original of Burns's fragmentary song of
same name (*Ald* 1839. ii, 155).

Your rosy cheeks are turn'd saw wan,
 Ye're greener than the grass, lassie,
Your coatie's shorter by a span,
 Yet deil an inch the less, lassie.

 Ye hae lien wrang, lassie,
  Ye've lien a' wrang,
 Ye've lien in some unco bed,
  And wi' some unco man.

Ye've loot the pounie o'er the dyke,
 And he's been in the corn, lassie;
For ay the brose ye sup at e'en,
 Ye bock them or the morn, lassie.

Fu' lightly lap ye o'er the knowe,
 And thro' the wood ye sang, lassie;
But herryin' o' the foggie byke,
 I fear ye've got a ftang, lassie.

WILL YE NA, CAN YE NA,
LET ME BE

TUNE: *I ha'e laid a herrin' in sa't*

From MMC. First lines paraphrased in 'Scroggam' (HH
iii, 192).

There liv'd a wife in Whistle-cockpen,
    Will ye na, can ye na, let me be,
She brews gude yill for gentleman,
    And ay she waggit it wantonlie.

The night blew sair wi' wind and weet,
    Will ye na, can ye na, let me be,
She shaw'd the traveller ben to sleep,
    And ay she waggit it wantonlie.

She saw a sight below his sark,
    Will ye na, can ye na, let me be,
She wadna wanted it for a mark,
    And ay she waggit it wantonlie.

She saw a sight aboon his knee,
    Will ye na, can ye na, let me be,
She wadna wanted it, for three,
    And ay she waggit it wantonlie.

O whare live ye, and what's your trade?
    Will ye na, can ye na, let me be,
I am a thresher gude, he said,
    And ay she waggit it wantonlie.

And that's my flail and workin' graîth,
    Will ye na, can ye na, let me be,
And noble tools, quo' she, by my faîth!
    And ay she waggît ît wantonlie.

I wad gie a browſt, the beſt I hae,
    Will ye na, can ye na, let me be,
For a gude darge o' graîth like thae,
    And ay she waggît ît wantonlie.

I wad sell the hair frae aff my tail,
    Will ye na, can ye na, let me be,
To buy our Andrew siccan a flail,
    And ay she waggît ît wantonlie.

ELLIBANKS

TUNE: *Gillicrankie*

From MMC. Original of song of same name attributed to
Burns (*B.Chr.* ii, 1893, 152). Burns in his *Journal of the
Border Tour* (ed. DLF 1943) with Robert Ainslie, records:

> Monday [14 May 1787] — Come to Inverleithing
> [Innerleithen, today] a famous Spaw, & in the vicinity of
> the palace of Traquair, where having dined, and drank
> some Galloway-whey, I here remain till to-morrow — saw
> Elibanks and Elibraes so famous in baudy song today — on
> the other side of Tweed.

In November 1791?, Burns wrote to Ainslie from
Dumfries (DLF. L ii, 99):

> ... When I tell you even c___* has lost its power to please,
> you will guess something of my hell within and all around
> me. I began 'Elibanks and Elibraes,' but the stanzas fell
> unenjoyed, and unfinished from my listless tongue.

Ellibanks and Ellibraes,
    My blessin's ay befa' them,
Tho' I wish I had brunt a' my claes,
    The first time e'er I saw them:
Your succar kisses were sae sweet,
    Deil d—n me gin I ken, man,
How ye gart me lay my legs aside,
    And lift my sark mysel, man.

* Scott Douglas's text in MMC, holograph addenda. Also JCE.

There's no a lass in a' the land,
  Can f—k sae weel as I can;
Louse down your breeks, lug out your wand,
  Hae ye nae mind to try, man:
For ye're the lad that wears the breeks,
  And I'm the lass that loes ye;
Deil rive my c—t to candle-wicks,
  Gif ever I refuse ye! ! !

I'll clasp my arms about your neck,
  As souple as an eel, jo;
I'll cleek my houghs about you're a—e,
  As I were gaun to speel, jo;
I'll cleek my houghs about you're a—e,
  As I were gaun to speel, jo;
And if Jock thief he should slip out,
  I'll ding him wi' my heel, jo.

Green be the broom on Ellibraes,
  And yellow be the gowan!
My wame it fiſtles ay like flaes,
  As I come o'er the knowe, man:
There I lay glowran to the moon,
  Your mettle wadna daunton,
For hard your hurdies hotch'd aboon.
  While I below lay panting.

COMIN' O'ER THE HILLS
O' COUPAR

TUNE: *Ruffian's Rant*

From MMC. Original of Burns's fragmentary song 'I met
a lass, a bonnie lass' (*Ald* 1839, ii, 156). In MMC, stanzas
iv–vi are incorporated in 'Blyth Will and Bessie's
Wedding.' We follow M'Naught in transplanting them.
As he says 'they seem to be... from another ditty much
resembling 'Comin' o'er the Hills o' Coupar.'

Donald Brodie met a lass,
  Comin' o'er the hills o' Coupar,
Donald wi' his Highland hand
  Graipit a' the bits about her.

  Comin' o'er the hills o' Coupar,
  Comin' o'er the hills o' Coupar,
  Donald in a sudden wrath
  He ran his Highland durk into her.

Weel I wat she was a quine,
  Wad made a body's mouth to water;
Our Mess John, wi's auld grey pow,
  His haly lips wad licket at her.

Up she started in a fright,
  Thro' the braes what she could bicker:
Let her gang, quo' Donald, now,
  For in him's nerse my shot is sicker.

*   *   *

Kate Mackie cam frae Parlon craigs,
    The road was foul twixt that an' Couper;
She shaw'd a pair o' handsome legs,
    When Highland Donald he o'ertook her.

Comin' o'er the moor o' Couper,
    Comin' o'er the moor o' Couper,
Donald fell in love wi' her
    An' row'd his Highland plaid about her.

They took them to the Logan steps
    An' set them down to rest thegither,
Donald laid her on her back
    An' fir'd a Highland pistol at her.

Lochleven Castle heard the rair,
    An' Falkland-house the echo sounded;
Highland Donald gae a stare,
    The lassie sigh'd, but was nae wounded.

ii, 3   MMC   misprints 'we's'

COMIN' THRO' THE RYE

From MMC. Original of Burns's song of same name (HH iii, 151). A pencilled note beside ſtanza iii reads: 'Written on a window of the Globe, Dumfries.'

O gin a body meet a body,
　　Comin throu the rye;
Gin a body f—k a body,
　　Need a body cry.

　　Comin' thro' the rye, my jo,
　　　　An' comin' thro' the rye;
　　She fand a ſtaun o' ſtaunin' graîth,
　　　　Comin' thro' the rye.

Gin a body meet a body,
　　Comin' thro' the glen;
Gin a body f—k a body,
　　Need the warld ken.

Gin a body meet a body,
　　Comin' thro' the grain;
Gin a body f—k a body,
　　C—t's a body's ain.

Gin a body meet a body,
　　By a body's sel,
What na body f—s a body,
　　Wad a body tell.

Mony a body meets a body,
　　They dare na weel avow;
Mony a body f—s a body,
　　Ye wadna think ît true.

AS I CAM O'ER THE
CAIRNEY MOUNT

TUNE: *Highland Laddie*

From MMC. Original of Burns's song of same name (HH iii, 171). A purified version by Allan Ramsay in TTM 1724 (169). Burns wrote to Thomson (Sept. 1793): 'The old Highland Laddie ... is sometimes called Ginglan Johnie; it being the air of an old humorous bawdy song of that name — You will find it in the Museum, vol; 4th P. 342.' (DLF, L ii, 201). Burns's note in the Interleaved SMM runs: 'The first and indeed the most beautiful set of this tune was formerly, and in some places is still known by the name of 'As I cam o'er the Cairney Mount,' which is the first line of an excellent but somewhat licentious song still sung to the tune.' (JCD. *N* 8).

As I cam o'er the Cairney mount,
    And down amang the blooming heather,
The Highland laddie drew his durk
    And sheath'd it in my wanton leather.

    O my bonnie, bonnie Highland lad,
        My handsome, charming Highland laddie;
    When I am sick and like to die,
        He'll row me in his Highland plaiddie.

With me he play'd his warlike pranks,
    And on me boldly did adventure,
He did attack me on both flanks,
    And push'd me fiercely in the centre.

A furious battle then began,
    Wi' equal courage and desire,
Altho' he ſtruck me three to one,
    I ſtood my ground and receiv'd his fire.

But our ammunîtion being spent,
    And we quîte out o' breath an' sweating,
We did agree with ae consent,
    To fight ît out at the next meeting.

JOHN ANDERSON, MY JO

From MMC. Basis for Burns's famous song of same name (HH iii, 63). The version in M'N agrees verbatim with MM27 where it is claimed to have been taken from a song-book of 1782. Other versions in *Philomel* (London 1744) and *The Masque* (London1768). Square brackets indicate torn page in MMC.

John Anderson, my jo, John,
　　I wonder what ye mean,
To lie sae lang I' the mornin',
　　And sit sae late at e'en?
Ye'll bleer a' your een, John,
　　And why do ye so?
Come sooner to your bed at een,
　　John Anderson, my jo.

John Anderson, my jo, John,
　　When first that ye began,
Ye had as good a tail-tree,
　　As ony ither man;
But now its waxen wan, John,
　　And wrinkles to and fro;
[I've t] wa gae-ups for ae gae-down,
　　[John] Anderson, my jo.

[I'm ba] ckit like a salmon,
    [I'm] breaſtit like a swan;
My wame it is a down-cod,
    My middle ye may span:
Frae my tap-knot to my tae, John,
    I'm like the new-fa'n snow;
And it's a' for your convenience,
    John Anderson, my jo.

O it is a fine thing
    To keep out o'er the dyke;
But its a meikle finer thing,
    To see your hurdies fyke;
To see your hurdies fyke, John,
    And hit the rising blow;
It's then I like your chanter-pipe,
    John Anderson, my jo.

When ye come on before, John,
    See that ye do your beſt;
When ye begin to haud me,
    See that ye grip me faſt;
See that ye grip me faſt, John,
    Until that I cry 'Oh!'
Your back shall crack or I do that,
    John Anderson, my jo.

John Anderson, my jo, John.
    Ye're welcome when ye please;
It's eïther in the warm bed
    Or else aboon the claes:
Or ye shall hae the horns, John,
    Upon your head to grow;
An' that's the cuckold's mallison,
    John Anderson, my jo.

DUNCAN DAVIDSON

From MMC. Basis of Burns's song of same name (HH iii, 19).

There was a lass, they ca'd her Meg,
    An' she gaed o'er the muir to spin;
She fee'd a lad to lift her leg,
    They ca'd him Duncan Davidson.

            Fal, lal, &c.

Meg had a muff and ît was rough,
    Twas black without and red within,
An' Duncan, case he got the cauld,
    He ſtole his highland p—e in.

            Fal, lal, &c.

Meg had a muff, and ît was rough,
    And Duncan ſtrak tway handfu' in,
She clasp'd her heels about his waiſt.
    'I thank you Duncan! Yerk ît in! ! !'

            Fal, lal, &c.

Duncan made her hurdies dreep,
    In Highland wrath, then Meg did say;
O gang he eaſt, or gang he weſt,
    His ba's will no be dry today.

THE PLOUGHMAN

From MMC. Original of Burns's song of same name (HH iii, 24). M'Naught's note reads: 'A purified version will be found in Herd [1769, 317].' Scott Douglas prints another version in his Kilmarnock edition (i, 222). The parable of the 'three owsen,' begun in the fourth stanza, is found in the 'Auld White Nag,' a licentious ditty current in Ayrshire to this day, the 'owsen' being changed into 'pownies.' It also is evidently old.

> Then he drew out his horses which were in number three,
> Three likelier pownies for to draw, their like ye ne'er did see;
> There was twa dun pownies on ahin', auld Whitey on afore,
> The muzzle-pin for a' the yirth was in the highest bore.
> Before he gat the hause-rig turned his horse began to sweat,
> And to maintain an open fur, he spurred wi' baith his feet,' &c.'

> The ploughman he's a bonnie lad,
>   His mind is ever true, jo;
> His garters knit below the knee,
>   His bonnet it is blue, jo.
>
>   Sing up wi't a', the ploughman lad,
>   And hey the merry ploughman;
>   O' a' the trades that I do ken,
>   Commend me to the ploughman.
>
> As wakin' forth upon a day,
>   I met a jolly ploughman,
> I tald him I had lands to plough,
>   If he wad prove true, man.

He says, my dear, tak ye nae fear,
　　I'll fit you till a hair jo;
I'll cleave it up, and hit it down.
　　And water-furrow't fair, jo.

I hae three ousen in my plough,
　　Three better ne'er plough'd ground, jo.
The foremost ox is lang and sma',
　　The twa are plump and round, jo.

Then he wi' speed did yoke his plough,
　　Which by a gaud was driven, jo!
But when he wan between the stilts,
　　I thought I was in heaven, jo!

But the foremost ox fell in the fur,
　　The tither twa did founder;
The ploughman lad he breathless grew,
　　In faith it was nae wonder.

But a sykie risk, below the hill,
　　The plough she took a stane, jo,
Which gart the fire flee frae the sock,
　　The ploughman gied a grane, jo.

I hae plough'd east, I hae plough'd west,
　　In weather foul and fair, jo;
But the sairest ploughing e'er I plough'd,
　　Was ploughing amang hair, jo.

　　　Sing up wi't a', and in wi't a',
　　　And hey my merry ploughman;
　　　O' a' the trades, and crafts I ken,
　　　Commend me to the ploughman.

ii 1　　wakin', i.e. walkin'

HOW CAN I KEEP MY MAIDENHEAD?

TUNE: *The Birks o' Abergeldie*

From MMC. Original of Burns's song 'O wat ye what my minnie did?' (*Ald* 1839, ii, 157).

How can I keep my maidenhead,
　　My maidenhead, my maidenhead;
How can I keep my maidenhead,
　　Among sae mony men, O.

The Captain bad a guinea for't.
　　A guinea for't, a guinea for't;
The Captain bad a guinea for't,
　　The Colonel he bad ten, O.

But I'll do as my minnie did,
　　My minnie did, my minnie did;
But I'll do as my minnie did,
　　For siller I'll hae nane, O.

I'll gie ît to a bonie lad,
　　A bonie lad, a bonie lad;
I'll gie ît to a bonie lad,
　　For juſt as gude again, O.

An auld moulie maidenhead,
　　A maidenhead, a maidenhead;
An auld moulie maidenhead,
　　The weary wark I ken, O.

The ſtretchin' o't, the ſtrivin' o't.
　　The borin' o't, the rivin' o't,
And ay the double drivin' o't,
　　The farther ye gang ben, O.

ANDREW AN' HIS CUTTIE GUN

From MMC. Original of Burns's song 'Blythe was she' (HH iii 29). Described by him in a letter to George Thomson (19 November 1794) as 'the work of a Master' (DLF, L ii, 276). 'Burns's song was modelled on the brilliant vernacular bacchanalian 'Andro and his cutty gun,' which is the original or a parody of verses in *The Merry Muse*.' (JCD. *N* 96). The drinking-song version appeared in TTM 1740 (423) and is indeed brilliant. It begins:

> Blyth blyth, blyth was she,
> Blyth was she butt and ben;
> And weel she loo'd a Hawick gill
> And leuch to see a tappit hen.

Hawick gills were renowned for their heroic proportions.

> When a' the lave gaed to their bed,
> And I sat up to clean the shoon,
> O wha think ye cam jumpin' ben,
> But Andrew and his cuttie gun.

> Blythe, blythe, blythe was she.
> Blythe was she but and ben,
> An' weel she lo'ed it in her neive.
> But better when it slippit in.

> Or e'er I wist he laid me back,
> And up my gamon to my chin,
> And ne'er a word to me he spak,
> But liltit out his cutty gun.

The bawsent bîtch she left the whalps,
  And hunted round us at the fun,
As Andrew fodgel'd wi his a—e,
  And fir'd at me the cuttie gun.

O some delights in cuttie ſtoup,
  And some delights in cuttie-mun,
But my delight's an a—elins coup,
  Wi' Andrew an' his cuttie gun.

O CAN YE LABOUR LEE, YOUNG MAN?

TUNE: *Sir Arch. Grant's Strathspey*

From MMC. Original of Burns's song of same name (HH
iii, 138).

I fee'd a man at Martinmas,
    Wi arle pennies three;
But a' the fau't I had to him,
    He coudna labour lee.

    O can ye labour lee, young man,
        O can ye labour lee;
    Gae back the road ye cam agin,
        Ye shall never scorn me.

A stibble rig is easy plough'd.
    An' fallow land is free;
But what a silly coof is he,
    That canna labour lee.

The spretty bush, an' benty knowe,
    The ploughman points his sock in.
He sheds the roughness, lays it by,
    An' bauldly ploughs his yokin'.

WAD YE DO THAT?

TUNE: *John Anderson, my jo*

From MMC. Original of Burns's song 'Lass, when your mither is frae hame' (*Ald* 1839, ii 156).

Gudewife, when your gudeman's frae hame,
  Might I but be sae bauld,
As come to your bed-chamber,
  When winter nights are cauld;
As come to your bed-chamber,
  When nights are cauld and wat,
And lie in your gudeman's stead,
  Wad ye do that?

Young man, an ye should be so kind,
  When our gudeman's frae hame,
As come to my bed-chamber,
  Where I am laid my lane;
And lie in our gudeman's stead,
  I will tell you what,
He f—s me five times ilka night,
  Wad ye do that?

THERE CAM A CADGER

TUNE: *Clout the Cauldron*

From MMC. Basis of Burns's fragmentary song, 'There came a piper out o' Fife.' (*Ald* 1839, ii, 159).

> There cam a cadger out o' Fife,
>   I wat na how they ca'd him;
> He play'd a trick to our gudewife,
>   When fient a body bad him.
>
> >   Fal lal, &c.
>
>
> He took a lang thing ſtout and ſtrang,
>   An' ſtrack ît in her gyvel;
> An' ay she swore she fand the thing
>   Gae borin' by her nyvel.
>
> >   Fal lal, &c.

JENNY MACRAW

TUNE: *The bonny moor-hen*

From MMC. Origin of Burns's fragmentary song of same
name. (*Ald* 1839, ii, 155).

Jenny Macraw was a bird o' the game,
An' mony a shot had been lows'd at her wame;
Be't a lang bearing arrow, or the sharp-rattlin' hail,
Still, whirr! she flew off wi' the shot in her tail.

Jenny Macraw to the mountains she's gaen,
Their leagues and their covenants a' she has taen;
My head now, and heart now, quo' she, are at reſt,
An' for my poor c—t, let the deil do his beſt.

Jenny Macraw on a midsummer morn,
She cut off her c—t and she hang't on a thorn;
There she loot ît hing for a year and a day,
But, oh! how look'd her a—e when her c—t was
away.

IV

COLLECTED BY BURNS

Notes in this section are by
SYDNEY GOODSIR SMITH
unless otherwise initialled

THE REELS O' BOGIE

TUNE: *Cauld Kail in Aberdeen*

From MM27. Not in MMC. Purified version in SMM (ii, 170) with words by the Duke of Gordon. This below is a very corrupt and anglicized text: for an idea of what the original was like, compare stanza iii with the old version known to Burns (in Section i B, 'There cam a Soger'). Another version in DH 1769 (314).

You lads and lasses all that dwell
    In the town of Strathbogie,
Whene'er you meet a pretty lass,
    Be sure you tip her cogie.
The lads and lasses toy and kiss,
    The lads ne'er think it is amiss
To bang the holes whereout they piss,
    And that's the reels o' Bogie.

There's Kent, and Keen, and Aberdeen,
    And the town of Strathbogie,
Where every lad may have his lass,
    Now that I've got my cogie.
They spread wide their snow-white thighs
    And roll about their wanton eyes,
And when they see your pintle rise
    They'll dance the reels o' Bogie.

A trooper going o'er the lea,
  He swore that he would steer me,
And long before the break of day,
  He giggled, goggled near me.
He put a stiff thing in my hand,
  I could not bear the banging o't
But long before he went away
  I suppled both the ends o't.

His pintle was of largest size,
  Indeed it was a banger,
He sought a prize between my thighs
  Till it became a hanger.
Had you but seen the wee bit skin
  He had to put his pintle in,
You'd sworn it was a chitterling
  Dancing the reels o' Bogie.

He turned about to fire again
  And give me t'other sally.
And as he fired I ne'er retired
  But received him in my alley.
His pebbles they went thump, thump,
  Against my little wanton rump,
But soon I left him but the stump
  To dance the reels o' Bogie.

Said I, young man, more you can't do,
    I think I've granted your desire,
By bobbing on my wanton clue,
    You see your pintle's all on fire.
When on my back I work like ſteel
    And bar the door wiſth my left heel,
The more you f— the less I feel,
    And that's the reels o' Bogie.

iv, I   MM27   (another edn.) ... largeish size.
v, 7   *Ibid*   ... with the ſtump.

JOCKEY WAS A BONNY LAD

TUNE: *John Roy Stewart's Strathspey*

From MMC. Another version in DH 1791 (ii, 325). The changes are all improvements poetically and were almost certainly made by Burns when transcribing the song.

My Jockey is a bonny lad,
A dainty lad, a merry lad,
A neat sweet pretty little lad,
 An' just the lad for me.
For when we o'er the meadows stray,
He's ay sae lively ay sae gay,
An' aft right canty does he say,
 There's nane he loes like me.

 An' he's ay huggin', ay dawtin',
 Ay clappin', ay pressin',
 Ay squeezin', ay kissin',
  An' winna let me be.

I met my lad the ither day,
Friskin' thro' a field o' hay,
Says he, dear Jenny, will ye stay,
 An' crack a while wi' me.
Na, Jockey lad, I darena stay,
My mither she'd miss me away;
Syne she'll flyte an' scauld a' day,
 An' play the diel wi' me.

 But Jockey still continued, &c.

Hoot! Jockey, see my hair is down,
An' look you've torn a' my gown,
An' how will I gae thro' the town,
　　Dear laddie tell to me.
He never minded what I said,
But wi' my neck an' bosom play'd;
Tho' I intreated, begg'd an' pray'd
　　Him no to touzle me.

　　But Jockey still continued
　　Huggin', dawtin', clappin', squeezin',
　　An' ay kissin', kissin', kissin'.
　　　　Till down cam we.

As breathless an' fatigued I lay,
In his arms among the hay,
My blood fast thro' my veins did play
　　As he lay huggin' me;
I thought my breath wou'd never last,
For Jockey danc'd sae devilish fast;
But what cam o'er, I trow, at last,
　　There diel ane kens but me.

　　But soon he weari'd o' his dance,
　　O' a' his jumpin' an' his prance,
　　An' confess'd without romance,
　　　　He was fain to let me be.

i, 5　　MMC　　misprints 'he' for 'we'
ii, 2　　MMC　　misprints 'a hay' for 'o' hay'

BLYTH WILL AN' BESSIE'S WEDDING

TUNE: *Roy's Wife*

From MMC. Stanza iv, says Scott Douglas in a pencilled note in MMC, is 'Burns's addendum.'

There was a weddin' o'er in Fife,
    An' mony ane frae Lothian at ît;
Jean Vernor there maiſt lost hir life,
    For love o' Jamie Howden at ît.

    Blyth Will an' Bessie's weddin',
    Blyth Will an' Bessie's weddin',
    Had I been Will, Bess had been mine,
    An' Bess an' I had made the weddin'.

Right sair she grat, an' wet her cheeks,
    An' naîthing pleas'd that we cou'd gie her;
She tint her heart in Jeamie's breeks,
    It cam nae back to Lothian wi' her.

[Tam]mie Tamson too was there,
    Maggie Birnie was his dearie,
He pat ît in amang the hair,
    An' puddled there till he was weary.

When e'enin' cam the town was thrang,
    An' beds were no to get for siller;
When e'er they fand a want o' room.
      They lay in pairs like bread an' butter.

Twa an' twa they made the bed,
    An' twa an' twa they lay the gíther;
When they had na room enough,
      Ilk ane lap on aboon the títher.

THE LASS O' LIVISTON

From MMC. There is a purified version by Allan Ramsay in TTM 1724 (99). Burns's note in the Interleaved Copy of SMM reads: '... The original set of verses to this tune is still extant, and have a very great deal of poetic merit, but are not quite ladies' reading.' (JCD. *N* 6). Scott Douglas, in a pencilled note in MMC, says 'Old song revised by Burns.'

> The bonny lass o' Liviston.
> > Her name ye ken, her name ye ken;
> And ay the welcomer ye'll be,
> > The farther ben, the farther ben.
> And she has it written in her contract
> > To lie her lane, to lie her lane,
> And I hae written in my contract
> > To claw her wame, to claw her wame.
>
> The bonny lass o' Liviston,
> > She's berry brown, she's berry brown;
> An' ye winna true her lovely locks,
> > Gae farther down, gae farther down.
> She has a black and a rolling eye,
> > And a dimplit chin, and a dimplit chin;
> And no to prie her rosy lips,
> > Wad be a sin, wad be a sin.

The bonny lass o' Liviston,
    Cam in to me, cam in to me;
I wat wi' baîth ends o' the busk,
    I made me free, I made me free.
I laid her feet to my bed-ſtock,
    Her head to the wa', her head to the wa';
And I gied her her wee coat in her teeth,
    Her sark an' a', her sark an' a'.

iii, 7   MMC   misprints 'wi' for 'wee'

SHE'S HOY'D ME OUT O'
LAUDERDALE

From MMC. Line 5, stanza iii, is incorporated in Burns's song 'The Deuk's Dang o'er my Daddie, O!' (HH iii, 139). Scott Douglas in a pencilled note in MMC says 'Old song revised by Burns.'

There liv'd a lady in Lauderdale,
    She lo'ed a fiddler fine;
She lo'ed him in her chamber,
    She held him in her mind;
She made his bed at her bed-stock,
    She said he was her brither;
But she's hoy'd him out o' Lauderdale,
    His fiddle and a' thegither.

First when I cam to Lauderdale,
    I had a fiddle gude,
My sounding-pin stood like the aik
    That grows in Lauder-wood;
But now my sounding-pin's gaen down,
    And tint the foot forever;
She's hoy'd me out o' Lauderdale,
    My fiddle and a' thegither.

First when I came to Lauderdale,
    Your Ladyship can declare,
I play'd a bow, a noble bow,
    As e'er was strung wi' hair;
But dow'na do's come o'er me now,
    And your Ladyship winna consider;
She's hoy'd me out o' Lauderdale,
    My fiddle and a' thegither.

ERROCK BRAE

TUNE: *Sir Alex. Don's Strathspey*

From MMC, where Scott Douglas comments 'Old song
revised by Burns.'

O Errock ſtane, may never maid,
  A maiden by thee gae,
Nor e'er a ſtane o' ſtanin' graîth,
  Gae ſtanin' o'er the brae.

And tillin' Errock brae, young man,
  An' tillin' Errock brae,
An open fur an' ſtanin' graîth,
  Maun till the Errock brae.

As I sat by the Errock ſtane,
  Surveying far and near,
Up cam a Cameronian,
  Wi' a' his preaching gear.

He flang the Bible o'er the brae,
  Amang the rashy gerse;
But the solemn league and covenant
  He laid below my a—e.

But on the edge of Errock brae,
  He gae me sic a ſten,
That o'er, and o'er, and o'er we row'd,
  Till we cam to the glen.

Yet ſtill his p—e held the grip,
        And ſtill his b—s hang;
That a Synod cou'd na tell the a—e
        To whom they did belang.

A Prelate he loups on before,
        A Catholic behin',
But gie me a Cameronian,
        He'll m—w a body blin'.

OUR GUDEWIFE'S SAE MODEST

TUNE: *John Anderson, my jo*

From MMC.

Our gudewife's sae modest,
    When she is set at meat,
A laverock's leg, or a tittling's wing,
    Is mair than she can eat;
But, when she's in her bed at e'en,
    Between me and the wa';
She is a glutton deevil,
    She swallows c—s and a'.

SUPPER IS NA READY

TUNE: *Clout the Cauldron*

From MMC.

Roseberry to his lady says,
    'My hinnie and my succour,
'O shall we do the thing you ken,
    'Or shall we take our supper?'

        Fal, lal, &c.

Wi' modest face, sae fu' o' grace,
    Replied the bonny lady;
'My noble lord do as you please,
    'But supper is na ready.'

        Fal, lal, &c.

YON, YON, YON, LASSIE

TUNE: *Ruffian's Rant*

From MMC, where Scott Douglas gives the tune as
'Cameron's got his wife again.'

I never saw a silken gown,
  But I wad kiss the sleeve o't;
I never saw a maidenhead
  That I wad spier the leave o't.

  O, yon, yon, yon, lassie,
    Yon, yon, yon;
  I never met a bonie lass
    But what wad play at yon.

Tell nae me, o' Meg my wife,
  That crowdie has na savour;
But gie to me a bonie lass
  An' let me steal the favour.

Gie me her I kis't yestreen,
  I vow but she was handsome,
For ilka birss upon her c—t,
  Was worth a royal ransom.

  An' yon, yon, yon, lassie,
    Yon, yon, yon,
  I never saw a bonie lass
    But what wad do yon.

THE YELLOW, YELLOW YORLIN'

TUNE: *Bonnie beds of roses*

From MMC, where Scott Douglas gives the tune as 'The Collier Laddie.'

It fell on a day, in the flow'ry month o' May,
    All on a merry merry mornin',
I met a pretty maid, an' unto her I said,
    I wad fain fin' your yellow yellow yorlin'.

O no, young man, says she, you're a ſtranger to me,
    An' I am aniſher man's darlin',
Wha has baiſh sheep an' cows, that's feedin' in the hows.
    An' a cock for my yellow yellow yorlin'.

But, if I lay you down upon the dewy ground,
    You wad nae be the waur ae farthing;
An' that happy, happy man, he never cou'd ken
    That I play'd wi' your yellow yellow yorlin'.

O fie, young man, says she, I pray you let me be,
    I wad na for five pound ſterling;
My miſher wad gae mad, an' sae wad my dad,
    If you play'd wi' my yellow yellow yorlin'.

But I took her by the waiſt, an' laid her down in haſte,
    For a' her squakin' and squalin';
The lassie soon grew tame, an' bade me come again
    For to play wi' her yellow yellow yorlin'.

SHE GRIPET AT THE GIRTEST O'T

TUNE: *East Nook of Fife*

From MMC.

> Our bride flate, and our bride flang,
> But lang before the laverock sang,
> She pay't him twice for every bang,
>   And gripet at the girtest o't.
>
> Our bride turn'd her to the Wa',
> But lang before the cock did craw,
> She took him by the b—ks and a',
>   And gripet at the girtest o't.

YE'SE GET A HOLE TO HIDE IT IN

TUNE: *Waukin' o' the Fauld*

O will ye speak at our town,
    As ye come frae the fair?
And ye'se get a hole to hide ît in,
    Ye'se get a hole to hide ît in;
Will ye speak at our town
    As ye come frae the fair,
Ye'se get a hole to hide ît in,
    Will haud ît a' and mair.

O haud awa your hand, Sir,
    Ye gar me ay think shame;
An' ye'se get a hole to hide ît in,
    Ye'se get a hole to hide ît in;
O haud awa your hand, Sir,
    Ye gar me ay think shame;
An' ye'se get a hole to hide ît in,
    An' think yoursel at hame.

O will ye let abee, Sir;
    Toots! now, ye've rivt my sark,
An' ye'se get a hole to hide ît in,
    Ye'se get a hole to hide ît in;
O will ye let abee, Sir;
    Toots! now, ye've reft my sark;
An' ye'se get a hole to hide ît in,
    Whare ye may work your wark.

O haud awa your hand, Sir,
 Ye're like to pît me daft;
And ye'se get a hole to hide ît in,
 Ye'se get a hole to hide ît in,
O had awa your hand, Sir,
 Ye're like to put me daft;
An' ye'se get a hole to hide ît in,
 To keep ît warm and saft.

O had ît in your hand, Sir,
 Till I get up my claes,
An' ye'se get a hole to hide ît in,
 Ye'se get a hole to hide ît in;
O had ît in your hand, Sir,
 Till I get up my claes;
An' ye'se get a hole to hide ît in,
 To keep ît frae the flaes.

i. 1   MMC   misprints 'As ye came...'

DUNCAN MACLEERIE

TUNE: *Jocky Macgill*

From MMC.

Duncan Macleerie and Janet his wife,
They gaed to Kilmarnock to buy a new knife;
But inſtead of a knife they coft but a bleerie;
We're very weel saird, quo' Duncan Macleerie.

Duncan Macleerie has got a new fiddle,
It's a' ſtrung wi' hair, and a hole in the middle;
An' ay when he plays on't, his wife looks sae cheary,
Very weel done, Duncan, quo' Janet Macleerie.

Duncan he play'd 'till his bow ît grew greasy;
Janet grew fretfu', and unco uneasy.
Hoot, quo' she, Duncan, ye're unco soon weary;
Play us a pibroch, quo' Janet Macleerie.

Duncan Macleerie play'd on the harp,
An' Janet Macleerie danc'd in her sark;
Her sark ît was short, her c—t ît was hairy,
Very weel danc'd, Janet, quo' Duncan Macleerie.

The time for an average four-part march is two minutes: a pibroch
12 minutes. [JB]

THEY TOOK ME TO THE HALY BAND

TUNE: *Clout the Cauldron*

From MMC.

They took me to the haly band,
　　For playing bye my wife, Sir;
And lang and sair they lectur'd me,
　　For hadin' sic a life, Sir.

I answer'd in na mony words,
　　'What deel needs a' this clatter;
'As lang as she cou'd keep the grip
　　'I aye was m—g at her.'

i, 2　　MMC　　misprints 'me.'

THE MODIEWARK

TUNE: *O for ane an' twenty, Tam*

From MMC.

The modiewark has done me ill,
And below my apron has biggīt a hill;
I maun consult some learned clark
About this wanton modiewark.

> An' O the wanton modiewark,
> The weary wanton modiewark;
> I maun consult some learned clark
> About this wanton modiewark.

O first īt gat between my taes,
Out o'er my garter niest īt gaes;
At length īt crap below my sark,
The weary wanton modiewark.

This modiewark, tho' īt be blin';
If ance īts nose you lat īt in,
Then to the hilts, wīthin a crack
It's out o' sight, the modiewark.

When Marjorie was made a bride,
An' Willy lay down by her side,
Syne nocht was hard, when a' was dark,
But kicking at the modiewark.

KEN YE NA OUR LASS BESS?

TUNE: *Auld Sir Symon*

From MMC.

O ken ye na our lass, Bess?
An' ken ye na our lass, Bess?
Between her lily white thies
She's bigget a magpie's nest.

An' ken ye na our lad, Tam?
An' ken ye na our lad, Tam?
He's on o' a three-fitted stool,
An' up to the nest he clamb.

An' what did he there, think ye?
An' what did he there, think ye?
He brak a' the eggs o' the nest,
An' the white's ran down her thie.

()

WHA THE DELL CAN HINDER THE WIND TO BLAW?

TUNE: *Wat ye wha I met yestreen*

From MMC.

It fell about the blythe new-year,
    When days are short and nights are lang,
Ae bonie night, the starns were clear,
    An' frost beneath my fit-stead rang;
I heard a carlin cry, 'relief!'
    Atweesh her trams a birkie lay;
But he wan a quarter in her beef,
    For a' the jirts the carlin gae.

She heav'd to; and he strak frae,
    As he wad nail'd the carlin thro';
An' ilka f—t the carlin gae,
    It wad hae fill'd a pockie fou;
Temper your tail, the young man cried,
    Temper your tail by Venus' law!
Double your dunts, the dame replied,
    Wha the deil can hinder the wind to blaw?

Stanza ii is a variant of stanzas 2 and 3 of 'Cumnock Psalms' (Section
I B).

WE'RE A' GAUN SOUTHIE, O

TUNE: *The Merry Lads of Ayr*

From MMC.

> Callum cam to Campbell's court,
>   An' saw ye e'er the make o't;
> Pay'd twenty shillings for a thing,
>   An' never got a straik o't.
>
>> We're a' gaun southie, O.
>> We're a' gaun there;
>> An' we're a' gaun to Mauchlin fair,
>> To sell our pickle hair.
>
> Pay'd twenty shillings for a quine,
>   Her name was Kirsty Lauchlan;
> But Callum took her by the c—t.
>   Before the laird o' Mauchline.
>
> Callum cam to Kirsty's door,
>   Says, Kirsty are ye sleepin'?
> No sac soun as ye wad trow.
>   Ye'se get the thing ye're seekin'.
>
> Callum had a peck o' meal,
>   Says, Kirsty, will ye draik it?
> She whippet off her wee white-coat,
>   An' birket at it nakit.

Bonie lassie, braw lassie.
  Will ye hae a soger?
Then she took up her duddie sark,
  An' he shot in his Roger.

Kind kimmer Kirsty,
  I loe wi' a' my heart, O,
An' when there's ony p—s gaun,
  She'll ay get a part. O.

iv. 3 MMC misprints 'of'

CUDDIE THE COOPER

TUNE: *Bonny Dundee*

From MMC.

There was a cooper they ca'd him Cuddy,
    He was the best cooper that ever I saw;
He cam to girth our landlady's tubbie,
    He bang'd her buttocks again the wa'.

Cooper quo' she, hae ye ony mony?
    The deevil a penny, quo' Cuddy, at a'!
She took out her purse, an' she gied him a guinea.
    For banging her buttocks again the wa'.

NAE HAIR ON'T

TUNE: *Gillicrankie*

From MMC, where Scott Douglas comments 'This is in the Dublin collection, 1769.'

Yestreen I wed a lady fair,
    An ye wad believe me,
On her c—t there grows nae hair,
    That's the thing that grieves me.

It vexed me sair, it plagu'd me sair,
    It put me in a passion,
To think that I had wad a wife,
    Whase c—t was out o' fashion.

THERE'S HAIR ON'T

TUNE: *Push about the jorum*

From MMC.

O, ere yestreen I stented graith,
  An' labor'd lang an' sair on't;
But fient a work, na work wad it,
  There's sic a crap o' hair on't.

  There's hair on't, there's hair on't,
  There's thretty thrave an' mair on't;
  But gin I live to anither year,
  I'll tether my grey naigs on't.

An' up the glen there rase a knowe,
  Below the knowe a lair on't,
I maist had perish'd, fit an' horse,
  I could na see for hair on't.

But I'll plant a stake into the flowe,
  That ploughmen may tak care on't;
An' lay twa steppin'-stanes below,
  An' syne I'll cowe the hair on't.

THE LASSIE GATH'RING NITS

TUNE: *O the broom*

From MMC.

There was a lass, and a bonie lass,
    A gath'ring nîts did gang;
She pu'd them heigh, she pu'd them laigh,
    She pu'd them whare they hang.

Till tir'd at length, she laid her down.
    An' sleept the wood amang;
Whan by there cam three lusty lads,
    Three lusty lads an' strang.

The first did kiss her rosy lips,
    He thought ît was nae wrang;
The second lous'd her bodice fair,
    Fac'd up wi' London whang.

An' what the third did to the lass,
    I's no put in this sang;
But the lassie wauken'd in a fright,
    An' says, I hae sleept lang.

THE LINKIN' LADDIE

TUNE: *Push about the jorum*

From MMC.

Waes me that e'er I made your bed!
　　Waes me that e'er I saw ye!
For now I've lost my maidenhead,
　　An' I ken na how they ca' ye.

My name's weel kend in my am countrie.
　　They ca' me the linkin' laddie;
An' ye had na been as willing as I,
　　Shame fa' them wad e'er hae bade ye.

JOHNIE SCOTT

TUNE: *O the broom*

From MMC.

Whare will we get a coat to Johnie Scott,
    Amang us maidens a'?
Whare will we get a coat to Johnie Scott,
    To mak the laddie braw:

There's your c—t-hair, and there's my c—t-hair.
    An' we'll twine ît wondrous sma';
An' if waft be scarce, we'll cowe our a—e,
    To mak him kilt an' a'.

MADGIE CAM TO MY BED-STOCK

TUNE: *Clout the Cauldron*

From MMC.

> Madgie cam to my bed-stock,
>   To see gif I was waukin;
> I pat my han' atweesh her feet,
>   An' fand her wee bît maukin.
>
>
>   Fal, lal, &c.
>
>
> C—t ît was the sowen-pat,
>   An' p—e was the ladle;
> B—ks were the serving-men
>   That waîted at the table.
>
>
>   Fal, lal, &c.

O GIN I HAD HER

TUNE: *Saw ye na my Peggy*

From MMC.

> O gin I had her,
> Ay gin I had her,
> O gin I had her,
>> Black altho' she be.
> I wad lay her bale,
> I'd gar her spew her kail;
> She ne'er soud keep a mail,
>> Till she dandl'd it on her knee.
>
> She says, I am light
> To manage matters right,
> That I've nae might or weight
>> To fill a lassie's ee;
> But wad she tak a yokin',
> I wad put a c—k in;
> A quarter o't to flocken,
>> I wad frankly gie.

---

i, 2   MMC   misprints 'Ae'
i, 7   mail,   *i.e.* meal.
i. 8   MMC   misprints 'Tell'

HE TILL'T AND SHE TILL'T

TUNE: *Maggie Lauder*

From MMC.

He till't, and she till't,
    An' a' to mak a lad again;
The auld held carl,
    Whan he wan on did nod again;
An' he dang, an' she flang,
    An' a' to mak a laddie o't;
But he bor'd and she roar'd,
    An' coudna mak a lassie o't.

Line 4 MMC reads   'When he wan on to nod again.'

V
ALIEN MODES

Notes in this section are by
SYDNEY GOODSIR SMITH
unless otherwise initialled

TWEEDMOUTH TOWN

From MMC.

Near Tweedmouth town there liv'd three maids,
    Who used to tope good ale;
An' there likewise liv'd three wives,
    Who sometimes wagged their tale;
They often met, to tope an' chat,
    And tell odd tales of men;
[Cr]ying, when shall we meet again, an' again,
    [Cr]ying, when shall we meet again.

Not far from these there liv'd three widows,
    With complexions wan an' pale,
Who seldom used to tope an' bouse,
    An' seldom wagged their tale.
They sigh'd, they pin'd, they griev'd, they whin'd,
    An' often did complain,
Shall we, quo they, ne'er sport or play
    Nor wag our tails again, an' again.

Nine northern lads with their Scots plaids,
    By the Union, British call'd,
All nine-inch men, to a bousing came,
    Wi' their brawny backs I'm tald.
They all agreed, to cross the Tweed,
    An' ease them of their pain;
They laid them all down,
    An' they f—k'd them all round,
An' cross'd the Tweed again, an' again.

i, 7, 8   Page cut. Maybe 'Saying...'
iii, 4   MMC reads 'backs an' tald.'

THE BOWER OF BLISS

TUNE: *Logan Water*

From MMC. In a letter to William Stewart, Closeburn
Castle, dated 'Ellesland, Wednesday even:' [?9 July, 1788],
Burns wrote: 'I inclose you the Plenipo. — You will see
another, The Bower of bliss; 'tis the work of a Revd
Doctor of the Church of Scotland — Would [to] Heaven
a few more of them would turn the[ir fie]ry Zeal *that way*!
There, they might *spend* their Holy fury, and shew the *tree*
by its *fruits*!!! There, the *in-bearing workings* might give
hopeful presages of a *New-birth*!!!! The other two are by
the author of the Plenipo, but 'The Doctor' is not half
there, as I have mislaid it. — I have no copies left of either,
so must have the precious pieces again.' (DLF.L i, 232).
M'Naught disingenuously remarks: 'This shows the part
played by the poet's boon companions in the
compilation of the Crochallan collection'; but this is the
only such contribution M'Naught points to — and an
utterly uncharacteristic one, at that. It also shows,
unfortunately, that the Bard really liked this sort of
drivel. The present editors agree entirely with M'Naught
when he says 'the 'high-kilted' muse does not become
drawing-room costume. The deliberate, downright,
mother-naked coarseness of the vernacular is infinitely
preferable to this sickening stuff, which is Greek to the
peasant, who calls a spade a spade because he has no other
word for it.'

Whilst others to thy bosom rise,
And paint the glories of thine eyes,
Or bid thy lips and cheeks disclose,
The unfading bloom of Eden's rose.
Less obvious charms my song inspire,
Which fell, not fear we most admire —
Less obvious charms, not less divine,
I sing that lovely bower of thine.

Rich gem! worth India's wealth alone,
How much pursued how little known;
Tho' rough its face, tho' dim its hue,
It soils the lustre of Peru.
The vet'ran such a prize to gain,
Might all the toils of war sustain;
The devotee forsake his shrine,
To venerate that bower of thine.

When the stung heart feels keen desire,
And through each vein pours liquid fire:
When with flush'd cheeks and burning eyes,
Thy lover to thy bosom flies;
Believe, dear maid, believe my vow,
By Venus' self, I swear, 'tis true!
More bright the higher beauties shine,
Illum'd by that strange bower of thine.

What thought sublime, what lofty strain
Its wond'rous virtues can explain?
No place how'er remote, can be
From its intense attraction free:
Tho' more elastic far than steel,
Its force ten thousand needles feel;
Pleas'd their high temper to resign,
In that magnetic bower of thine.

Irriguous vale, embrown'd with shades,
Which no intrinsic storm pervades!
Soft clime, where native summer glows,
And nectar's living current flows!
Not Tempe's vale, renowned of yore,
Of charms could boast such endless store;
More than Elysian sweets combine,
To grace that smiling bower of thine.

O, may no rash invader stain,
Love's warm, sequestered virgin fane!
For me alone let gentle fate,
Preserve the dear august retreat!
Along its banks when shall I stray?
Its beauteous landscape when survey?
How long in fruitless anguish pine,
Nor view unvail'd that bower of thine?

O! let my tender, trembling hand,
The awful gate of life expand!
With all its wonders feast my sight;
Dear prelude to immense delight!
Till plung'd in liquid joy profound,
The dark unfathom'd deep I sound;
All panting on thy breast recline,
And, murmuring, bless that bower of thine.

Last line MMC has 'bliss'

THE PLENIPOTENTIARY

TUNE: *The Terrible Law* or *Shawnbuee*

From MM27. Not in MMC. Enclosed in same letter as 'The Bower of Bliss'; it is certainly a cut above that horror. It was composed by Captain Morris, an ornament of the Carlton House set and author of *Songs Drinking, Political and Facetious*. (*c*.1790).

> The Dey of Algiers, when afraid of his ears,
> A messenger sent to our court, sir,
> As he knew in our state the women had weight,
> He chose one well hung for the sport, sir.
> He searched the Divan till he found out a man
> Whose b—— were heavy and hairy,
> And he lately came o'er from the Barbary shore
> As the great Plenipotentiary.
>
> When to England he came, with his p—— in a flame,
> He showed it his Hostess on landing,
> Who spread its renown thro' all parts of the town,
> As a pintle past all understanding.
> So much there was said of its snout and its head,
> That they called it the great Janissary;
> Not a lady could sleep till she got a sly peep
> At the great Plenipotentiary.

As he rode in his coach, how the whores did approach,
And stared, as if stretched on a tenter;
He drew every eye of the dames that passed by,
Like the sun to its wonderful centre.
As he passed thro' the town not a window was down,
And the maids hurried out to the area,
The children cried, 'Look, there's the man with the cock,
That's the great Plenipotentiary.'

When he came to the Court, oh, what giggle and sport,
Such squinting and squeezing to view him,
What envy and spleen in the women were seen,
All happy and pleased to get to him.
They vowed from their hearts, if men of such parts
Were found on the coast of Barbary,
'Tis a shame not to bring a whole guard for the King,
Like the great Plenipotentiary.

The dames of intrigue formed their c—— in a league.
To take him in turns like good folk, sir;
The young misses' plan was to catch as catch can,
And all were resolved on a stroke, sir.
The cards to invite flew by thousands each night,
With bribes to the old secretary,
And the famous Eclipse was not let for more leaps
Than the great Plenipotentiary.

When his name was announced, how the women all bounced,
And their blood hurried up to their faces;
He made them all itch from navel to breech,
And their bubbies burst out all their laces;
There was such damned work to be f—— by the Turk.
That nothing their passion could vary;
All the nations [? matrons] fell sick for the Barbary p——
Of the great Plenipotentiary.

A Duchess whose Duke made her ready to puke,
With fumbling and f—— all night, sir,
Being first for the prize, was so pleased with its size.
That she begged for to stroke its big snout, sir.
My stars! cried her Grace, its head's like a mace,
'Tis as high as the Corsican Fairy;
I'll make up, please the pigs, for dry bobs and frigs.
With the great Plenipotentiary.

And now to be bor'd by this Ottoman Lord
Came a Virgin far gone in the wane, sir,
She resolved for to try, tho' her c—— was so dry.
That she knew it must split like a cane, sir.
True it was as she spoke, it gave way at each stroke.
But oh, what a woeful quandary!
With one terrible thrust her old piss-bladder burst
On the great Plenipotentiary.

The next to be tried was an Alderman's Bride,
With a c—— that would swallow a turtle,
She had horned the dull brows of her worshipful spouse,
Till they sprouted like Venus's myrtle.
Thro' thick and thro' thin, bowel deep he dashed in.
Till her c—— frothed like cream in a dairy.
And expressed by loud farts she was strained in all parts
By the great Plenipotentiary.

The next to be kissed, on the Plenipo's list,
Was a delicate Maiden of Honor,
She screamed at the sight of his p—— in a fright,
Tho' she'd had the whole Palace upon her.
O Lord, she said, what a p—— for a maid!
Do, pray, come look at it, Cary!
But I *will* have one drive, if I'm ripped up alive,
By the great Plenipotentiary.

Two sisters next came, Peg and Molly by name,
Two ladies of very high breeding,
Resolved one should try, while the other stood by
And watch the amusing proceeding.
Peg swore by the gods that the Mussulman's cods
Were as big as both buttocks of Mary;
Molly cried with a grunt, he has ruined my c——
With his great Plenipotentiary.

The next for this plan was an old Haridan,
Who had swallowed huge p—— from each nation,
With over much use she had broken the sluice
'Twixt her — and its lower relation.
But he stuck her so full that she roared like a bull,
Crying out she was bursting and weary,
So tight was she stuck by this wonderful f——
Of the great Plenipotentiary.

The next for a shag came the new Yankee flag;
Tho' lanky and scraggy in figure,
She was fond of the quid, for she had been well rid
From Washington down to a nigger.
Oh my! such a size! I guess it's first prize,
It's a wonder, quite next Ni-a-gary;
W-a-l-l, now I'm in luck, stranger, let's f——,
Bully for the great Plenipotentiary.

All heads were bewitched and longed to be stitched,
Even babies would languish and linger,
And the boarding-school Miss, as she sat down to piss,
Drew a Turk on the floor with her finger.
For fancied delight, they all clubbed for a shite,
To frig in the school necessary,
And the Teachers from France f—— a la distance
With the great Plenipotentiary.

Each sluice-c—d bawd, who'd been s——d abroad
Till her premises gaped like a grave, sir,
Found luck was so thick, she could feel the Turk's p——,
Tho' all others were loſt in her cave, sir.
The nymphs of the ſtage did his ramrod engage,
Made him free of their gay seminary;
And the Italian Signors opened all their back doors
To the great Plenipotentiary.

Then of love's sweet reward, measured out by the yard,
The Turk was moſt bleſt of mankind, sir,
For his powerful dart went right home to the heart,
Whether ſtuck in before or behind, sir.
But no pencil can draw this great-pintled Bashaw,
Then let each c—— loving contemporary,
As cocks of the game, let's drink to the name
Of the great Plenipotentiary.

UNA'S LOCK

From MM27. Not in MMC. Included in *The Giblet Eye*
(*c*.1806). Burns wrote to George Thomson in September
1794 (DLF, *L* ii, 256), enclosing the song 'Sae flaxen were
her ringlets' (HH iii, 160):

> Do you know … a blackguard Irish song called 'Oonagh's
> Waterfall, or The lock that scattered Oonagh's p—ss'? … —
> I have often regretted the want of decent verses to ſt you
> may be pleased to have some verses to ſt … that you may
> sing ſt to the Ladies.

'Twas on a sweet morning,
  When violets were a-springing,
The dew the meads adorning,
  The larks melodious singing;
The rose-trees, by each breeze,
  Were gently wafted up and down,
And the primrose, that then blows,
  Bespangled nature's verdant gown.
The purling rill, the murmuring ſtream,
  Stole gently through the lofty grove:
Such was the time when Darby ſtole
  Out to meet his barefoot love.

    Tol, lol, &c.

Sweet Una was the tightest,
  Genteelest of the village dames;
Her eyes were the brightest
  That e'er set youthful heart in flames.
Her lover to move her
  By every art in man essay'd
In ditty, for pity,
  This lovely maid he often prayed,
But she, perverse, his suit deni'd.
  Sly Darby, being enraged at this,
Resolv'd when next they met to seize
  The lock that scatters Una's piss.

    Tol, lol, &c.

Beneath a lofty spreading oak
  She sat with can and milking pail;
From lily hands at each stroke
  In flowing streams the milk did steal.
With peeping, and creeping,
  Sly Darby now comes on apace;
In raptures the youth sees
  The blooming beauties of her face.
Fir'd with her charms, he now resolv'd
  No longer to delay his bliss,
But instantly to catch the lock
  That scatters pretty Una's piss.

    Tol, lol, &c.

Upon her back he laid her,
        Turned up her smock so lily white;
With joy the youth surveyed her,
        Then gaped with wonder and delight.
Her thighs they were so snowy fair,
        And just between appeared a crack;
The lips red, and overspread
        With curling hair of jetty black.
Transported now, Darby beholds
        The sum of all his promised bliss,
And instantly he caught the lock
        That scatters pretty Una's piss.

        Tol, lol, &c.

Within his arms he seized her,
        And pressed her to his panting breast;
What more could have appeased her,
        But oaths which Darby meant in jest.
He swore he'd but adore her,
        And to her ever constant prove;
He'd wed her, he'd bed her,
        And none on earth but her he'd love.
With vows like those he won her o'er,
        And hoped she'd take it not amiss
If he presumed to catch the lock
        That scatters pretty Una's piss.

        Tol, lol, &c.

His cock it stood erected,
 His breeches down about his heels,
And what he long expected
 He now with boundless rapture feels.
Now entered, and concentrated.
 The beauteous maid lay in a trance,
His bullocks went like elbows
 Of fiddlers in a country dance.
The melting Una, now she cries,
 I'd part with life for joy like this;
With showers of bliss they jointly oiled
 The lock that scatters Una's piss.

Tol, lol, &c.

VI

LIBEL SUMMONS

LIBEL SUMMONS

The British Museum has three MSS of this poem, known also as 'The Court of Equity' and 'The Fornicator's Court.' MS A — Egerton MS 1656, folios 8a-10a — has the fullest text, totalling 160 lines. MS B — Egerton MS 1656, folio 11a-b — is a fragment, containing only the first 57 lines of the poem. MS C — Additional MS 22307: the Hastie Collection of Burns MSS, folios 176a-177b — is a shorter version of only 110 lines.

The present text is Hans Hecht's collation of the three MSS, as printed in *Archiv für das Studium der Neueren Sprachen und Literaturen*, Vol. cxxx (1913), pp. 67ff. It follows MS A, with one couplet from MS B inserted in brackets. The most important variants in MS C are given in foot-notes. [DLF]

Written by Burns for the Tarbolton Bachelors' Club in 1786. A version is included as MS addendum by Scott Douglas in MMC. [SGS]

In Truth and Honor's name, AMEN.—
Know all men by these presents plain.—

This twalt o' May at M[auchli]ne given;
The year 'tween eighty five an' seven;
We, FORNICATORS by profession,
As per extractum from each Session;[1]

---

[1]   In MS C this couplet follows here:
    In way and manner here narrated
    Pro bono Amor congregated

And by our BRETHREN conſtituted,
A COURT of Equity deputed:
Wīth special authoris'd direction,
To take beneath our ſtrict protection,
The ſtays-unlacing, quondam maiden,
Wīth growing life and anguish laden;
Who by the Scoundrel is deny'd
Who led her thoughtless ſteps aside.—[2]

The knave who takes a private ſtroke
Beneath his sanctimonious cloke:
(The Coof wha ſtan's on clishmaclavers
When lasses hafflins offer favors)[3]

All who in any way or manner
Distain the FORNICATOR'S honor,
We take cognisance there anent
The proper Judges competent.—

Firſt, Poet B[urns], he takes the CHAIR,
Allow'd by all, his tītle's fair;
And paſt nem. con. wīthout dissension,
He has a DUPLICATE pretension.—

[2] In MS C the next eight lines read as follows:
> He who disowns the ruin'd Fair-one,
> And for her wants and woes does care none;
> The wretch that can refuse subsiſtence
> To those whom he has given exiſtence;
> He who when at a lass's by-job,
> Defrauds her wi' a fr—g or dry—b—b;
> The coof that ſtands on clishmaclavers.
> When women haflins offer favors:—

[3] From MS B.

The second, Sm[i]th, our worthy FISCAL,
To cowe each pertinacious rascal;
In this, as every other ſtate,
His merît is conspicuous great;
R[ichmo]nd the third, our truſty CLERK,
Our minutes regular to mark,
And sît dispenser of the law,
In absence of the former twa.—
The fourth, our MESSENGER AT ARMS,
When failing all the milder terms,
Hunt[e]r, a hearty willing Brother,
Weel skill'd in dead an' living leather.—

Wîthout preamble less or more said,
We, BODY POLITIC aforesaid,
Wîth legal, due WHEREAS and WHEREFORE,
We are appointed here to care for
The int'reſts of our Conſtîtuents,
And punish contravening Truants;
To keep a proper regulation
Wîthin the liſts of FORNICATION.

WHEREAS, Our FISCAL, by petîtion,
Informs us there is ſtrong suspicion
YOU, Coachman DOW, and Clockie BROWN,
Baîth residenters in this town,
In other words, you, Jock and Sandie
Hae been at wark at HOUGHMAGANDIE;
And now when ît is come to light,
The matter ye deny outright.—

You CLOCKIE BROWN, there's witness borne,
And affidavît made and sworne,
That ye hae rais'd a hurlie-burlie
In Maggy Mîtchel's tirlie-whurlie.—
(And blooster'd at her regulator,
Till a' her wheels gang clîtter-clatter.—)[4]

An' farther ſtill, ye cruel Vandal,
A tale might e'en in Hell be scandal.
Ye've made repeated wicked tryals
Wîth drugs an' draps in doctor's phials,
Mix'd, as ye thought, wi' fell infusion.
Your ain begotten wean to poosion.
An' yet ye are sae scant o' grace.
Ye daur set up your brazen face,
An' offer for to tak your aîth,
Ye never lifted Maggie's claîth.—
But tho' by Heaven an' Hell ye swear.
Laird Wilson's sclates can wîtness bear,
Ae e'enin of a M[auchli]ne fair,
That Maggie's maſts, they saw them bare,
For ye had furl'd up her sails,
An' was at play at heads an' tails.—

4   From MS C.

You COACHMAN DOW are here indicted
To have, as publickly ye're wyted,
Been clandeſtinely upward-whirlan
The petticoats o' Maggie Borlan;
An' gied her caniſter a rattle,
That months to come ît winna settle.—
An' yet ye offer your proteſt,
Ye never harry'd Maggie's neſt;
Tho' ît's weel-kend that, at her gyvle.
Ye hae gien mony a kytch an' kyvie.—

Then BROWN & DOW, above-design'd.
For clags and clauses there subjoin'd,
We COURT aforesaid, cîte & summon,
That on the fourth o' June in comin.
The hour o' Cause, in our Courtha'
At Whîteford's arms, ye answer LAW!

But, as reluctantly we punish.
An' rather, mildly would admonish:
Since Better Punishment prevented,
Tham OBSTINANCY sair repented.—

Then, for that *ancient Secret's sake*,
Ye have the honor to partake;
An' for that *noble Badge* you wear,
You, SANDIE DOW, our BROTHER dear,
We give you as a MAN an' MASON,
This private, sober, friendly lesson.—

Your crime, a manly deed we view ît.
As *man alone* can only do ît;
But, in denial, persevering,
Is to a *Scoundrel's name* adhering.
The beſt of *men* hae been surpris'd:
The beſt o' *women* been advis'd:
Nay, *cleverest Lads* hae haen a trick o't.
An' *bonnieſt Lasses* taen a lick o't.—
Then Brother Dow, if you're asham'd
In such a QUORUM to be nam'd,
Your conduct much is to be blam'd.—
See, ev'n *himsel* — there's godly BRYAN,
The auld *whatreck* he has been tryin;
When such as he put to their han',
What man or character need ſtan'?
Then Brother dear, lift up your brow,
And, like yoursel, the truth avow;
Erect a dauntless face upon ît,
An' say, 'I am the man has done ît;
'I Sandie Dow gat Meg wi' wean,
'An's fît to do as much again.'

Ne'er mind their solemn rev'rend faces,
Had they — in proper times an' places,
But *seen & fun'* — I muckle dread ît,
They juſt would done as you & we did.—
To tell the truth's a manly lesson,
An' doubly proper in a MASON.—

You MONSIEUR BROWN, as ſt is proven,
Meg Mſtchel's wame by you was hoven;
Wſthout you by a quick repentence

Acknowledge Meg's an' your acquaintance,
Depend on't, this shall be your sentence.—
Our Beadles to the Cross shall take you,
And there shall mſther naked make you;
Some canie grip near by your middle,
They shall ſt bind as tight's a fiddle;
The raep they round the pump shall tak
An' tye your hans behint your back;
Wi' juſt an ell o' ſtring allow'd
To jink an' hide you frae the croud.
There ye shall ſtan', a legal seizure,
Induring Maggie Mſtchel's pleasure;
So be, her pleasure dinna pass
Seven turnings of a half-hour glass:
Nor shall ſt in her pleasure be
To louse you out in less than three.—
This, our futurum esse DECREET,
We mean ſt not to keep a secret;
But in OUR SUMMONS here insert ſt,
And whoso dares, may controvert ſt.—
This, mark'd before the date and place is;
Subsignum eſt per B[urns] the Praeses.

L.S.B.

This summons & the Signet mark
Extractum eſt per R[ichmon}d, Clerk.—

R ... d.

At M[auchli]ne twenty fifth o' May,
About the twalt hour o' the day,[1]

You two in propria personae
Before design'd Sandie & Johnie,
This SUMMONS legally have got,
As vide witness underwrote;
Within the house of John D[ow], Vintner,
Nunc facio hoc—

                    Gullelmus Hun[te]r.

[1]   In MS C these lines read:

        At MAUCHLINE, idem date of June,
        Tween six & seven, the afternoon,

and the date in line 3 (p.171) is 'This fourth o' June.'

SONGS BY BURNS, WITH MUSIC
By Valentina Bold

I'LL TELL YOU A TALE OF A WIFE

TUNE: *Auld Sir Symon*

Andante

I'll tell you a tale of a Wife, And she was a Whig and a Saunt;

She liv'd a most sanc- ti- fy'd life, But whyles she was fash'd wi' her —

'I'LL TELL YOU A TALE OF A WIFE'
TUNE: *'Auld Sir Symon'*

This tune is also known as 'Auld Sir Simon the King'. It is
shown here as it appears in James C. Dick *The Songs of Robert
Burns. Now First Printed with the melodies for which they were written*
(London: Henry Frowde, 1903): no.248 where it is used to
set the recitative 'Sir Wisdom's a fool' in 'The Jolly Beggars'.
Dick uses, as his source text, *Wit and Mirth; or Pills to Purge
Melancholy* vol iii (London: J. Tonson, 1719): 143 and see too
his notes to the song; Donald Low *The Songs of Robert Burns*
(London: Routledge, 1993): songs 33 and 120.

BONIE MARY

TUNE: *Minnie's ay glowering o'er me*

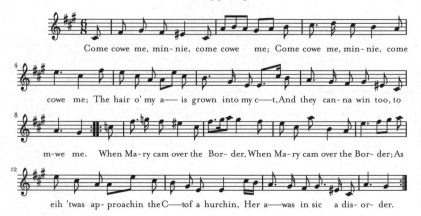

Come cowe me, min-nie, come cowe me; Come cowe me, min-nie, come cowe me; The hair o' my a— is grown into my c—t, And they can-na win too, to m-we me. When Ma-ry cam over the Bor-der, When Ma-ry cam over the Bor-der; As eih 'twas ap-proachin the C—t of a hurchin, Her a—was in sic a dis-or-der.

'BONIE MARY'

TUNE: *'Minnie's ay glowering o'er me'*

This tune is taken from James Johnson *The Scots Musical Museum* 6 vols in 3 (Edinburgh: J. Johnson, 1787–1803): song 180 (where it is used to set 'Katy's Answer'). See too Donald Low *The Songs of Robert Burns* (London: Routledge, 1993): no.253.

ACT SEDERUNT O' THE SESSION

TUNE: *O'er the moor amang the heather*

In Edin-burgh town they've made a law, In Edin-burgh at the Court o Ses -

sion, That stand-ing pr—cks are fau-teors a, And guil-ty of a high trans-gres-sion.

'ACT SEDERUNT OF THE SESSION'

TUNE: *O'er the muir amang the heather'*

This tune is from James Johnson *The Scots Musical Museum* 6 vols in 3 (Edinburgh: J. Johnson, 1787–1803): song 328 where it is used for the song of the same title. See too James C. Dick *The Songs of Robert Burns. Now First Printed with the melodies for which they were written* (London: Henry Frowde, 1903): no.356 and his notes to this song. This is an often reprinted tune and can, in addition, be found in many modern collections including *The Gow Collection of Scottish Dance Music* ed Richard Carlin (London: Oak Publications, 1986), no.382. There is a note on the song, too, in John Glen *Early Scottish Melodies* (Edinburgh: Glen, 1900): 74.

WHEN PRINCES AND PRELATES

TUNE: *The Campbells are Coming*

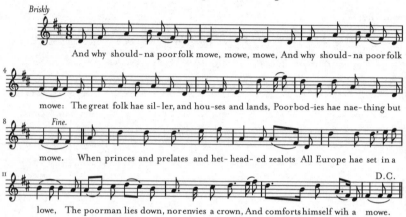

And why should-na poor folk mowe, mowe, mowe, And why should-na poor folk

mowe: The great folk hae sil-ler, and hou-ses and lands, Poor bod-ies hae nae-thing but

mowe. When princes and prelates and het-head-ed zealots All Europe hae set in a

lowe, The poor man lies down, nor envies a crown, And comforts himself wih a mowe.

'WHEN PRINCES AND PRELATES'
TUNE: *'The Campbells are Coming'*

This very well known tune is given here from James C. Dick
*The Songs of Robert Burns. Now First Printed with the melodies for which
they were written* (London: Henry Frowde, 1903): no.336
where it is used for 'Upon the Lowlands I Lay, I Lay' and
see Dick's notes, along with Donald Low *The Songs of Robert
Burns* (London: Routledge,1993): no.223 and James
Johnson *The Scots Musical Museum* 6 vols in 3 (Edinburgh: J.
Johnson, 1787–1803): song 299. Again, it appears in
numerous modern publications, particularly those aimed at
instrumentalists, including *Melodius Scotland* (London:
George Newnes, 1925–29) vol 3: 116 and George F. Farnell
Songs of Bonnie Scotland (Glasgow: Collins, 1934): 11.

WHEN PROSE-WORK AND RHYMES

TUNE: *The Campbells are Coming*

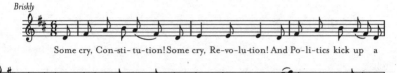

Some cry, Con-sti- tu-tion! Some cry, Re-vo-lu-tion! And Po-li-tics kick up   a

rowe;   But Prince and Re- pub- lic, A- gree on the Subject, No trea- son is in a good

—.   While Prose-work and rhymes Are hunted for crimes, And things are the devil knows

how;   A-ware o' my rhymes, In these kit- tle times, The subject I chuse is a—.

'WHILE PROSE-WORK AND RHYMES'

TUNE: *'The Campbells are Coming'*

NINE INCH WILL PLEASE A LADY

TUNE: *The Quaker's Wife*

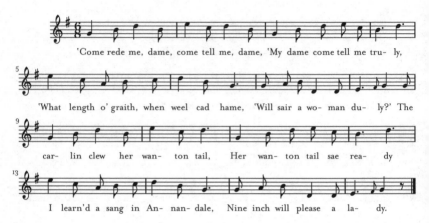

'Come rede me, dame, come tell me, dame, 'My dame come tell me tru- ly,

'What length o' graith, when weel cad hame, 'Will sair a wo- man du- ly?' The

car- lin clew her wan- ton tail, Her wan- ton tail sae rea- dy

I learn'd a sang in An- nan- dale, Nine inch will please a la- dy.

'NINE INCH WILL PLEASE A LADY'
TUNE: 'The Quaker's Wife'

The tune here is from *The National Melodies of Scotland; united to the songs of Robert Burns, Allan Ramsay, and other eminent lyric poets* (London: Jones and Company, 1934: 120. See too Donald Low *The Songs of Robert Burns* (London: Routledge, 1993): no.110.

ODE TO SPRING

TUNE: *The tither morn*

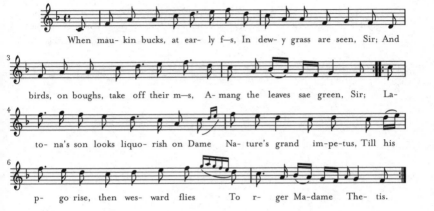

When mau- kin bucks, at ear- ly f—s, In dew- y grass are seen, Sir; And

birds, on boughs, take off their m—s, A- mang the leaves sae green, Sir; La-

to- na's son looks liquo- rish on Dame   Na- ture's grand   im- pe-tus, Till his

p-   go rise, then wes- ward flies   To   r-   ger Ma-dame   The-   tis.

'ODE TO SPRING'

TUNE: *The tither morn*

The tune here is taken from James Johnson *The Scots Musical Museum* 6 vols in 3 (Edinburgh: J. Johnson, 1787–1803): song 345. See too Donald Low *The Songs of Robert Burns* (London: Routledge, 1993): no.275.

SAW YE MY MAGGIE

TUNE: *Saw ye na my Peggy*

Saw ye my Mag- gie? Saw ye my Mag- gie?

Saw ye my Mag- gie? Co- min oer the lea?

'O SAW YE MY MAGGIE?'

TUNE: *O saw ye na my Peggy?*

The tune here is taken from *A Selection of the most Favourite Scots Songs Chiefly Pastoral. Adapted for the Harpsichord with an Accompaniment for the Violin by Eminent Masters* (London: William Napier, 1795) vol 2: 57. Compare to the tune in Donald Low *The Songs of Robert Burns* (London: Routledge, 1993): no. 366.

THE FORNICATOR

TUNE: *Clout the Cauldron*

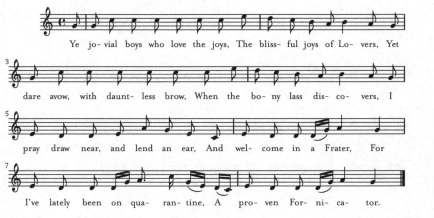

Ye jo-vial boys who love the joys, The bliss-ful joys of Lo-vers, Yet

dare avow, with daunt-less brow, When the bo-ny lass dis-co-vers, I

pray draw near, and lend an ear, And wel-come in a Frater, For

I've lately been on qua-ran-tine, A pro-ven For-ni-ca-tor.

'THE FORNICATOR'
TUNE: *'Clout the Cauldron'*

The air is taken from James Johnson *The Scots Musical Museum*
6 vols in 3 (Edinburgh: J. Johnson, 1787–1803): song 23.
It also appears in William Thomson *Orpheus Caledonius. Or a
Collection of scots Songs* 2nd ed (London: William Thomson,
1733) which is now available on CD-rom as a facsimile copy
(Retford, Nottinghamshire: Nick Parkes, 2003). See too
Donald Low *The Songs of Robert Burns* (London: Routledge,
1993): no.25 and James C. Dick *The Songs of Robert Burns. Now
First Printed with the melodies for which they were written* (London: Henry
Frowde, 1903): no.251 where it is used to set 'My bonie lass I
work in brass' from 'The Jolly Beggars. The tune is also
known as 'The Blacksmith and his Apron'.

MY GIRL SHE'S AIRY

TUNE: *Black Joke*

My Girl she's ai- ry, sh' s bu- xom and gay, Her breath is as sweet as the

blos- soms in May; A touch of her lips I ra- vi- shes quite; She's always good na- tur'd, good

hu- mor'd and free: She dan- ces, she glan- ces, she smiles with a glee; Her

eyes are the lightenings of joy and de- light: Her slen- der neck, her handsome waist, Her

hair well buck-l'd, her stays well lac'd, Her taper white leg, with an et, and a, c, For her

a, b, e, d, and her c, u, n, t, And Oh, for the joys of a long win- ter night!

'MY GIRL SHE'S AIRY'
TUNE: *'Black Joke'*

This tune, which is still popular for performance, is available at a number of traditional music websites, including www.folktunefinder.com, www.traditionalmusic.co.uk/irish-folk-music/ and sniff.numachi.com/pages/tiBLCKJKE; ttBLCKJKE.html. See too the version, adapted for performance by David Johnson in Donald Low *The Songs of Robert Burns* (London: Routledge,1993): no.25 and that in R. Maver *Collection of Genuine Irish Melodies and Songs* (Glasgow: 1877). It is also available on-line at

THERE WAS TWA WIVES

TUNE: *Take your auld cloak about you*

There was twa wives, and twa witty wives, As e'- er play'd hough-

ma-gan-die, And they coos out, u- pon a time, Out o'er a drink o' brandy;

'THERE WAS TWA WIVES'

TUNE: *'Take your auld cloak about you'*

The tune here, which appears in many instrumental
collections, is taken from *The National Melodies of Scotland; united to
the songs of Robert Burns, Allan Ramsay, and other eminent lyric poets*
(London: Jones and Company, 1934: 187. See too Donald
Low *The Songs of Robert Burns* (London: Routledge, 1993): no.167.

FURTHER READING:
A SELECTED LIST

Editions of *The Merry Muses* (most are available in the National Library of Scotland)

Anon, *The merry muses of Caledonia: a collection of favourite Scots songs, ancient and modern; selected for the use of the Crochallan Fencibles* [Edinburgh?: no publisher.], Printed in the year 1799. Reproduction Edinburgh: National Library of Scotland, 1958. NLS Mf.1059.

_____, *The merry muses : a choice collection of favourite songs* (Dublin: Printed for the booksellers, [1804?]).

Burns, Robert, *The merry muses, etc.* (no place of publication: no publisher). Privately printed, '1827'.

_____, *The merry muses a choice collection of favourite songs* (London: no publisher, 1843), c.192?.

_____, *The merry muses : a choice collection of favourite songs gathered from many sources / by Robert Burns, to which is added two of his letters and a poem—hitherto suppressed and never before printed* (no place of publication: no publisher). Privately printed (not for sale), '1827' [c.1847 or later].

_____, *The merry muses of Robert Burns* (no place of publication: no publisher). Privately printed, for the Caledonian Society of London, 19?).

_____, *The merry muses of Caledonia : a collection of favorite Scots songs ancient and modern, selected for use of the Crochallan fencibles, with introd., notes, and glossary* (no place of publication: no publisher). Privately printed for subscribers only, [19?]. 750 numbered copiees for America.

_____, *The merry muses : a choice collection of favourite songs gathered from many sources. by Robert Burns, to which is added two of his*

letters and a poem — hitherto suppressed and never before printed
(no place of publication: no publisher), 90 copies
1827. Privately printed, *c.*1910.

_____, *The merry muses : a choice collection of favourite songs gathered
from many sources / by Robert Burns, to which is added two of his
letters and a poem — hitherto suppressed and never before printed*
(no place of publication: no publisher). Privately
printed (not for sale), 1827 [1910]. 90 copies.

_____, *The merry muses of Caledonia (original edition) a collection of
favourite Scots songs ancient and modern, selected for use of the
Crochallan Fencibles. A vindication of Robert Burns in connection
with the above publication and the spurious editions which succeeded
it* (Kilmarnock: Burns Federation, 1911). For
subscribers only.

_____, *The merry muses : a choice collection of favourite songs gathered
from many sources / by Robert Burns, to which is added two of his
letters and a poem — hitherto suppressed — and never before printed*
(no place of publication: no publisher). Privately
printed: A gentleman of London, 1930. 100 copies.

_____, *The merry muses of Caledonia.* Edited by James Barke
and Sydney Goodsir Smith, with a prefatory note and
some authentic Burns texts contributed by J.
DeLancey Ferguson (Edinburgh: M. Macdonald,
1959) For private distribution to members of the Auk
Society only.

_____, *The merry muses: a selection of favorite songs gathered from many
sources. Originally collected by Robert Burns; to which are added one
of his letters — formerly suppressed — and a group of merry toasts and
sentiments* (San Francisco: City Lights Books, 1962).

_____, *The merry muses of Caledonia,* edited by James Barke
and Sydney Goodsir Smith, with a prefatory note and

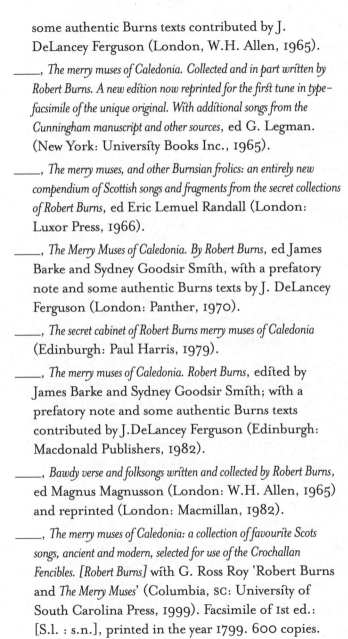

some authentic Burns texts contributed by J.
DeLancey Ferguson (London, W.H. Allen, 1965).

____, *The merry muses of Caledonia. Collected and in part written by Robert Burns. A new edition now reprinted for the first tune in type-facsimile of the unique original. With additional songs from the Cunningham manuscript and other sources*, ed G. Legman.
(New York: University Books Inc., 1965).

____, *The merry muses, and other Burnsian frolics: an entirely new compendium of Scottish songs and fragments from the secret collections of Robert Burns*, ed Eric Lemuel Randall (London:
Luxor Press, 1966).

____, *The Merry Muses of Caledonia. By Robert Burns*, ed James
Barke and Sydney Goodsir Smith, with a prefatory
note and some authentic Burns texts by J. DeLancey
Ferguson (London: Panther, 1970).

____, *The secret cabinet of Robert Burns merry muses of Caledonia*
(Edinburgh: Paul Harris, 1979).

____, *The merry muses of Caledonia. Robert Burns*, edited by
James Barke and Sydney Goodsir Smith; with a
prefatory note and some authentic Burns texts
contributed by J.DeLancey Ferguson (Edinburgh:
Macdonald Publishers, 1982).

____, *Bawdy verse and folksongs written and collected by Robert Burns*,
ed Magnus Magnusson (London: W.H. Allen, 1965)
and reprinted (London: Macmillan, 1982).

____, *The merry muses of Caledonia: a collection of favourite Scots songs, ancient and modern, selected for use of the Crochallan Fencibles. [Robert Burns]* with G. Ross Roy 'Robert Burns
and *The Merry Muses*' (Columbia, SC: University of
South Carolina Press, 1999). Facsimile of 1st ed.:
[S.l. : s.n.], printed in the year 1799. 600 copies.

ON THE MERRY MUSES AND BURNS'S EROTIC AND BAWDY WRITING

Adams, James 'Deîty or Dirt? A Review of an Old Controversy on Robert Burns', *Burns Chronicle* IV, Jan 1895: 17-27.

Beaty, Frederick L., 'Burns's Comedy of Romantic Love', *Proceedings of the Modern Language Association (PMLA)* 83 (2): May 1968, pp.429–38.

Ferguson, J. De Lancey, 'The Suppressed Poems of Burns', *Modern Philology* 30 (1): 1932: 53–60.

____, 'Some new Burns letters', *PMLA* 3: 1936: 975–84.

____, 'Burns and The Merry Muses', *Modern Language Notes*, Nov 1951: 471–73.

M'Naught , D., 'The Merry Muses of Caledonia', *Burns Chronicle* III, February 1894: 24–45.

____, 'The "Merry Muses" Again', *Burns Chronicle* XX, 1911: 105–19.

MacDonald, Hugh, 'The Rev. George Gilfillan versus Robert Burns (Reprinted from a very rare pamphlet', *Burns Chronicle* IV, Jan 1875: 28–40.

'The Rev. George Gilfillan versus Robert Burns. (Reprinted from a very rare Pamphlet', *Burns Chronicle* IV, Jan 1895: 28–40.

Pearl, Cyril, *Bawdy Burns. The Christian Rebel*. London: Frederick Muller: 1958.

Roy, G. Ross, 'The "1827" Edition of Robert Burns's Merry Muses of Caledonia', *Burns Chronicle* 4th series XI, 1986: 32–44.

RELATED READING

Ashe, Geoffrey, *Sex, Rakes and Libertines. The Hell-Fire Clubs.* Revised edition, first published W.H. Allen, 1974. (Stroud: Gloucestershire, 2005).

Bold, Alan, ed., The *Sexual Dimension in Literature* (London: Vision Press, 1982).

Dick, James C., *The Songs of Robert Burns. Now first printed with the melodies for which they were written: A study in tone-poetry with bibliography, historical notes and glossary* (London: Henry Frowde, 1903).

Dollimore, Jonathan, *Sex, Literature and Censorship* (Cambridge: Polity Press, 2001).

Farmer, John S., ed, *Merry Songs and Ballads prior to the year A.D. 1800* (London?: no publisher, 1895). Privately printed for subscribers only.

Foxon, David, *Libertine Literature in England. 1660–1745* (New York: University Books, 1965).

The Giblet Pye, being the Heads, Tails, Legs and Wings, of the Anacreontic songs of the celebrated R. Burns, G.A. Stevens, Rochester, T. L—tle, and others (Shamborough: John Nox, 1806).

Hunt, Lynn and Margaret Jacob, 'The Affective Revolution in 1790s Britain', *Eighteenth-Century Studies* 34 (4), 2001: 491–521.

Legman, G., *The Horn Book. Studies in Erotic Folklore and Bibliography*. First published 1964 (New York: University Books, 2nd printing), 1966.

Lord, Evelyn, *The Hell-Fire Clubs. Sex, Satanism and Secret Societies* (New Haven: Yale University Press, 2008).

Low, Donald, *The Songs of Robert Burns* (London: Routledge, 1993).

Rousseau G.S., and Roy Porter, eds., *Sexual Worlds of the Enlightenment* (Manchester: Manchester University Press, 1987).

Stevenson, David, *The Beggar's Benison. Sex Clubs of the Scottish Enlightenment* (East Linton: Tuckwell Press, 2001).

RECORDINGS

Bowman, Gill, Tich Frier, Fiona Forbes, Robin Laing et al, *Robert Burns — The Merry Muses* (Glasgow: Iona Records, 1996) IRCD035.

MacColl, Ewan, *Songs from Robert Burns' Merry Muses of Caledonia*. Sung by Ewan MacColl. Edited and annotated by Kenneth S. Goldstein (no place of publication: Dionysus, 1962). DI.

Burns, Robert, *The Complete Songs of Robert Burns*. Vols 1-12, produced by Fred Freeman (Eaglesham, Glasgow: Linn Records, 1995–2002). Linn Records CDK 047, 051, 062, 083, 086, 099, 107, 143, 156, 199, 200 and 201.

Reader, Eddi, *Eddi Reader sings the songs of Robert Burns* (London: Rough Trade Records, 2003). RTRADECD 097.

Redpath, Jean, *Songs of Robert Burns*. Arranged by Serge Hovey, 7 vols. First published 1976–1990. Rereleased on 4 CDs (USA: Rounder; Cockenzie: Greentrax, 1990–1996). CDTRAX 029, 114–16.

RESOURCES

James Barke Papers, the Mitchell Library, Glasgow.

Sydney Goodsir Smith papers, Edinburgh University
Library Gen 1773.

Sydney Goodsir Smith papers, University of Delaware
MSS 226.

Sydney Goodsir Smith papers, National Library of
Scotland ACC 10397/44; 103972.

'The merry Muses of Caledonia', bound volume
including transcript and notes by J.C. Ewing, Andrew
Carnegie Library, Local Studies, 1247a.

GLOSSARY

A

A', all
Abee, me be
Aboon, above
Ae, one; only
Aff, off
Afore, before
Aften, often
Aiblens, perhaps
Aik, an oak
Ain, own
Aith, an oath
Aits, pats
Alane, alone
An, if
Ance, once
Ane, one
An's, and is; and his
As due as, whenever
Atweesh, between
Auld, old
Awa, away
Awe, to owe
Awee, a little time
Ay or **aye**, always
Ayont, beyond

B

Bad, bid
Bade endured; desired; persuaded
Bairn'd, got with child
Baith, both
Bann'd, cursed
Bane, bone
Bang, a stroke

Bauld, bold
Be, by
Bear, barley
Bed-stock, bedside; wood bar at front of box bed
Befa', befall
Behint, behind
Belang, belong to
Beld, bald
Belyve, by and by
Ben, inside
Bends, bounds
Benty, grassy
Be't, be it
Bicker, beaker
Bide, to stand, to endure
Bien (of a person) well-to-do; (of a place) comfortable
Bigget, build
Biggit, built
Birkie, fellow
Birss, hair; bristle
Blatter, attack
Blaw, to blow; to brag
Bleerie, bleary-eyed
Blin', blind
Bluid, blood
Blyth, happily
Bock, to spew; to vomit
Boddle, one-sixth of a penny
Boost, must needs
Bort, bored
Bousing, drinking
Bowe, bowl
Brae, slope of a hill
Braid, cloth

Brak, did break
Braw, fine; handsome
Brawlies, splendidly
Brawly's, finely as
Broads, shutters
Brose, porridge
Browſt, a brewing
Brunt, burnt
Bruſt, burſt
Busk, bush
Buskît, dressed; decked
But, wíthout; wanting
Buttock-hire, penance
Byre-en', cowshed end

C
Ca', to drive; a call
Ca'd, summoned; driven; drove
Ca' throu', to push forward
Cadger, a carrier
Caller, fresh
Cam, came
Cameronian, Presbyterian sect
Canie, careful
Canna, cannot
Canty, cheerful
Carl, a man
Carlin, an old woman
Cauld, cold
Chaup, a blow
Chearie, cheery
Chiel, young fellow
Chuckies, chickens
Claes, clothes; covers
Claise, clothes
Claîth, cloth
Clappin', fondling
Clash, gossip; to talk
Clatter, to talk idly

Claught, clutched
Claut, to sweep; to snatch at
Claw, to scratch; to fondle
Cleek, hook
Clegs, spurs
Clew, scratched; fondled
Clishmaclavers, idle talks
Clocken-hen, broody hen
Cloot, hoof
Clout, mend; patch
Clouts, clothes
Coal-riddle, sieve
Coft, bought
Coggin', wedging
Cogie, a small wooden pail
Coof, a fool
Cooſt, did caſt off
Cooſt out, quarrelled
Coup, to overturn
Courtha', court hall
Cow, cowered
Cowe, crop; horror
Cow'd, cropped
Crack, gossip
Crap, crept; a crop
Craw, to crow
Creel, a basket
Crowdie, porridge; gruel
Cuttie, líttle
Cuttie-mun, old song
Cuttie ſtoup, short drinks

D
Dae, do
Daffin, sporting
Dang, pushed; knocked
Darge o' graîth, day's work
Daud, a lump
Daught na, dared not

Daur, dare
Dawtin', petting
Deevil's dozen, 13 inches
Deil, the devil
Dibble, tool
Dilly, toying
Ding, to shove; to hit
Dinna, do not
Ditty, indictment
Dizzen, dozen
Docht, could
Dock, tail
Dockies, tails
Dockins, dock leaves
Doit, mite
Dool, blow; sorrowful
Doudled, dandled
Dow, do, can
Dow, a pigeon
Down-cod, feather pillow
Draik, to soak
Dree, to bear; to endure
Dreep, to drip
Druken, drunken
Dub, a shift
Dud, short
Duddie, little
Duntie, thump
Dunts, strokes; blows; knocks
Durk, a dagger
Dyke-back, back of the wall

E
Eastlin, eastern
Ee, eye; to watch
E'en, evening
Een or **sin**, eyes
Eith, easy
Elekit, of the Elect

En', end
Enow, enough

F
Fa', enjoy
Fae, foe
Fa'en, fallen
Fairin', food
Fand, found
Fash, heed
Fash'd, vexed
Fauld, folded; a fold
Fauteors a', offenders all
Fau't, faulted
Fau'tor, offender
Fants, faults
Fee, wage
Fee'd, hired
Feetie, feet
Fidge, to exert
Fient a, devil a
Fin', find
Fistles, fizzes
Fit, foot
Fit-man, footman
Fitstead, footstep
Flaes, fleas; flies
Flang, struggled; heaved
Flate, protested
Fley'd, afraid
Flowe, morass
Fly'd, frightened
Flytin, scolding
Foggie, mossy
Foot, speed
Forbye, besides
Forgat, forgot
Fou, full; drunk
Frae, from

Fu', full; drunk
Fun', found
Fur or **furr**, furrow

G
Gae, go; gave
Gaed or **gade**, went
Gain', against
Gair, gusset
Gamon, petticoat
Gang, to go
Gang ben, to go in
Gar, to make; to compel
Gard, made
Garse, grass
Gart it clink, made it chime
Gart me, got me to
Gat, got
Gaud, goad; the plow shaft
Gaun, going
Gavel, gable
Gear, wealth; goods; harness
Gerse, grass
Gets, children
Gie, give
Gied me the glaiks, jilted me
Gie'n, given
Gif, if
Gin, if
Girden, exercise
Girdin', driving
Girt, girdled
Girtest, greatest
Girt's, wide as
Gizzen, dry up
Glaur, muck
Gled, buzzard; kite
Glowran, gazing
Goosset, gusset

Goud or **gowd**, gold
Gowan, daisies
Garipit, groped
Graith, equipment, gear
Grane, groan
Grat, wept
Gravat, muffler
Greetie, crying
Gripet, grasped
Groazle, grunt
Gyvel or **gyvle**, gable

H
Ha', hall
Had, hold
Hadin', leading
Haen, had
Hafflins, partially; half
Haly, holy
Haly band, kirk session
Hame, home
Han', hand
Hanger, dagger
Haud, hold
Heigh, high
Her lane, alone
Herryin', robbing
Hie, high
Hing, hang
Hinnie, honey
Hissle or **hizzie**, girl; hussie
Holland-sark, linen shift
Hotch'd, shoved
Hough, thigh
Houghmagandie, fornication
Hoven, swollen
Howe, hollow
Howk, dig
Hoy'd, hailed

Hurdies, buttocks
Hurdies fyke, buttocks in action
Hurly, storm

I
Ilk, each
Ilka, every
Ither, each one; other
Ither, adder
I's no, I'll not
Itsel, itself

J
Jad, a jade
Jander, to chatter
Jimp, slender
Jink, to dodge
Jirts, jerks
Jo, sweetheart; joy

K
Kail, soup; broth
Kecklin, cackling
Ken, know
Kend, known
Kill, kiln
Kimmer, a married woman; a
  gossip
Kimmerland, womankind
Kintra, country
Kipples, couples
Kirst'nln', christening
Kittle, ticklish; difficult;
  dangerous; tricky
Knocking-stone, stone mortar
  for hulling barley
Knowe, knoll, hillock
Koontrie, country
Kye, cattle

Kytch, toss
Kyvie, swindle

L
Labour lee, plow grassland
Labster, lobster
Laft, left
Laigh, low
Laik, lack
Lair, bog
Laithron doup, lazy rump
Lane, alone
Lang's, long as
Langsyne saunts, saints of long
  ago
Lap, leapt
Lat, let
Lave, the rest
Laverock, the lark
Lea's, leaves
Lee-rig, untilled field
Leuch or **leugh**, laughed
Licket, lick; a beating
Lien, lain
Liltit, pulled
Linkin', sprightly
Links, locks
Loan, lane
Lo'ed, loved
Loon, fellow; lad
Loot, let
Loups, leaps
Lous'd, loosened
Louse, to loosen
Lowe, blaze
Lown, lad
Lowse, to loosen
Lucky, goodwife
Lucky land, alewife

Lug, to pull
Lugs, ears

M
Mae, more
Mail, meal; male
Mair, more
Maiſt, almoſt
Mak, make
Make, like
Mallison, curse
Mane, moan
Mantie, cloth
Margh, marrow
Ma't, malt
Maukin, a hare
Maun, muſt
Maunna, muſt not
Meal-pocks, meal bags
Meikle, much
Mess, miniſter
Midden wa', dunghill wall
Mim-mou'd, mealymouthed
Minnie, mother
Misca'd, abused
Modeworck or **modiewark**, mole
M—e, mowe
Mou', mouth
Moulie, soft; earthy
Muckle, bigger; much
Muir, moor

N
Nae, not; no
Naething, nothing
Naigs, nags
Na mony, few
Nane, none

Neebor, neighbor
Neep, turnip
Neiſt, next
Neive, fiſt
Nerse, tail
Nicher, whinny
Nidge't, squeezed
Nine, nine inches long
Nîts, nuts
Nocht, nothing
Nyvel, navel

O
O', of
Onie or **ony**, any
Or, before
O't, of ît
Ousen, oxen
Owsen-ſtraw, ox ſtall

P
Pat, put
Pat in my will, gave me my way.
Pegh, puff
Pickle, little
Pickle hair, laſt corn cut
Pît, put
Pîth, ſtrength
Plack, a third of a penny
Playing bye, being false to
Pock, bag
Pockie, sack
Poosion, poison
Pounie, pony
Pow, the head; to pull
Prie, to accept; to taſte
Pry, to try; to taſte
Pu'd, pulled

Q

Quarter, one-quarter yard; 9 inches

Quine, lass; wench

Quo', quoth

R

Raep, rope

Rair, roar

Rase, rose

Rashes, rushes

Rashy, rushy

Raxin, reaching

Rede, advise

Reek, smoke

Ring, reign

Ripples, backache

Rive, tear

Rivt, torn

Roaring-pin, rolling pin

Rock, a diſtaff

Row, roll up; wrap

Rowted, bellowed

Rowth, plenty

Rug, tug

Runt, cabbage ſtalk

S

Sae, so

Saft, soft

Sair, to serve; sorely; severe; very much

Saird, served

Saireſt, hardeſt

Sangs, songs

Sark, shift; shirt; chemise

Sa'tty, salty

Saunt, saint

Scauld, scold

Scauls, scolds

Solates, slates

Sel, self

Sell'd, sold

Shaw'd, showed

Shawn, shown

Sheds, divides

Sherra, sheriff

Shillin hill, winnowing hill

Shoon, shoes

Sic, such

Siccan a, such a

Sicker, sure

Side and wide, large and low-hung

Siller, money

Sin, since

Sinners, sinews

Sinsyne, since then

Skelpît droup, slapped rump

Sma', small

Sock, plowshare

Sodger or **sojer**, soldier

Sonsy, healthy

Soud, should

Souple, to make supple

Sowen, pat; gruel pot

Spak, spoke

Speel, climb

Spier, ask

Spier'd at, asked

Spretty, rushy

Stane, ſtone

Stane o' ſtanin' graîth, set of good equipment

Stung, ſting

Stanin', ſtanding; hesîtantly

Stan't themlane, ſtand by themselves

Stark, ſtrong

Starns, ſtars

Staund, set

Staunin', ſtanding; erect

Steer, ſtir; arouse

Stell'd, braced

Stented graith, harnessed the plow

Steward, housekeeper

Stibble, ſtubble

Stilts, shafts

Stown't, ſtolen ît

Strack, ſtruck

Stralk o't, shot at ît

Straik't, ſtroked

Strung, ſtrong

Strunt, spirîts

Succar, sugar

Succour, sugar

Sykie risk, watery mark

Sync, then; since

T

Tae, too

Taen, taken

Taes, toes

Tald, told

Taper, shapely

Tappît en, large jug

Tell'd, told

Tent, attend

Tham, them

Theekît, thicket

Thegîther, together

Thie, thigh

Thirl, thrill

Thole, endure

Thrang, full; thronged

Thrave, 24 sheaves of grain

Thretty, thirty

Thumpin, buxom

Till, to

Till't, tilled; 'went to ît'

Tinkler, tinker

Tint, loſt

Tirliewirlies, ornaments

Tîttling, sparrow

Titty, siſter

Tocher, dowry

Todlen, toddling

Toop-horn, ram's horn

Tope, good ale

Touzle, dishevel

Trams, shafts

Trogger, a peddler

Trow, to swear

Trow'd, rolled

Twa, two

Twalt, twelfth

Tway thumb-bread, two thumbs broad

Twynin', working

U

Unco, uncommon; great; strange

Unkenned, unknown

Upo', upon

V

Vera, very

Verra crack, inſtant

W

Wa', a wall

Wad, would; would have

Wad airt, would direct

Wadna, would not

Wadna daunton, was dauntless
Wadna wanted it, wouldn't have lost it
Wae gae, woe to
Waes me, alas
Waery fa', curses on
Waft, to weave; wool
Waigles, waggles
Wakin', walking
Waled, picked
Waly, well
Wame, belly
Wan, won
Want, lack
Wants the, has no
Wap, wrap
Wark, work
Warld, world
Warst, worst
Wast, west
Wat, know; wet
Wauken'd, wakened
Waukin, awake
Waulies, the buttocks
Waur, worth
Waur't, worried
Waxen wan, grown feeble
Wean, child
Wearin', using
Webster, weaver
Wee, little; a bit; a short period of time
Wee coat, petticoat
Weel, well
Weel-knoozed, well-kneaded
Weel kend, well-known
Weet, splash-board; wet
Weetin', wetting
Weir, war; might

Whang, tape; lace; a large slice
Whatreck, weasel
What she could bicker, an fast as she could
Whittle, knife
Whyles, sometimes
Wi'a, who'll
Wight, brisk
Wi little wark, easily
Wimble bores, small holes
Win', wind
Wind-wa's, windy walls; a boaster
Winna, will not
Winna true, will not believe
Wordy, worthy
Wyte, blame

Y

Yeard, yard
Yerk, to drive; to jerk
Ye'se, you shall, you will
Yill, ale
Yin, one
Yokin', a stint; a bout
Yorlin, a finch

The Luath Kilmarnock Edition: *Poems, Chiefly in the Scottish Dialect* by Robert Burns
Illustrations by Bob Dewar, Introduction by John Cairney, Afterword by Clark McGinn

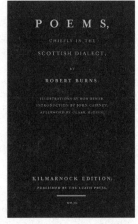

This special illustrated edition celebrates the 250th anniversary of the birth of Robert Burns, probably the world's favourite poet. *Poems, Chiefly in the Scottish Dialect*, the only book of his poetry published in his short lifetime, is probably the most significant book ever published from Scotland.

A limited Subscriber Edition of *Poems, Chiefly in the Scottish Dialect* is available exclusively from Luath Press, priced £40. The first Kilmarnock Edition, published 1786, was a Subscriber Edition of 612 copies, the Luath Subscriber Edition is also limited to 612 copies. Each volume is signed and numbered by John Cairney, 'The Man Who Played Burns', and attractively presented in a numbered slipcase.

A bookshop edition is also available, priced £15.

Subscriber Edition, £40, ISBN 978-1-906817-08-4, for enquiries call 0131 225 4326 or email sales@luath.co.uk.

Bookshop Edition, £15, ISBN 978-1-906307-67-7, is available at all good bookshops or direct from www.luath.co.uk.

Luath Press Limited
committed to publishing well written books worth reading

LUATH PRESS takes its name from Robert Burns, whose little
collie Luath (*Gael.*, swift or nimble) tripped up Jean Armour at a
wedding and gave him the chance to speak to the woman who
was to be his wife and the abiding love of his life. Burns called
one of 'The Twa Dogs' Luath after Cuchullin's
hunting dog in Ossian's *Fingal*. Luath Press was
established in 1981 in the heart of Burns
country, and is now based a few steps up the
road from Burns' first lodgings on Edinburgh's
Royal Mile.

Luath offers you distinctive writing with a hint
of unexpected pleasures.

Most bookshops in the UK, the US, Canada,
Australia, New Zealand and parts of Europe either
carry our books in stock or can order them for you.
To order direct from us, please send a £sterling cheque,
postal order, international money order or your credit
card details (number, address of cardholder and expiry
date) to us at the address below. Please add post and pack-
ing as follows: UK – £1.00 per delivery address; overseas surface
mail – £2.50 per delivery address; overseas airmail – £3.50 for the
first book to each delivery address, plus £1.00 for each additional
book by airmail to the same address. If your order is a gift, we will
happily enclose your card or message at no extra charge.

Luath Press Limited
543/2 Castlehill
The Royal Mile
Edinburgh EH1 2ND
Scotland
Telephone: 0131 225 4326 (24 hours)
Fax: 0131 225 4324
email: sales@luath.co.uk
Website: www.luath.co.uk

ILLUSTRATION: IAN KELLAS